D

The Genealogist's Question & Answer Book

THE *genealogist's* question &answer BOOK

Marcia Yannizze Melnyk

BETTERWAY BOOKS
CINCINNATI, OHIO

www.familytreemagazine.com

Other fine Betterway Books are available from your local bookstore or on our Web site at www.familytreemagazine.com. To subscribe to Family Tree Magazine Update, a free e-mail newsletter with helpful tips and resources for genealogists, go to http://newsletters.fwpublicat ions.com.

06 05 04 03 02   5 4 3 2 1

Library of Congress Cataloging-in-Publication Data

Melnyk, Marcia Yannizze
  The genealogist's question & answer book / Marcia Yannizze Melnyk.
    p. cm.
  Includes bibliographical references and index.
  ISBN 1-55870-590-2 (alk. paper)
    1. Genealogy—Miscellanea. 2. United States—Genealogy—Miscellanea. I. Title:
  Genealogist's question & answer book.
  CS21 .M37 2002
  929′.1—dc21
                                        2001052808
                                              CIP

Editor: Sharon DeBartolo Carmack, CG
Production editor: Brad Crawford
Production coordinator: Mark Griffin
Cover designer: Brian Roeth
Interior designer: Sandy Conopeotis Kent
Icon designer: Cindy Beckmeyer

DEDICATION

I would like to dedicate this book to the following people:

To my mother, Shirley Diana Rogers Pike, who has given me support and encouragement, and whose excitement in my search for ancestors makes it all worthwhile.
To my husband, Jim, for his continuing support; frequent "find what you can" dinners; and patience when I am frustrated, unable to write, or angry with my computer.

To my friends Dawn and Steve Rockwell for allowing me to borrow their kids, Jacob and Joseph, when I needed a reality check or a break from writing. They have made me laugh and relax— something that every author needs at one time or another during the arduous process of putting together a manuscript.

Acknowledgments

There are so many people to thank not only for all of their assistance with this book, but also for their emotional support and assistance with my research and ongoing education.

To my friend, fellow genealogist, author, and editor, Sharon DeBartolo Carmack, who has provided guidance, support, suggestions, and the occasional reminders of my deadlines. She has been there for emotional support when the words just wouldn't come and has been an example of someone who is even busier than I am yet still gets it all done. Most of all I want to thank her for setting such high standards with her writing and giving me a goal to reach for!

To my friend, teacher, and mentor, Walter Hickey, at the National Archives regional facility in Waltham, Massachusetts, for letting me pick his brain every week regarding research, records, and laws affecting federal records and for proofreading and setting me straight on my immigration and census chapters. He never ceases to amaze me with his knowledge and his willingness to share it. He even lets me volunteer at the archives!

To my fellow Betterway authors Maureen Taylor, Kathleen Hinckley, Christine Crawford-Oppenheimer, Katherine Scott Sturdevant, Sharon DeBartolo Carmack, and Emily Anne Croom, who have expanded my knowledge of genealogy and all its related subjects through their books. I consider myself fortunate to count myself among these talented women.

Last, but certainly not least, I wish to thank my family. My husband, Jim, and daughters, Diana and Kate, have provided support and encouragement in all my efforts. And to my wonderful ancestors, who have given me a reason to love history, dusty courthouses, horrendous handwriting, and microfilm machines. I am here because of them—I hope they are as proud of me as I am of them.

About the Author

Marcia Yannizze Melnyk is a professional genealogist, lecturer, and author of *The Weekend Genealogist*, *The Genealogist's Handbook for New England Research*, and *The Ancestors and Descendants of Annabelle Whitehead and Anthony Pedro*. She is the creator of the New England Historic Genealogical Society's popular "Genealogy 101" course, which she has taught for seven years. She is a member of the Genealogical Speakers Guild and the Association for Professional Genealogists and is president of the Italian Genealogical Society of America.

Icons Used in This Book

Case Study
Examples of this book's advice at work

Notes
Thoughts, ideas, and related insights

Citing Sources
Reminders and methods for documenting information

Oral History
Techniques for getting family stories

\di'fin *vb*
Definitions
Terminology and jargon explained

Printed Source
Directories, books, pamphlets, and other paper archives

For More Info
Where to turn for more in-depth coverage

Reminder
"Don't-Forget" items to keep in mind

Hidden Treasures
Family papers and home sources

Research Tip
Ways to make research more efficient

Idea Generator
Techniques and prods for further thinking

See Also
Where in this book to find related information

Important
Information and tips you can't overlook

Sources
Where to go for information, supplies, etc.

Internet Source
Where on the Web to find what you need

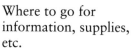 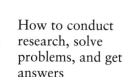
Technique
How to conduct research, solve problems, and get answers

Library/Archive Source
Repositories that might have the information you need

Timesaver
Shaving minutes and hours off the clock

Microfilm Source
Information available on microfilm

Tip
Ways to make research more efficient

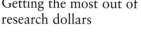
Money Saver
Getting the most out of research dollars

Warning
Stop before you make a mistake

Table of Contents At a Glance

Table of Contents

Introduction

Genealogy is a fast-growing, educational, and thought-provoking pastime, albeit sometimes a frustrating one. In the twenty-first century, individuals just starting to trace their families have more resources available to them than ever before. While this can be a benefit to the researcher, it can also be a hindrance.

One hundred years ago, in what is sometimes considered the first "genealogy boom," there were few secondary sources (published books, indexes, abstracts) available, and researchers had to use the original records wherever they might find them. This made research prohibitive unless a person lived near the court or agency that housed the records she needed because the researcher had to use original records instead of someone else's transcribed or abstracted version. Accurate copying of the information was just as critical then as it is today. The added problem researchers had in that time was that everything had to be hand copied. There were no photocopiers, only typewriters and pens—fountain pens at that.

Today we have the opposite problem: too much information from too many sources. It can be overwhelming to the beginning or intermediate researcher as to where to begin, what to believe, and what to do next. I hope this book will answer many of your questions regarding record types, documentation, computer resources, research facilities, and terminology. The questions presented here come from my nearly ten years of teaching classes and lecturing in the genealogical field. I asked librarians, lecturers/teachers, and archivists what questions genealogists ask them most frequently. Amazingly, the same questions showed up over and over again, indicating that they are not adequately addressed in many genealogy books.

As with any hobby, profession, or pastime, there is a specialized language used by seasoned researchers that is often confusing or misleading to newer family historians. We as professionals need to remember that when we talk to less experienced researchers, whether as reference librarians, instructors, or volunteers at research facilities, we should be aware that the terms we use might not be generally known. I attended a lecture entitled "Duh! I Thought You Knew That!" at one of the national genealogical conferences. The presenter pointed out many of the terms and records that we use on a regular basis that baffle new researchers. She also pointed out our responsibility to teach and share with these individuals. Whenever a librarian, instructor, or volunteer uses a term you do not understand, ask about it. There are no dumb questions, and the odds are that if you need the answer to that question, others need it as well. It also helps remind those of us in the field to slow down and make sure we don't fall into the "I thought you knew that" mentality.

I hope you will bear that responsibility in mind as you learn in this book many of the things you have wondered about and will need to know while tracing your family. I thoroughly enjoyed writing it and getting to know the many people who contributed their expertise and time. Most of all, thank you to the millions of beginning family historians who keep asking those great questions!

—Marcia Yannizze Melnyk

ONE

General Genealogical Questions

There are probably almost as many questions regarding genealogical research as there are genealogists. Even those of us who are considered professionals in the field must continually learn, ask questions, and tackle new records as part of our daily research. Sometimes people think that an "expert" or "professional" knows the answer to every question in his field of expertise. While there are some pros out there who constantly amaze me with their knowledge, most will readily admit that they do not know everything about every record or source. My definition of an expert is someone who may not know everything but knows where to find the answer.

There are so many research facilities, societies, and organizations to help researchers that it is often difficult to know where to start. There are national, state, county, and town record repositories as well as organizations and societies at all of these levels. See page 18 for a thorough breakdown.

Where do I start finding records or information on my family?
The first place to start is at home with family records, documents, and the personal knowledge of your closest relatives. Many researchers are so eager to get started that they often overlook these valuable sources until it is too late. Records get thrown away or destroyed, and relatives pass away or can become incapacitated. When older members of the family die, entire life histories disappear. Their memories may extend as far back as their great-grandparents, and every piece of information they can provide is a valuable clue in your research.

Hidden Treasures

Once you begin to gather information, from either oral histories (see chapter two), accumulation of family papers, or personal knowledge, it is important that you document all of your sources (see chapter nine) and compile the information on standard genealogical forms (see chapter twelve). You will need to verify any dates, locations, and names provided by other relatives, since memories are fallible and others can innocently pass on inaccurate information.

What other steps can I take to get started?

Another helpful strategy is to send letters or questionnaires to all of your relatives to let them know that you are researching the family. Other individuals may have some accumulated data, papers, or Bibles belonging to the family, or photo albums with ancestors' pictures, and they may be able to supply you with additional information and clues. One may even have a great-aunt's genealogical research papers from the previous century! You will never know until you ask. Be sure to send self-addressed, stamped envelopes for their replies.

How do I track down long-lost relatives?

With the many online telephone directories and other resources, you can locate not only long-lost relatives, but also others with the same surname who might turn out to be relatives. There are many Web sites that help track classmates from high school or college that you can register on or use to search for old friends or relatives. Checking with high schools or colleges on upcoming reunions can also put you back in touch with individuals, especially around notable graduation anniversaries such as the fifth, tenth, or twenty-fifth.

Several books can also assist you in tracking down long-lost relatives and friends: *Locating Lost Family Members & Friends*, by Kathleen W. Hinckley, *How to Find Almost Anyone, Anywhere*, by Norma Mott Tillman, and *How to Locate Anyone Who Is or Has Been in the Military*, by Richard S. Johnson and Debra Johnson Knox, are just a few of the many books available. There are also many organizations such as U.S. Search, <http://www.ussearch.com>, that will search for an individual for a fee. Private detectives and these professional researchers have databases at their disposal that are not accessible to the average person. Posting a query on a county or state Web page on the USGenWeb at <http://www.usgenweb.com> can also bring results. Be creative: Contact mutual friends and other relatives, or read obituaries for their family members to see if their names and residences are listed. The possibilities are limited only by your imagination.

After I have accumulated all of the family records, what records should I use next?

Most researchers will find themselves with at least several generations filled in on a pedigree chart (see chapter twelve) after reviewing all of the information provided by family members. If the information was passed on to you verbally, you should verify the dates and places for the events. You can do this by obtaining copies of birth, marriage, and death records for the individuals on the pedigree chart. To do this, you need to know where the events occurred, what the rules are governing your access to the records, and where to go or write to obtain them. In some localities you can look up the records yourself—either at the office holding the records or on microfilm in a research library—and hand-copy them or purchase copies from the office.

Many reference books (see list at end of this chapter) will help you determine where to go next based on your geographic area of interest, time period, and research needs. Each individual research project will be slightly different depending on the time period and geographic location.

How do I locate a facility that has research materials I might need?

The first thing a researcher must do is determine when and where the ancestor in question lived. Records are held at many different governmental levels including town, county, state, and even federal. Knowing which governmental level created or holds each type of record will save you many frustrating hours of futile research. Research the record before you use the record to research!

Many reference books detail where records are stored, and others explain in depth all of the individual types of records. There are books on census records (both federal and state), military records, land and probate records, church records, vital records, and others. Today's genealogists have a wealth of material available to guide them in their searches. The wise researcher takes the time to read a good beginner book about genealogical research, and then about the specific types of records she will be using. Time taken to understand the subject matter is time well spent.

Books such as *The Source, Ancestry's Red Book, The Genealogy Sourcebook*, and *The Genealogist's Companion & Sourcebook* (see list at end of chapter) make finding records a little easier.

What types of facilities will I use?

While you will certainly need to use the state, county, and town vital records offices for some of the more recent records, most records one hundred years old and older are usually available in abstracted, microfilmed, or transcribed form at state and local archives, libraries, and genealogical societies. Many records are also held by the federal government in federal archives and libraries. Determine what agency (federal, state, county, or town) has authority over the record of interest to you, and then look for the archive or library that houses those records. The following facilities house a variety of records necessary for your research.

FEDERAL AND STATE ARCHIVES
National Archives and Records Administration (NARA)

The main NARA facility is located in Washington, DC, and houses microfilm copies of records as well as many original records that have not yet been microfilmed, including Civil War pension and service records for Union soldiers. Indexes to many of the paper records stored in Washington, DC, are available at one of the sixteen regional facilities around the United States (see the list on page 6). Using the indexes in the regional centers will enable you to obtain photocopies of the original documents by mail through NARA for a fee.

Central Facility

700 Pennsylvania Ave. NW, Washington, DC 20408; (202) 501-5400.

This is the central location for all records held by NARA. Indexes to many of these records—including census, Revolutionary War and Civil War pensions,

For More Info

RESEARCH FACILITIES TO CONSIDER

- local or county libraries
- local/county historical and genealogical societies
- county and state archives
- county courthouses and records offices
- military archives
- National Archives and Records Administration facilities
- Family History Library and the Family History Centers

service records, draft registrations, naturalizations, and passenger lists—have been microfilmed and are available at most of the regional offices. The paper copies of the pension records are available only at the Washington, DC, facility.

The Sixteen Regional NARA Facilities

Each of these regional facilities has all of the U.S. federal census schedules for the entire country, as well as the Revolutionary War pension records and other microfilmed military records. Each facility holds unique records for the geographical area it serves. These records include naturalization records, federal court records, passenger lists, and other records pertaining to that region.

Southeast Region (Atlanta)

1557 St. Joseph Ave., East Point, GA 30344-2593; (404) 763-7474. Serves Alabama, Florida, Georgia, Kentucky, Mississippi, North Carolina, South Carolina, and Tennessee.

Northeast Region (Boston)

Frederick C. Murphy Federal Center, 380 Trapelo Rd., Waltham, MA 02452-6399; (781) 647-8104. Serves Connecticut, Maine, Massachusetts, New Hampshire, Rhode Island, and Vermont.

Northeast Region (Pittsfield)

10 Conte Dr., Pittsfield, MA 01201-8230; (413) 445-6885. Microfilm reading room serves primarily the Northeast, but has census, military, and other records of national scope. (Has Port of New York passenger lists.)

Northeast Region (New York City)

201 Varick St., New York, NY 10014-4811; (212) 337-1300. Serves New Jersey, New York, Puerto Rico, and the U.S. Virgin Islands.

Mid-Atlantic Region (Center City Philadelphia)

900 Market St., Philadelphia, PA 19107-4292; (215) 597-3000. Serves Delaware, Maryland, Pennsylvania, Virginia, and West Virginia.

Mid-Atlantic Region (Northeast Philadelphia)

14700 Townsend Rd., Philadelphia, PA 19154-1096; (215) 671-9027. Serves Delaware, Maryland, Pennsylvania, Virginia, and West Virginia.

Great Lakes Region (Chicago)

7358 S. Pulaski Rd., Chicago, IL 60629-5898; (773) 581-7816. Serves Illinois, Indiana, Michigan, Minnesota, Ohio, and Wisconsin.

Rocky Mountain Region (Denver)

Bldg. 48, Denver Federal Center, W. Sixth Ave., and Kipling St., P.O. Box 25307, Denver, CO 80225-0307; (303) 236-0804. Serves Colorado, Montana,

North Dakota, South Dakota, Utah, and Wyoming, and holds most New Mexico records.

Southwest Region (Fort Worth)
501 W. Felix St., Bldg. 1, Fort Worth, TX 76115-3405; (817) 334-5525; P.O. Box 6216, Fort Worth, TX 76115-0216. Serves Arkansas, Louisiana, New Mexico, Oklahoma, and Texas.

Central Plains Region (Kansas City)
2312 E. Bannister Rd., Kansas City, MO 64131-3011; (816) 926-6272. Serves Iowa, Kansas, Missouri, and Nebraska.

Pacific Region (Laguna Niguel, California)
24000 Avila Rd., First Floor, East Entrance, Laguna Niguel, CA 92677-3497; (949) 360-2641. Serves Arizona, Clark County, Nevada, and Southern Califonia.

Pacific Region (San Francisco)
1000 Commodore Dr., San Bruno, CA 94066-2350; (650) 876-9009. Serves American Samoa, Hawaii, Nevada (except for Clark County), northern California, and Trust Territory of the Pacific Islands.

Pacific Alaska Region (Seattle)
6125 Sand Point Way NE, Seattle, WA 98115-7999; (206) 526-6501. Serves Idaho, Oregon, and Washington.

Pacific Alaska Region (Anchorage)
654 W. Third Ave., Anchorage, AK 99501-2145; (907) 271-2443. Serves Alaska only.

Great Lakes Region (Dayton)
3150 Springboro Rd., Dayton, OH 45439-1883; (937) 225-2852. Serves Indiana, Michigan, and Ohio.

Central Plains Region (Lee's Summit, Missouri)
200 Space Center Dr., Lee's Summit, MO 64064-1182; (816) 478-7079. Serves New Jersey, New York, Puerto Rico, and the U.S. Virgin Islands.

Note: Each of these facilities also has a booklet describing its holdings. You can write or e-mail to request one of these informative booklets for the regional office of interest. You can also visit the NARA Web site at <http://www.nara .gov> and click on "Nationwide Facilities" then "Regional Records Services Facilities" to see what specific records a facility holds.

State Archives and Libraries
Each state maintains an archive and/or a library that houses a wide variety of records that pertain to the state and its government. These records may include

state census, state military, naturalization, and passenger records, to name just a few. Some state archives and libraries are also repositories for many types of records, both microfilmed and original, that have been deposited there for safekeeping. The holdings vary from state to state. To locate these facilities, consult reference books (see list at end of chapter) such as *Long-Distance Genealogy*, which lists the state archives and libraries throughout the United States. You can also find these facilities on the Web at Cyndi's List <http://www.cyndis list.com> or through the USGenWeb <http://www.usgenweb.com>.

NATIONAL LIBRARIES OR LIBRARIES WITH COLLECTIONS OF NATIONAL SCOPE

Library of Congress

This library has perhaps one of the most extensive collections of family histories and U.S. city directories and has copies of every book that has been copyrighted in the United States. Several books deal with the Library of Congress collections and using the facility; these include *The Center* and *The Library of Congress* (see end of chapter for more details). The Library of Congress has an online catalog available at <http://catalog.loc.gov>.

DAR Library

This library is maintained by the National Society, Daughters of the American Revolution (DAR) and contains materials of interest to individuals wishing to document their ancestry for membership in the DAR society. Family Bible transcriptions are one of the many record types the DAR has compiled over the years that are of value to the researcher. You can access its online catalog at <http://www.dar.org/library/onlinlib.html>.

Allen County Public Library

This public library in Fort Wayne, Indiana, may at first not pique your interest, but the Historical Genealogical Department has one of the largest collections of genealogical materials in North America. It holds massive collections of censuses; city directories; family histories; state, county, and town histories; passenger lists from more than seventy ports in the United States, Canada, and Germany; and one of the most complete collections of genealogical periodicals in the country. The staff is also responsible for the *Periodical Source Index* (PERSI), which indexes subjects in the periodical collection. You can access the Allen County Public Library online at <http://www.acpl.lib.in.us/>. Follow the link to its online library catalog.

Family History Library and Its Worldwide Family History Centers

The Church of Jesus Christ of Latter-day Saints' Family History Library (FHL), located in Salt Lake City, Utah, holds one of the largest collections of micro-filmed records in the world. These records are from thousands of locations worldwide and cover a wide range of time periods. Anyone may use these records free of charge in Salt Lake City and, for a small rental fee, at any of the thousands of Family History Centers around the world.

The Church of Jesus Christ of Latter-day Saints (the Church), or Mormon Church, makes these records available at the local branch libraries, called Family History Centers (FHCs). To determine the nearest FHC location, visit the FamilySearch Web site at <http://www.familysearch.org> and look up the locations around the world. Each FHC will have varying hours since all are staffed by volunteers. You can also look up film availability on the Web site by using the Family History Library Catalog. Once you have determined what films you may need, you can order them through your local FHC. The films will be sent from Salt Lake City to the local FHC, where you can look at the films and make copies. After a specified period of time, the films will be sent back to Salt Lake City, or you can renew them (again for a small fee) to stay in the local FHC for a longer period of time. This is especially helpful with films from foreign countries, as the language barrier may make searching the record more tedious and time consuming.

The FamilySearch Web site and the local Family History Centers have many useful tools for the researcher. In addition to the millions of rolls of microfilm, they also have many useful aids and resource guides.

Family History Library Catalog

The catalog, available online or in a Family History Center, lists all of the millions of rolls of microfilm, microfiche, and books available at the Family History Library in Salt Lake City. The catalog lists the films by locality or record type. While the books do not circulate, many of them have been microfilmed, and most records in microfilm format can be rented for use at your local FHC. The microfiche version of this catalog (available at the FHL and at local FHCs) can also be searched by author and subject. This is a great tool to determine what books might be in print for your specific research subject but might not be widely available. Knowing specific titles, you will search more efficiently for books.

Resource Guides

There is a published (in printed format as well as printable from the Web site) resource guide for every U.S. state and most foreign countries. The resource guides explain the records available and what microfilms the Church has in its collection. These resource guides are divided by place (U.S. states and foreign countries), title, subject matter (pensions, periodicals, probate records, immigration, etc.), and specific document type (mostly blank data extraction forms). To access these, go to the FamilySearch Web site at <http://www.familysearch .org> and click on "View maps, forms, guides, and other research helps."

Foreign Word Lists

In addition to the resource guides for foreign countries, word lists that provide you with translations for some of the words in a country's records are helpful tools. Many of these words are antiquated and do not appear in a current

Sources

For detailed information on using the Family History Library in person, online, and at one of its worldwide centers, see *Your Guide to the Family History Library*, by Paula Stuart Warren and James W. Warren.

translation dictionary. The words included in the foreign word lists are specific to those in records used by genealogists. I have found the word lists to be extremely helpful when I use foreign records.

International Genealogical Index (IGI)

This database, available online as well as in the FHCs (in CD and microfiche format), is a compilation of records (excluding death records) that have been gleaned from microfilms of vital records as well as family group sheets submitted by Church members over the years. While there is no guarantee that the data are correct, the IGI is a valuable tool for the researcher. When you find a name of interest to you on the IGI, you can determine the source of the submission. If the record was abstracted from a microfilm (perhaps of the town records), you can order the roll of film and review the record yourself. When the record comes from an individual's submission, you can order a copy of the original submission to determine what sources supplied the data. While the Church makes no attempt to prove the information provided, that information may still provide valuable clues to further research.

Ancestral File

This file is a compilation of family group sheets and pedigree files submitted by other genealogical researchers as well as Church members. It is available online as well as on CD-ROM at the local FHC. The files provide not only valuable clues but also the name and address for the submitter of any particular data. Again, the FHC makes no attempt to verify the information provided, and any individual, Church member or not, can submit his information for inclusion in the Ancestral File database.

U.S. Social Security Death Index

This database, available in the FHL and FHC facilities, is a listing of individuals whose deaths were reported to the Social Security Administration from approximately 1962 to the present. An entry usually includes the individual's name, birth date, death date, Social Security number and its state of issuance, and residence at the time of death. This database can also be accessed free at <http://www.ancestry.com> and other sites.

Scottish Old Parochial Registers (OPR)

Available only at the FHL and the local FHCs but not on the FamilySearch Web site. The OPR are abstracts of the parish registers from the Church of Scotland (Presbyterian) that groups surnames as well as given names indicating which parish register contained the information. The index covers the time period from 1500 to 1854 and the information included is given name, surname, parents or spouse, gender, christening or marriage date and place, and the source information. The actual parish registers are also available on microfilm. The OPR are a valuable resource for the pre-1855 time period when there was no civil registration in Scotland.

U.S. Military Index

Available at the FHL and FHCs but not online. This index provides a listing of servicemen who died in the Korean War (1950–53) and The Vietnam War (1954–75). The indexes provide the serviceman's birth and death dates, place of last residence, place of death, rank, and serial number. In addition to this information, the Vietnam index also includes the serviceman's religious affiliation, race, and marital status.

LIBRARIES AND GENEALOGICAL SOCIETIES

An overwhelming number of libraries and genealogical societies that may have valuable information to further your research are scattered all over the United States and the rest of the world. Information on such facilities and groups can be found in books like *The Genealogist's Address Book*, current edition, and *Ancestry's Red Book*. Locating these facilities and groups has become easier because of the Internet. The Web site for the USGenWeb <http://www.usgenweb .com> is broken down by state, then by county, and in some cases by town. Local societies and libraries that can assist you are listed, and most have links to use to learn what records the facility holds, hours of operation, and rules for use. Genealogical societies usually list the membership requirements and benefits as well as publications that they may have produced that are for sale. These genealogical societies sometimes offer newsletters that you can post queries in; free lookup service, for members, in local records or books; and lists of books pertaining to their area of research. Many actually maintain research libraries.

University libraries should not be overlooked as a source for research. State and county histories, social histories, manuscript collections, alumni lists and biographies, and other historical papers and information can be found at these facilities. If the college or university offers a degree in history, the wealth of information contained in the library can be extensive. The other nice thing is that during the academic year most of these libraries are open for the better part of each day. I once visited a college library that is open until midnight every night of the week!

Library/Archive Source

COUNTY COURTHOUSES

While every state differs as to which records are created and/or stored at the state, county, or town level, most states have at least some records at the county level. You first need to determine what level of government had jurisdiction over the specific records you need. Once you have determined who created the record, you need to determine if those records are still in the county courthouse or have been transferred to a state or county archive. Many indexes have been created over the years to make locating these records a little easier for you.

Once you determine where the original records or microfilmed copies are located, you can use the resources to further your research. Books such as *The Source, Ancestry's Red Book, The Genealogist's Address Book, The Handy*

Book for Genealogists, and *County Courthouse Book* are just a few of the many resources for locating these facilities and learning about their holdings.

VITAL RECORDS BUREAUS

Every state in the United States has, at one time or another, required local (town or county) records to be sent to the state agency governing the documentation of vital events—births, marriages, deaths—within the state. While the time periods these records cover vary greatly (with some states not requiring statewide registration until well into the twentieth century), the state agencies can be valuable to the researcher. Since the statewide records and indexes can, in most cases, provide you with information as to what town or county submitted a record, you can compare the state record with the original record once you know where the original is located. If your ancestors moved around within a state, these statewide indexes can be real time-savers since you can determine what records were reported from what locations. Always keep in mind that some states only required that records from a specific date forward be sent to the state, while other locations copied and sent all records in their possession to the state record office.

The official state record office might be called the Department of Health, the Department of Vital Records, the State Board of Health, etc. To locate the office and determine the time frame that the records cover, consult one of the many reference books that list state records repositories. *International Vital Records Handbook*, current edition, has not only the information as to where to write and what records are held, but also an official form to copy, fill in, and send to request a record. The USGenWeb at <http://www.usgenweb.com> and Cyndi's List at <http://www.cyndislist.com> on the Internet also provide addresses and information regarding vital records offices and requirements for obtaining documents.

How do I determine relationships between cousins, etc.?

Many books on genealogy provide a chart to help you determine exactly how you are related to your collateral relatives (aunts, uncles, cousins, etc.). When using these charts, you must first determine the common ancestor of the individuals. The chart on page 13 is from the book *Unpuzzling Your Past*, 4th edition, by Emily Anne Croom.

Example

My "cousin" Bud and I have a common ancestor—Orville Rounds. Orville is my great-grandfather, and he is Bud's grandfather. Using the chart, look at the left column and see that Orville's grandson (Bud) is in row number two. Going across the top of the chart, look for great-granddaughter (me); it appears in column number three. Follow column number three down to its intersection with row number two; Bud is my first cousin once removed, that is, one generation removed. Two individuals who are grandchildren of the same individual are first cousins. The charts make this determination easy and straightforward.

	1	2	3	4	5	6	7	8	9
	COMMON ANCESTOR	SON / DAU.	GRAND-SON	GREAT GRAND-SON	G-G GRAND-SON	G-G-G GRAND-SON	4G GRAND-SON	5G GRAND-SON	6G GRAND-SON	7G GRAND-SON
1	SON / DAU.	BRO / SIS.	NEPHEW / NIECE	GRAND NEPHEW	GREAT GRAND-NEPHEW	G-G GRAND-NEPHEW	G-G-G GRAND-NEPHEW	4G GRAND-NEPHEW	5G GRAND-NEPHEW	6G GRAND-NEPHEW
2	GRAND-SON	NEPHEW / NIECE	1ST COUSIN	1 COU 1 R	1 COU 2 R	1 COU 3 R	1 COU 4 R	1 COU 5 R	1 COU 6 R	1 COU 7 R
3	GREAT GRAND-SON	GRAND NEPHEW	1 COU 1 R	2ND COUSIN	2 COU 1 R	2 COU 2 R	2 COU 3 R	2 COU 4 R	2 COU 5 R	2 COU 6 R
4	G-G GRAND-SON	GREAT GRAND-NEPHEW	1 COU 2 R	2 COU 1 R	3RD COUSIN	3 COU 1 R	3 COU 2 R	3 COU 3 R	3 COU 4 R	3 COU 5 R
5	G-G-G GRAND-SON	G-G GRAND-NEPHEW	1 COU 3 R	2 COU 2 R	3 COU 1 R	4TH COUSIN	4 COU 1 R	4 COU 2 R	4 COU 3 R	4 COU 4 R
6	4G GRAND-SON	3G GRAND-NEPHEW	1 COU 4 R	2 COU 3 R	3 COU 2 R	4 COU 1 R	5TH COUSIN	5 COU 1 R	5 COU 2 R	5 COU 3 R
7	5G GRAND-SON	4G GRAND-NEPHEW	1 COU 5 R	2 COU 4 R	3 COU 3 R	4 COU 2 R	5 COU 1 R	6TH COUSIN	6 COU 1 R	6 COU 2 R
8	6G GRAND-SON	5G GRAND-NEPHEW	1 COU 6 R	2 COU 5 R	3 COU 4 R	4 COU 3 R	5 COU 2 R	6 COU 1 R	7TH COUSIN	7 COU 1 R
9	7G GRAND-SON	6G GRAND-NEPHEW	1 COU 7 R	2 COU 6 R	3 COU 5 R	4 COU 4 R	5 COU 3 R	6 COU 2 R	7 COU 1 R	8TH COUSIN

RELATIONSHIP CHART ABBREVIATIONS

BRO = brother
SIS = sister
DAU = daughter
COU = cousin
R = removed (generations removed)

G-G = great-great
GRANDSON = grandson or granddaughter
SON = son or daughter
NEPHEW = nephew or niece

The chart may be extended in either direction for identifying more distant relationships.

From Unpuzzling Your Past, *4th ed., by Emily Anne Croom. Used with permission.*

Some of the genealogical computer programs on the market will also determine these relationships for you.

Definitions

What is a pedigree chart?

This term refers to a chart where you record your direct-lineage ancestors—that is, your parents, grandparents, great-grandparents, etc.—and does not include the names or information for your siblings or those of your parents, grandparents, etc. The pedigree chart contains the names of individuals who are directly responsible for your existence. If any one of the people on your pedigree chart did not exist, neither would you!

How does the pedigree chart numbering system work?

The numbering system for pedigree charts is probably one of the most baffling subjects to beginning researchers. How the chart is numbered is determined by the number of generations (three, four, five, etc.) included on the pedigree chart you are using.

Let's use a four-generation chart as an example. Person number 1 is the root person, or the person whose pedigree is being documented. Person number 1 may be male or female, but from this point on males are always even numbers and females are odd (who decided this, anyway?). Person number 1's parents are number 2 (father) and number 3 (mother). Person number 2's parents are numbers 4 and 5. To continue the chart beyond the last column (which in this case contains eight names), number the additional charts consecutively. The first chart is chart number 1; you fill in the continuing charts beginning with person number 8 from chart number 1's right-hand column. The chart this individual continues to is chart number 2. Number the charts continuing from the remaining seven individuals in this column as charts three through nine. Notice that the males continue on an even-numbered chart and the females on an odd-numbered one.

Using this system of numbering the charts, you can determine the chart continuation numbers by simply multiplying the chart number (chart number 2, for example) by the number of individuals in the far right column (in this case, eight people) and adding 1. For chart number 2, the resulting number is 17. Begin assigning the chart continuation numbers at the bottom of the far right column and work your way up. The ancestors for chart number 2 would continue on charts 10 through 17.

One problem with most computer programs that handle a genealogical database is they fail to assign a number to the continuing chart if there is no data in the field. (Typing "unknown" in the field avoids this.) For this reason I prefer to hand-number my charts rather than let the program do it for me.

How does an Ahnentafel chart numbering system work?

Since the Ahnentafel (German for "ancestor chart or table") is a list of ancestors rather than a more extensive chart, the numbering system is a little easier. (See pages 204 and 205) You again begin with individual number 1. The parents of number 1 are number 2 (father) and number 3 (mother). To determine the

Pedigree Chart

Chart no. 1
No. 1 on this chart is the same
as no. 1 on chart no. 1

8 Abiah CARPENTER   cont. 2
B: 9 Apr 1643
P: Weymouth, Norfolk, MA
M: abt 1665
P: Pawtuxet, Providence, RI
D: 13 Sep 1729
P: Providence, Prov., RI

4 Oliver CARPENTER
B: abt 1675
P: Pawtuxet, RI ?
M:
P: RI
D: 24 Jul 1727
P: N. Kingston, Wash., RI

9 Mary REDWAY (?)   cont. 3
B: 27 May 1646
P: Rehoboth, Bristol, MA
D:
P:

2 Thomas CARPENTER
B: abt 1709
P: W. Greenwich, Kent, RI ?
M: 4 Jul 1737
P: W. Greenwick/Westerly, RI
D:
P:

10 UNKNOWN O'KILLEY (?)   cont. 4
B:
P:
M:
P:
D:
P:

5 Sarah O'KILLEY (?)
B:
P:
D:
P:

11 UNKNOWN   cont. 5
B:
P:
D:
P:

To override the numbering problem, type unknown as the persons' name.

1 Beriah CARPENTER
B: abt 1745
P: RI
M: 1773
P: RI
D: Apr 1834
P: S. Huntington, Chitt., VT [newspaper]

12 Unknown PAGE   cont. 6
B:
P:
M:
P:
D:
P:

Elizabeth "Betsey" BABCOCK
Spouse

6 John PAGE
B:
P:
M:
P:
D: bef 6 Jul 1763
P: RI

13 UNKNOWN   cont. 7
B:
P:
D:
P:

3 Elizabeth PAGE
B:
P:
D:
P:

14 UNKNOWN   cont. 8
B:
P:
M:
P:
D:
P:

7 Sarah UNKNOWN
B:
P:
D:
P:

15 UNKNOWN   cont. 9
B:
P:
D:
P:

Prepared 6 Aug 2000 by:
Marcia D. Melnyk
10 Genealogy Drive
Anytown, USA

1

number for any individual's father, simply double the individual's number. To determine the number for the mother, double the individual's number and add 1 (e.g., person number 10's father is number 20, and his mother is number 21). Remember that with the exception of person number 1, males are always even numbers and females are always odd numbers.

How do I properly store my records and documents?

Let's face it, genealogical research is a lot of work. If you are going to put so much effort into documenting your ancestors, you should also put some time into proper storage and preservation to assure that all of your hard work survives into the next generations. While many researchers use photocopies as part of their daily research, photocopies are highly acidic. Currently the photocopy process uses chemicals to adhere toner to the paper to create the copy. While you may not currently have a way to produce an acid-free photocopy, **you can protect the other papers and the copy by encapsulating it in an acid-free sheet protector.** These sheet protectors are readily available for a nominal cost at most office supply stores, and you should look for the words *archival safe* on the packaging. By inserting each photocopy in a protector, you not only protect that document but also any others that might come in contact with it in your files or binders. Sometimes I think I should buy stock in the companies that make the sheet protectors since I use so many.

Tip

Many companies produce genealogical forms for handwritten charts. Keep in mind that your permanent copies should be on acid-free paper and printed in acid-free ink. Before purchasing such forms, you should determine if both the paper and ink used to print them are acid free. You can even find permanent, acid-free rollerball pens for writing on these forms.

Where can I find such forms?

Several companies produce forms for the family historian, but one of the major ones is Everton Publishers in Logan, Utah, (800) 443-6325. Others include Ancestry in Salt Lake City, (800) 531-1790, and Genealogy Unlimited in Victoria, British Columbia, (800) 747-4877. All of these companies produce catalogs, and a simple call will put you on their mailing lists. Make sure to determine if the forms you are buying are on acid-free paper and printed with acid-free ink.

The Unpuzzling Your Past Workbook: Essential Forms and Letters for All Genealogists by Emily Anne Croom is chock-full of many types of forms that you can use, as well as examples of creative ways to use such forms. This is an excellent book to help you understand and use forms in your genealogical research. Croom also includes blank copies of these forms that you can tear out and photocopy for your own use. Once you have used a form during actual research, you will know if it suits your specific needs. If it does not, having used the form and determining what is missing or needs to be changed can help you create your own forms to fit your specific research needs. Trial and error is the best way to learn about and create forms that will make your research more efficient.

Another source for forms is your genealogical computer program. Most, if not all, programs allow you to print out both blank and completed forms from the program. You can also create many individualized forms using spreadsheet programs (such as Microsoft Excel), word processing programs (by inserting a table), or one of the many forms programs currently available. I use one that is called Cosmi Forms Maker & Filler (sometimes marketed under the Swift or Cosmi name), which is inexpensive and easy to use. It costs less than twenty dollars and creates any type of form I can think up. I use it constantly and have streamlined my research notes by creating specialized forms.

One such form is for extracting vital records from an index. In Massachusetts the vital records indexes are in five-year increments in book form. I looked at one of the index books to see how the index was set up and then created a form following that setup. The form includes a column for each of the following facts: the individual's name, the year of the record, the town submitting the record to the state, the volume number, and the page number. It also includes a column to check off when I have looked at a specific record. This makes doing the indexing so much easier since I can do all of the indexing at the library and then take my worksheet to the vital records office to look up the actual records.

*What should I do with old records that were passed
down to me from previous generations?*

If the original documents you have were printed in the last one hundred years or so, they are probably on highly acidic paper and should also be encapsulated to protect all other papers that come in contact with them. Also the oils from your hands can speed up the decay of the document itself, so encapsulating it will help preserve it for future generations. Original photographs and documents should never be framed and placed where sunlight can fade and destroy them. Make a color photograph or photocopy of the document or picture to frame, and store the original in a protective sleeve away from light, humidity, and any possible water damage. Documents and photographs should not be stored where the temperature and humidity fluctuate widely. These are precious keepsakes that must be preserved for future generations.

ENCAPSULATION VS. LAMINATION

For any of your precious photographs or documents, you want to protect them by encapsulating the item within acid-free sheet protectors. This allows the historical item to "float" freely and can easily be removed. Lamination, on the other hand, will damage photographs and documents, since it involves heating and melting a plastic coating over the item. This process is irreversible and not recommended for anything.

\di'fin\ *vb*

Definitions

Genealogists obtain their supplies from several archival supply companies including Gaylord Brothers and Light Impressions. Search for these on the Internet under the keywords "archival supplies," or ask the staff at a local library or archives what supplier they use.

WHERE TO LOOK FOR RECORDS

Records at the town level and in local libraries

- cemetery and tombstone records

- city directories

- newspapers

- school records

- tax lists

- town records

- vital records

- voter registration records

Records at the county level or county libraries

- county and state census records

- county histories

- deed (land and property records)

- naturalization records

- newspaper collections

- vital records

- wills, estates (probate records)

Records at the state level or in state archives

- archived historical documents

- immigrant and passenger manifest documents (pre-federal period)

- manuscript collections

- newspaper collections

- state census records

- state land grants

- state military records

Records at the federal level

- census (federal only)

- immigrant and passenger manifest documents

- military records (for federal military service)

- naturalization records (after INS establishment in 1922)

- pension records (federal military service)

Records in church archives or offices

- church histories, anniversary histories

- church records pertaining to the purchase of pews, donations, membership lists, etc.

- lists of clergymen who served in the parish or church

- sacrament records regarding baptisms, marriages, deaths/burials

You can also consult several great books outlining how to care for and preserve family photographs and documents, including *Preserving Your Family Photographs* by Maureen A. Taylor. Many photographers are now restoring and duplicating treasured family photographs, and they can create a negative for a picture so additional copies can be made and shared with other relatives. Distributing copies of these one-of-a-kind photographs is one way of assuring that at least some photographs will survive for future generations to enjoy. If there is only one copy, it is at risk of destruction from many sources including fire, flood, neglect, and misplacement. It is also important to purchase a pen or marker that is safe for photographs and then label every picture you can. Note who is in the photo, the date (or approximate date) the photo was taken, and the occasion (if known) so that future generations won't inherit boxes of unidentified photographs. These usually end up in garage sales and flea markets and are then lost to the family's future generations.

Sources

FURTHER READING

American Genealogical Research at the DAR, Washington, D.C., by Eric G. Grundset and Stephen B. Rhodes. Washington, D.C.: DAR, 1997.

Ancestry's Red Book: American State, County & Town Sources, rev. ed., by Alice Eichholz. Salt Lake City, Utah: Ancestry, Inc., 1992.

The Center: A Guide to Genealogical Research in the National Capital Area, by Christina K. Schaefer. Baltimore, Md.: Genealogical Publishing Co., Inc., 1996.

A Complement to Genealogies in the Library of Congress: A Bibliography, by Marion J. Kaminkow. Supplements for 1972–1976 and 1976–1986. Baltimore, Md.: Magna Carta Book Co., 1972, 1977, 1987–2001.

County Courthouse Book, 3d ed., by Elizabeth Petty Bentley. Baltimore, Md.: Genealogical Publishing Co., Inc., 1995.

Genealogies in the Library of Congress: A Bibliography, by Marion J. Kaminkow. Baltimore, Md.: Magna Carta Book Co., 1981.

The Genealogist's Address Book, 4th ed., by Elizabeth Petty Bentley. Baltimore, Md.: Genealogical Publishing Co., Inc., 1998.

The Genealogist's Companion & Sourcebook, by Emily Anne Croom. Cincinnati, Ohio: Betterway Books, 1994.

The Genealogy Sourcebook, by Sharon DeBartolo Carmack. Los Angeles, Calif.: Lowell House, 1997.

Guide to Genealogical Research in the National Archives of the United States, 3d ed. Washington, D.C.: National Archives Trust Fund Board, 2000.

The Handy Book for Genealogists, 9th ed., by George B. Everton. Logan, Utah: Everton Publishers, 1999.

How to Find Almost Anyone, Anywhere, by Norma Mott Tillman. Nashville, Tenn.: Rutledge Hill Press, 1998.

How to Locate Anyone Who Is or Has Been in the Military, 8th ed., by Richard S. Johnson and Debra Johnson Knox. Spartanburg, S.C.: Military Information Enterprises, 1999.

International Vital Records Handbook, 4th ed., by Thomas Jay Kemp. Baltimore, Md.: Genealogical Publishing Co., Inc., 2000.

The Library of Congress: A Guide to Genealogical and Historical Research, by James C. Neagles. Salt Lake City, Utah: Ancestry, Inc., 1996.

Locating Lost Family Members & Friends, by Kathleen W. Hinckley. Cincinnati, Ohio: Betterway Books, 1999.

Long-Distance Genealogy, by Christine Crawford-Oppenheimer. Cincinnati, Ohio: Betterway Books, 2000.

The Researcher's Guide to American Genealogy, 3d ed., by Val D. Greenwood. Baltimore, Md.: Genealogical Publishing Co., Inc., 2000.

The Source: A Guidebook of American Genealogy, rev. ed. Salt Lake City, Utah: Ancestry, Inc., 1997.

United States Local Histories in the Library of Congress: A Bibliography, by Marion J. Kaminkow. Baltimore, Md.: Magna Carta Book Co., 1975.

Unpuzzling Your Past, 4th ed., by Emily Anne Croom. Cincinnati, Ohio: Betterway Books, 2001.

The Unpuzzling Your Past Workbook: Essential Forms and Letters for All Genealogists, by Emily Anne Croom. Cincinnati, Ohio: Betterway Books, 1996.

TWO

Oral History and Home Sources

ORAL HISTORY—the recording (written, audio, or video) of memories and facts pertaining to an earlier era or place.

Recording an oral history can be a special way to preserve someone's thoughts, ideas, and memories of another time and place. It is also a unique way to hold on to your relatives, to hear their voices and laughter many years from now. We would all like to avoid the realization that our loved ones will not always be with us. We have the opportunity to do what our parents and grandparents could not do. With the invention of audio and video recorders we can preserve for our children and future generations that which made our relatives the special individuals that they are. **Do not wait for an "opportune time."** Illness and death happen without notice and can wipe out an entire generation of memories in an instant. We can also record and save our own memories.

Important

How can I begin to record my memories for future generations?

Whether you are twenty-nine or ninety-two, you can record or write your memories down for future generations. Think of how excited you would be to find a recording of or journal written by your great-grandmother. Preserving memories is a very old tradition. Some cultures hand down information in the form of family stories recounting ancestors' lives. This type of oral tradition is especially important in some cultures such as Native Americans and African Americans and may be the only family information available to the descendant.

To begin recording your own memories can be difficult. Where do you start? I have found many published books that can help you overcome the initial uncertainty of where to start. Many of these books are referred to as grandparent's books, books for your daughters or sons, and books intended for general family information. These books usually have pages with questions that prompt the memory retrieval process and get you to start writing down your thoughts. You will be amazed at the many wonderful memories that will come back to you once you begin. It is important to record some of the negative memories as well, since these events shaped your life and the lives of your family. Perhaps your memories of the death of a sibling, your grandparents, or parents will provide future generations with insight into the cultural and social aspects of a different time. Everything you write will be important to those reading it years from now. You need not worry about correct punctuation, grammar, or even chronological order. If you had the opportunity to read something written by your great-great-grandparents, would you be critical of misspelled words or no punctuation? Probably not.

What if I cannot find such books to record my thoughts?

Many people over the years have avidly kept journals or diaries. Both of my daughters have kept journals since their preschool years, something that a preschool teacher initiated. Each child would draw a picture and then narrate the story about that picture to the teacher, who would write it down. As my daughters became more proficient at writing words, they began to record part and then all of their stories by themselves. This simple school exercise has steered them on a path to write daily or weekly in a journal. To encourage this habit, I always purchase blank books for them to write in. One Christmas I gave each of my daughters a standard-size leather journal cover (to easily obtain refills), so now all of their journals are the same size. By encouraging children to write at an early age, you may ensure that future generations will have a record of family memories like you had hoped for.

Idea Generator

Another way to begin writing down your memories is to perform the following exercise. If time travel were possible and someone told you that you could go back in time to talk to any one of your ancestors for just one hour, what would you ask them? Remember you have only one hour. Make a list of the questions you would want to ask. Pick your questions carefully because once the hour is up, you are done. Put that list aside and then several days later review it. Perhaps you will need to adjust the list, adding questions that you think of later. Once you are comfortable with your list of questions, answer them as they pertain to you. Remember that what you want to know about your ancestors your descendants will want to know about you. Your life, thoughts, and dreams will mean as much to your descendants when you are gone as your ancestors' mean to you.

What types of things are children most interested in?

Over the years I have presented many talks about oral histories to audiences varying from elementary school students to junior and senior high school students to senior citizens. I have noticed a similarity in the types of information they find interesting. Stories about how their parents or grandparents met and courted seem to hold the most attention. Younger children want to hear about their parents. Their grandparents can tell them about their parents as young children. What mischief did they get into? Did they have a favorite toy? What activities did they participate in? Funny stories will delight the children more than anything else and make the interaction a memorable one. It also helps to encourage the awareness that even their parents were children once, a concept usually hard for young children to grasp.

What steps should I take to prepare for an interview?

The previous exercise of listing questions you would like to ask is always a good idea. Having a specific direction in your questioning will help you stay on track and focused. While having a list of questions will get you started, always allow for new thoughts and queries that will pop up as stories are related to you. Since it is impossible to predict the direction the interview will take, be flexible as well as focused. Lists of questions pertaining to various subjects appear later in this chapter. You can use these questions as a starting point, and many more will come to mind as you read the lists. If specific questions are most important to you, put them on a separate sheet of paper as well as on your master list. Another method I have used is to create just one list and use a colored highlighter to mark the most important questions. This helps keep me focused on the questions I want to ask before time runs out.

What steps should I take for conducting the actual interview?

When conducting an interview, make sure that both you and your subject are comfortable. One on one, with no distractions or other people listening, is the only way to conduct the interview. Let your subject know that he has the right to answer or not answer any question asked. If he does not feel comfortable answering a question, *do not* push; simply move on to the next one. Let him know that you appreciate and value his time.

Some people are nervous about being recorded (either audio or especially video). Remember that recorders were not as commonplace to older family members as they are to you. Assure the subject that she can stop the interview whenever she wishes simply by asking. Don't place the recording device where the interviewee can see it as she is speaking. This might make her nervous or inhibit her. Be sure, however, it is near enough to catch both your voice and hers. Since most people will look directly at you when responding to a question, having the recording device off to the side and out of the direct line of vision is a good idea. **Have extra tapes at hand, and try to make the transition from one tape to another as seamless as possible.** Know the time length of each tape and keep an eye on the time so you can change the tape before it runs out. I use the stopwatch feature on my watch as my guide. I can easily tell at a glance how much time has elapsed and conduct the interview accordingly. I often offer the interviewee a glass of water or ask if she needs to stand up and stretch when we are nearing the end of the recording time. This is a good time to swap tapes without distracting the person being interviewed or placing too much focus on the recording device.

Tip

Are there specific questions that I should start with?

The order of your questions can assist you in placing your subject at ease. By beginning with very simple, fact-based questions that are nonthreatening and easy to answer, you can get your subject past that initial uneasiness. By the time you come to the more difficult, thought-provoking questions both you and your subject should be at ease with each other and may be even oblivious to being recorded. Always pause after asking a question; give your subject time to think and respond. Be careful not to interrupt the interviewee in the middle of his answer as it will break his train of thought. Be patient if he is slow to answer, as he may be pondering how he wishes to word something or recalling a memory that will relate to the question. Keep in mind that in most cases, the interview can be done in multiple sittings. This gives the person time to reflect on some of your questions, which may spark memories and reflections that will enhance the next interview.

What should I do if the interviewee does not want to answer a question?

Never press an issue that makes the person uncomfortable. Drop the question and perhaps ask it again in a reworded form later in the session. I have found that many times the interviewee will state that he doesn't know the answer to a specific question. I pass over that question, marking it on my list with a colored highlighter, and then interject the reworded question if a related topic comes up later. Many times this strategy is successful.

Example

When interviewing my elderly aunt, I asked if she knew anything about siblings of her father (my grandfather). She stated that he had at least two sisters and one brother but she did not know their names. Later in the interview she mentioned something about her aunt living in the apartment above them in Italy. When I asked her who that aunt was, she stated that it was my grandfather's sister. I simply asked what the aunt's name was. My aunt replied that she did not know her aunt's name but that she was married to a Belcastro. When I then asked if she knew Mr. Belcastro's first name she said, "No, but his daughter, Rose Napoli, lives on Lake Street in Arlington." I then contacted Rose, and she provided all of the missing names of siblings, their spouses, and many of the grandchildren who all lived in the Arlington area. By approaching the question from another angle, I was successful in ultimately obtaining the desired information.

How do I begin?

To begin your session, always state the date and subject's name, as well as your name and where you are. For example, "This is November 15, 2001, and I am in Rowley, Massachusetts, talking with Mrs. Shirley Diana Rogers Yannizze, my mother. My name is Marcia Diane Yannizze Melnyk." Then move right on to the first question. Keep the pace slow, giving your subject time to reflect on the questions, and most of all be a good listener! Have fun!

What can I do if a face-to-face interview is not possible?

Interviews can be conducted over the phone or by mail. Make a list of questions for your interview subject to review. Ask her to tape-record her answers or even write down the memories and answers for you. Keep in mind that handwritten letters may be few and far between for future generations due to the Internet and e-mail. Having something written in her handwriting can be pre-

Technique

cious. In some cases you may have to provide the subject with a small, easy-to-use tape recorder or ask a relative living near the subject to do the actual interview using your questions. Do not let distance stop you from gathering this information.

What tools can I use to enhance the interview?

Many books currently on the market include historical photos of towns or areas and can evoke wonderful memories. These collections of photographs from the early years of the twentieth century are thought provoking; giving one to your interview subject before your interview can jump-start the process. Family photographs can also be utilized in the same way. Photographs of people and events will trigger memories of family times, both happy and sad.

You should also go through any family papers in advance to develop additional questions. Asking in your interview about items like photo albums, letters, newspaper clippings, certificates (graduation, religious, marriage, divorce, etc.), baby books, family Bibles, naturalization papers, passports, fraternity membership papers, military records, diaries, and cemetery papers can lead to valuable information. This is an opportunity to ask questions about why particular documents were saved and what their significance is.

One important tool to enhance an interview is social histories. Try to read about the time and place your subject lived. Understanding the social aspects of the lives of your research subjects will better prepare you for the interview. Know what local and world events were taking place around them. This will help you put the subjects in a social context and provide many additional questions. Remember to ask questions about how these events affected the individuals and their families.

What if I have no living older relatives to interview?

If all of your older relatives have passed away or are unable, through illness or loss of memory, to be interviewed, look to their peers as possible subjects. **Are some of their lifelong friends still living as senior members of the community?** Local senior citizens groups can be a treasure trove of information. You may not be able to get your ancestor's personal information, but you certainly can get a feeling for what the world was like for your ancestor. Social histories again can be a valuable tool to learn what daily life was like for any of our ancestors. If you can contact an individual who lived in the same town at the same time as your ancestor, information is available for you to get a pretty good idea of your ancestor's life.

Idea Generator

Diaries can also provide valuable information. Diaries of not just your ancestors but others living in the same locale and time can be insightful. If your ancestors were some of the many who traveled west in the large westward migration, read one of the many books and diaries about the journey as seen through the eyes of others who endured it. Several books have also been transcribed from diaries of women who suffered through the migration. They will give you an appreciation of your ancestors' struggles and obstacles and make you realize how strong and resilient they were.

If your ancestor was a New England farmer in the 1800s, look for diaries of other farmers in that geographic area to create a picture of the time. You may be surprised and find your ancestor's name mentioned in the diary of another local farmer or merchant. These are the gold mines that are hidden in social histories and diaries.

Another tool that can help you understand the time frame of your subject's life is newspaper collections. Each U.S. state has an official repository for newspapers, so you can read both local and national news from any given period in history. Look at the news items, the social columns, the advertising, and the editorials. You will come to understand and appreciate the time frame more clearly and be better able to adapt your questions to pertinent subject matter. I have a very vivid memory of where I was, exactly what I was doing, and how I felt when I heard the news of President Kennedy's assassination. This world event affected my life as a young teenager in the 1960s. Such events are valuable tools to take your subject back to another time and place. One memory will lead to another and open up new avenues of discussion.

How do I locate such materials as diaries and social histories?

Diaries are held by many libraries and historical societies. They are usually part of a manuscript collection since they are one-of-a-kind, handwritten records of individuals. **Try searching the *National Union Catalog of Manuscript Collections* (NUCMC) for manuscript collections.** Some of the reference books, like *Ancestry's Red Book*, list manuscript collections in each state. Begin with the state where your ancestor resided. Look not only for your individual but also for her contemporaries.

Library/Archive Source

College and university libraries are wonderful places to look for social histories. Michigan State University (in East Lansing, Michigan) has an online catalog with nearly 250 entries under the oral history topic alone. You can usually find libraries listed on the USGenWeb state pages. Most colleges and universities have their catalogs online where you can use them to search for books about your subject of interest. Once you have the title and author of a book you are interested in, try to locate it through a library in your area. For books not available locally, check out the interlibrary loan policies at your public and college libraries.

Bringing Your Family History to Life Through Social History by Katherine Scott Sturdevant is an excellent place to learn about social history and its benefits to the family history researcher. Sturdevant offers many tips and insights into using historical documents and oral histories as a basis for a more complete family history. Always keep in mind that our ancestors were not just dates and places, but living, feeling human beings who were shaped by their world and then shaped ours.

How can I document family heirlooms for future generations?

This question comes up more often today as we become more aware of archival preservation of artifacts and documents. All framed and unframed photographs should be labeled on the back using an acid-free pen especially designed for photos. It is better not to write directly on the photo but to attach a label (acid free, please) naming the time and place the picture was taken, the subjects, and their relationship to the family. If the picture is framed, make sure all materials used in the framing are acid free as well. Then place an acid-free label on the back of the frame, not on the photo itself.

For artifacts such as jewelry and furniture, take several close-up pictures of the article from several different angles. Then record, either on a label or paper, to whom the article originally belonged, how it came into your possession, and any stories that are associated with it. If you have several items, you can create a photo album of all of the historical items. It is also wise to make multiple copies of the photos and information (for genealogical and insurance purposes) and store one copy out of your home (safe deposit box, a relative's house, etc.) so that should a fire or flood occur, you will still have the documentation. Another tip is to attach a label or tag to each item to identify it as an heirloom. Unfortunately many personal items and furniture are sold at yard sales and estate auctions long before the surviving relatives find out about the pieces' history. By labeling each individual piece, you may be able to prevent this from happening, like it almost happened to me.

I attended an auction at a cousin's home several years ago and was overwhelmed with all of the items being auctioned. As I helped him get items ready for bid, I came across a marble box that was partially covered in maroon velvet. Inside were old coins, military medals, and political memorabilia. I asked him if he wanted to sell the contents along with the box or as separate items. He replied that the box had been his grandmother's jewelry box. Further conversation revealed that the grandmother he was referring to was my great-grandmother! Needless to say, I kept the jewelry box. He didn't think anyone in the family would be interested in it, so he was going to sell it. He had completely forgotten that his grandmother was an ancestor to my family as well as his. I shudder to think of all of the other items that may have been sold at this or other auctions that may have had family significance.

What can I do with all of the old photographs that are not labeled or are glued into photo albums?

Several books on the market address proper care and preservation of photographs, such as Maureen A. Taylor's *Preserving Your Family Photographs*. Many of these books also address the problems that may occur with photographs that have become stuck in albums that are not acid free.

Many of our grandparents used albums with black construction paper pages. Some albums have the pictures tucked into photo corners, while other photos are glued onto the pages. **Do not try to remove the glued ones from these albums as you may destroy the picture or damage it beyond repair.** One thing you can do to slow the deterioration of the attached photos is to insert a sheet of acid-free tissue paper between the pages of the book. This prevents the photos and black paper from touching photos on the opposite page. Preventing further damage to the photographs is important.

Posing similar problems are the albums with "magnetic" pages that were

Warning

popular in the second half of the 1900s. The glue on the pages, while initially allowing the pictures to be removed, becomes permanent over time. I have several albums that are about twenty-five years old that refuse to release any pictures. The first thing I did was remove the clear plastic coverings on the photos since this plastic is most likely acidic. I then placed acid-free paper between the pages (the glue around the pictures had no stickiness left). Until I find some way to remove the photos without damaging them, I can at least slow down the deterioration. When the pages were still tacky around the pictures, I slipped the pages into acid-free sheet protectors. Sheets of acid-free Mylar for larger albums are available through archival supply companies.

Can I do anything about torn, faded, or otherwise damaged photographs?
Many companies specialize in restoring old photographs. While they can at times seem to work miracles, they cannot replace lost portions of the picture. Photos that are very faded can, in most cases, be restored to good contrast without damaging the original copy. I have had several photographs enhanced and the contrast increased with wonderful results. Many computer programs can "repair" photos after they are scanned into the computer. Never do anything to an original photo that cannot be undone!

If you have the only copy of a family photograph and it is in good condition, you can have a photographer take a photo of it and make a negative. You can then have copies made from the negative to share with other relatives or to frame for display. Be careful to avoid hanging original photographs where the sun can fade or damage them. I have even had color laser photocopies made of some old photographs and framed the copies. You cannot tell the difference between the original and a copy once it is framed. Even old photographs that are black and white have some sepia tones, or an aged patina to them. A color copy will look as old as the original.

Oral History

THE INTERVIEW
Here are some questions to get you started.

Family Facts
- How old are you? When and where were you born?
- How many brothers and sisters are in your family? What is their order of birth?
- What is your first memory as a child? Why do you think that memory is so vivid?
- What type of child were you (happy, shy, outgoing, etc.)?

Parents and Grandparents
- Who were your parents/grandparents? What did you call them?
- What was your mother's maiden name? What were her parents' names?
- What was your mother's given name? Did she have a nickname? What was it? Do you know the story behind how she got the nickname?

- Did your mother have brothers and sisters? How many? What were their names?
- Do you know who the first person in your family was to come to the United States?
- What country did that person emigrate from? When? Did that person say why he or she emigrated?
- Do you remember that person? What was he like? What were his occupations?
- Do you recall what that person looked like (tall, short, thin, heavyset, bald, bearded, etc.)?
- Does anything in particular stand out about that person (sense of humor, etc.)?
- Do you know when or how your parents/grandparents met? Did they ever talk about their courtship or the early days of their marriage?
- Where did they live? Did they move around much? If so, why (e.g., work, military, etc.)?
- What do you recall about the house that you grew up in?
- What did it look like? Were there many other families on the street?
- What schools did you attend? What special friends did you have in school?
- Were there any special places in the neighborhood (corner store, playground, etc.)?
- Did your mother work outside of the home? Doing what? If she didn't work outside the home, what kind of things did she do?
- Did she like to cook? Was she a good cook? What were your favorite foods that she made? Why?
- Did she ever let you help with the chores? Which ones did you particularly like to help with? Why? Which ones did you dislike? Why?
- What family traditions do you remember from your childhood? Have they continued on to your generation?
- Have any family heirlooms or property been handed down from your grandparents to the current generation? If so, what? To whom did they first belong? Did they hold some special meaning or significance in your grandparents' lives? To whom will they be passed? Is there a special significance to this choice (first son, youngest daughter, etc.)?

Teenage Fads, Dress Styles, and Slang
- What were some of the fads or styles among young people when you were a teenager?
- What were some of the slang expressions used?
- How did the girls and boys wear their hair?
- What were the fads or trends that your parents did not like or approve of?
- Who were your best friends?
- What movies and music were popular?
- What was an average day like when you were a teenager?
- When did you start your first job? What was it like?

Personal Opinions and Outlook

- What everyday conveniences do we have today that were not available when you were a child/young adult/newlywed?
- What were the major issues and worries that faced you then? How were they different from today's problems?
- What world or local event affected your life the most?
- Were you as aware of the events in the world as we are today?
- What were your major concerns for the future?
- What dreams or expectations for the future did you have? Which came to pass and which did not?
- What events in your life, if any, caused you to change your expectations or goals? Were the changes for the better, or do you have regrets?
- Do you think it was easier then or is easier now to reach the goals we set for ourselves? Why?
- If you could go back in time knowing what you know now, what, if anything, would you change? Why?
- What was the most rewarding time or event in your life? Why?
- What single piece of advice would you like to give me?

Try to make the interview enjoyable time spent together. *Always* remember to thank your subject when you are through. If need be, you can schedule another interview date at this time.

Sources

FURTHER READING

Bringing Your Family History to Life Through Social History, by Katherine Scott Sturdevant. Cincinnati, Ohio: Betterway Books, 2000.

Family Tales, Family Wisdom, by Robert U. Akeret, Ed.D. Paperback. New York: Henry Holt & Co., 1991. Hardcover. New York: William Morrow & Co., Inc., 1991.

A Genealogist's Guide to Discovering Your Female Ancestors, by Sharon DeBartolo Carmack. Cincinnati, Ohio: Betterway Books, 1998.

How to Outlive Your Lifetime, by Timothy W. Polk. Sunnyvale, Calif.: Family Life International, 1994.

Keeping Family Secrets Alive, 2d ed., by Vera Rosenbluth. Port Roberts, Wash.: Hartley & Marks Pub., 1997.

Once Upon a Memory, by Jean Alessi and Jan Miller. White Hall, Va.: Betterway Publications, 1987.

Our Grandmothers: Loving Portraits by 74 Granddaughters, edited by Linda Sunshine. New York: Welcome Enterprises, Inc., 1998.

Preserving Your Family Photographs, by Maureen A. Taylor. Cincinnati, Ohio: Betterway Books, 2001.

Recording Your Family History, by William Fletcher. New York: Dodd, Mead & Co., 1986.

The Tape-Recorded Interview, by Edward D. Ives. Knoxville: University of Tennessee Press, 1995.

Touching Tomorrow, by Mary LoVerde. New York: Fireside Books, 2000.

Transcribing and Editing Oral History, by Willa K. Baum. Nashville, Tenn.: AltaMira Press, 1991.

Uncovering Your Ancestry Through Family Photographs, by Maureen A. Taylor. Cincinnati, Ohio: Betterway Books, 2000.

Unlocking the Secrets of Your Childhood Memories, by Dr. Kevin Leman and Randy Carlson. Nashville, Tenn.: Thomas Nelson Publishers, 1982.

Women's Diaries of the Westward Journey, by Lillian Schlissel. New York: Schocken Books, Inc., 1992.

Writing the Family Narrative, by Lawrence P. Gouldrup, Ph.D. Salt Lake City, Utah: Ancestry, Inc., 1987.

THREE

Vital Records and Church Records

Reminder

V ital records and church records are perhaps the most sought-after genealogical records. These records are considered more reliable than many
other types of records. While they may be the "official" records of
events, their accuracy depends on the care and attention of the original authors.
Was the information provided by the person involved in the event truthful and
accurate? Did the clerk understand the presented information and interpret
what he or she heard correctly? Was the event recorded when it happened or
later as an afterthought? These are all questions that must be asked, even though
you may not be able to answer them, before taking any vital record or church
record as "gospel."

**Many states did not require birth, marriage, or death records to be registered
until well into the late 1800s and in some cases not until the mid 1900s.** While some
New England states kept town and county records as early as the 1600s, some
key states such as New York did not begin until 1847. Even though the law
requiring school districts to keep a record of births, marriages, and deaths was
passed in 1847, compliance was not the general rule. That law was repealed in
1853 and another law took its place in 1880, with compliance being less than
100 percent in the earliest years.

I use the New York example to show how these vital records, considered
standard practice today, were not viewed in the same manner before the twentieth century. Just because a state passed a law requiring the records to be kept
does not mean the towns or counties complied. Because of this, the records for
the earliest years after institution of a law are far from complete. This applies
even more so for church records. Remember the First Amendment and separating church and state?

Church records are more complete for certain religions and nearly nonexis-
tent for others. In the earliest days of the English Colonies and the United States,
many clergymen were itinerant ministers. This term applies when a clergyman
traveled across a geographic area tending to the religious needs of members of

his faith. He may or may not have had a home church but would travel from one small-town church to another. Because of this type of ministry, the records did not have one set place for storage. Many of the clergymen considered the records to be their own personal possessions and took them when they moved away or headed west. These records often turn up in manuscript collections or personal papers thousands of miles away from where they were originally recorded. While the records may be more complete for some denominations, finding them can be difficult.

VITAL RECORDS

What constitutes a vital record?

A record of birth, marriage, death, etc., created by a division of government to maintain documentation of the population under its jurisdiction is referred to as a *vital record*. Some of these records are considered primary sources, while others are secondary at best. These records can be recorded at any level of government, depending on the state and local laws governing them. Some states began recording these events at the town level, while territories and states that joined the union later might have recorded them at the county level.

What kind of record constitutes a primary source?

A primary (meaning first) source is any record that is created at or close to the time of the event being documented. It is the first record of the event. Usually, one or more of the parties involved provides information for the record. However, just because it is considered a primary source does not ensure its accuracy.

\di'fin\ *vb*

Definitions

Example

Consider marriage records and death records. A marriage record or license is created when the two parties concerned answer questions pertaining to themselves. This type of record is quite reliable since the information is firsthand from the people it is about. Although a death record can be a primary source record, obviously the person the information pertains to did not provide it.

When you use town or county vital records books, it is sometimes difficult to determine if the records are actually primary sources. Regardless, these may be the closest you will get to the first record of an event. To illustrate, if a state or county did not require a civil marriage license, the church record might be the primary source. If a state or county license was required before the marriage actually took place, the county/town record of the marriage license would be the primary source record.

How do I know if the record I am looking at is
the original or primary source record?

You must first determine when the records were created in that state or territory. Are you looking at records that are in chronological order, or are records from many different time periods mixed together? Why was the record created? What level of government had control over those records originally? In many areas the church or local government produced the original record to keep track of its population. These records were, in most cases, then required to be sent to the next level of government. This can mean that the original record is at the town or church level, with copies being sent to the county or state level. Vital records in the United States are for the most part town, county, or state records and therefore are not under federal government jurisdiction.

Are vital records ever federal records or documents?

My first response to this question would be no, the federal government's NARA does not have vital records. As with most "rules," this one certainly has exceptions, but they are few and do not pertain to the majority of researchers. The only times the federal government or one of its official authorities creates or maintains such a record are

1. When an American citizen living overseas gives birth to a child, marries, or dies, the record might be recorded with the U.S. Consulate in that country. Additional research and consultation with a NARA employee are necessary to determine if such a record was created and where it might be found.

2. When such an event occurs on a U.S. military base on foreign soil (rarely before the 1900s), the record might be considered a federal document. Even if the marriage, birth, or death occurs overseas and is recorded at the military base, it may also be recorded in the official town of residence of the parties concerned. Always look for the town, county, or state record first. Records generated on military bases are official records of the branch of the military (e.g., army, navy, marines, etc.) whose jurisdiction the base is under.

Besides some birth dates listed in some federal censuses, in some obscure occasions, a vital record may be included in federal government records. For the average genealogical researcher, looking to the federal government or the NARA for such information will prove futile.

When might I find a vital record included in a federal record?

The answer to this question can be misleading, so I will preface the answer by stressing that the inclusion of a vital record within a federal document does not mean that the included record is a federal document. Such a record is included only as information or proof of the event for the purposes of the federal document. For instance, Civil War and Revolutionary War pension applications often include original or transcribed marriage records. A veteran's widow who applied for a pension based on her husband's military service had to prove that she was actually married to the veteran in question. I have seen Bible pages, samplers, church marriage certificates, and the like included in pension files as documentation of marriage.

Always keep in mind the original purpose of the record. Records of individuals within the United States fall into two basic categories: (1) that individual's interaction with the state, county, or local government and (2) the interaction of that individual with the federal government. Determining what level of government controlled or governed the record at the time it was created is imperative to research success.

How do I locate an original vital record?

Research the state or territory history to determine where the original records were created in any given time period. The laws changed many times in almost every jurisdiction. Many genealogical reference books (see reading list at the end of the chapter) list the dates of inception for vital record maintenance in any given geographic area. Research the record before you try to use the record for research. In many cases statewide or countywide indexes were created to make access to the local records easier for government purposes. Use these indexes only to determine who submitted the original record and to do a cursory review of the record. In many cases the state or county record has enough information to rule the record in or out for your research, especially when you are dealing with a common surname.

WHERE TO FIND VITAL RECORDS

Vital records (birth, marriage, death records) may be found at the local (town), county, and state levels. Most state recordings of such records are submitted by other jurisdictions (church, town, etc.) and so can be used to determine the location of the original, or primary, record. See Kemp's *International Vital Records Handbook* and *Where to Write for Vital Records*, available online at <http://www.cdc.gov/nchs/howto/w2w/w2welcom.htm> from the National Center for Health Statistics.

Sources

If the town or county record lists a church that submitted the record to them, look at that church record as well. In such cases you may have two "original records" to obtain. The local government office may have the original marriage license, while the church may have the actual marriage record.

Most birth records before the 1920s were submitted to the town or county clerks by doctors, midwives, or even family members. In most cases the record will not indicate who reported the birth or death, and the information is only as good as the person presenting it—but that record is all you have. Many doctors and midwives kept small books that they recorded all such records in, and these books would actually be the primary, or first, record. The odds that you will find such a book are extremely slim, but these books do occasionally show up as diaries or in manuscript collections.

Why do I need to go to the original record if the state or county one lists all of the information I need?

Many of these records were kept at the local level first, and laws requiring them to be reported to the county or state were passed much later. Some laws required that all records created from a specific date forward be sent, while others required that transcriptions of all previous records be sent as well. Compliance to these new laws was uneven to say the least. In many cases a specific form was provided to town or county clerks to record and send information to the new governing office. The original may have had more information than there was space for on the form, but the clerks only filled in what was required. Many original records also have information that was never transcribed onto the newer form. In some cases the clerks left spaces blank, even though the information appeared on the original record. Since in most cases there was no follow-up or review of these transcriptions, much information was lost in the transfer. Some records were not sent at all! Also keep in mind that any time a record is transcribed, there is a chance for errors. Clerks and other officials are human, and mistakes are inevitable when copying. **The more generations away from the original record you are, the less reliable the information is.** I have seen the husband's name listed on a transcription as being the father of a woman and the father's name listed as the husband. This mistake was cleared up by looking at the original record rather than depending on the copy that was sent to another jurisdiction.

Reminder

What other problems should I watch out for?

Transcription errors might include miscopied or transposed dates, names, or other information copied from the wrong line in the record book to simple misinterpretation of handwritten names. One important skill to develop as a researcher is skepticism. Never take a record at face value, and question every aspect of it. This will result in more accurate data for your family history.

One example of a problem I ran into took me several years to sort out, because I took the vital record entry as I found it without questioning the data. The town of Clarendon reported to the state of Vermont the birth records for the children of James and Urana (Cole) Rounds. Having used the state copy, I mistakenly assumed that the children were born in Clarendon, Vermont, between 1763 and about 1790. At that time it did not occur to me that 1763 was pretty early for Vermont records. (Vermont was not a state until 1791, and settlement was not widespread until around the 1780s.) Years later, when working on records in western Massachusetts and Gloucester, Rhode Island, I came across the birth record for one of James and Urana Rounds' children. Comparing it to the Clarendon record, I found them to be exactly the same. What was going on? I decided to look at the original entry in the Clarendon records rather than rely on the state copy. Imagine my surprise when I discovered that the Clarendon records clearly stated that some of the births took place in Scituate and Gloucester, Rhode Island—a minor detail left off the state copies! Further research turned up several entries for one of the children in towns from Rhode Island, Connecticut, Massachusetts, New York, and Vermont. It appeared that James or Urana Rounds recorded the births of their children in every town they resided in (or even passed through), and most of the clerks neglected to note that the birth did not take place there. At least the Clarendon clerk was on top of things!

One more thing to do (isn't there always something else?) is to **determine**

when the town, county or state was created or became a separate entity. If a town separated from a larger town or county, the records created before the division will most likely be in the parent town or county. Separating the records physically would have been impossibly complicated at best, so only records created after the separation should be in the new town or county. Knowing what governmental division had control of the record *at the time it was created* will save you many frustrating hours of futile research. (See page 145.)

Do state or county laws affect the reliability of the vital records?

Absolutely! Many states have laws that affect the records for adopted children and illegitimate children born to a married woman. Many states create a new birth certificate showing the adopted parents as the birth parents when an adoption is finalized. This can mislead a researcher who has no knowledge of the adoption. During certain time periods, if a married woman gave birth to a child that she knew was not her husband's child, the husband's name still had to be put on the birth certificate as the father.

I encountered all of this when researching birth parents for an adoptee who was born in 1947 in Massachusetts. I found her original birth record as well as the falsified one showing her adoptive parents as the birth parents. The "true" certificate listed the birth mother and her husband as the parents. Upon further research and conversations with the birth mother, I learned that her husband was not and could not have been the biological father. Her husband had been overseas in the military for almost two years when the child was born. Massachusetts law at that time required that if a child was born to a married woman her husband's name must go on the certificate. The birth mother said that she informed the hospital and doctor that her husband was not the biological father but was told that it didn't matter; legally he was considered the biological parent. This misinformation would not have been discovered if the birth mother had been deceased at the time of the research.

Are there any clues to when a certificate might be a falsified one?

When you look at a certificate, compare it to others of the same time period. Knowing what information should be included will help you determine when information is missing. In the previous example, where the falsified birth certificate listed adoptive parents as biological parents, the thing that made the certificate stand out was the absence of a doctor's name on the certificate. The original certificate contained the delivering doctor as part of the information. This may not be true for all certificates, but if something is missing you should ask questions. When was the date of recording on the certificate? False birth certificates are usually recorded and filed at the time of the adoption, although they can be backdated, so they may be filed out of sequential date order. Also look at the name of the recording clerk. Is it the same person as other records for the same time period and location? Again, when you look at every aspect of the document, things might stand out as odd. You should always follow up on any suspect information.

I actually proved one certificate to be a falsified one by using the recording

Research Tip

Signs a birth record might
be falsified:
No doctor's name
Filing date is much later
than the birth date (usually
two years or more)

clerk's name as the research tool. When I found the birth certificate (early-1920s time frame), I suspected it might not be the original since there was no doctor or midwife named on the certificate. Upon looking at other certificates before and after it, I found that the doctors or midwives were not named on every certificate, so I could not base my assumption of adoption on that. I then focused on the recording clerk. The town reports listing town employees, services, etc., showed that the clerk who signed the certificate was sworn into office three years after the birth. Another clerk was listed for the year prior to and for two years after the birth date. Further research in the court and probate files confirmed that the individual whose birth I was researching was in fact adopted.

Many times when you look for a certificate, you may be told that it is "restricted" for one reason or another. In some states if a birth certificate does not list a father, the child was stillborn, the child was subsequently adopted, or a correction was made to any of the information, the record may be classified as restricted. These restrictions vary from state to state and for different time periods.

How can I be sure a certificate is true and accurate?

In most cases you cannot with all certainty say a certificate is completely accurate. With all the examples that I have provided throughout this book, you should realize that a certificate is only as accurate as the memories and communication of the parties involved, the laws governing the creation of the record, and the accuracy of the clerk recording it.

Sometimes information may have been intentionally falsified by the involved parties. I once had found a baptismal certificate that listed the baptismal date as 18 October 1909. When recording it into the family database, I discovered a discrepancy with that date: I had a birth certificate listing the birth date as 16 October 1910. Since the baptismal certificate was an original, signed by the priest and both of the child's sponsors, I knew something was wrong. Could two children of the same name have been born a year apart? Unlikely, but certainly not impossible. Research, again in the town reports, showed the birth of Joseph Anthony Burkhart in 1909. The parents, listed as Anthony Burkhart and Emily Foley, were the telling part. The mother was the same person listed on both the 1909 and 1910 records, but the father was not! The 1910 birth certificate listed the parents as William Bond and Emily Foley. Further research showed that the mother had married William Bond in 1910. But how did Joseph get a certificate listing his birth with William and Emily as parents?

Research was inconclusive as to whether William Bond had adopted the child as his own, so I went back to the 1910 entry in the birth registers. It was noted that this was a "late filing," meaning that it was recorded after the fact. In this case the record was entered into the books in 1942! It seems that Joseph A. Burkhart went to the town hall to get a copy of his birth record for the purpose of entering the military. Apparently Joseph's mother told him he was born in 1910. No record was found, so the mother went to the town hall and signed a sworn affidavit that Joseph was born in October 1910 and that William Bond was his father. Even Joseph's tombstone lists his date of birth as 1910. Again I state that information is only as accurate as the memory or communication of the person providing it!

If the father's name does not appear on a birth record, how can I find out who he was?

Short of DNA testing, you have no surefire way to determine this fact. Since most of the records genealogists work with are for nonliving people, you may never discover this piece of the puzzle. But this does not mean that you shouldn't try. **While the individual's birth record might not list the father, check the individual's marriage record and death record.** If a person listed his father on these records, you might at least be able to narrow down the possibilities. In one case of an illegitimate birth, no father's name was on the certificate. The child's marriage license listed her father, so I looked for information on him at the time period of her birth. He is also listed in the census and other records from the time period of her birth. The marriage record for the woman's parents shows that they were married after her birth. At the time of the woman's birth, the man was in the process of divorcing his first wife. Does this prove the parentage? No, it only shows the possibility that he is the father.

Research Tip

In another case, I found a birth record for an illegitimate child, Daniel Pope, that listed only the mother's name, Amelia Pope; the child was given her surname. Dead end? Not in this case: I found a death record for Daniel Pope, who died when he was four months old, listing Amelia Pope and Daniel Freed as his parents. Since most certificates do not indicate whether the parents were married to each other, further research was needed. I located Daniel Freed and Amelia Freed in the next census; they are listed as married and having two other children. Their marriage record shows that the marriage took place the month after the birth of Daniel.

You must always look for additional ways to obtain or verify every piece of information—being in print once does not make it accurate. Someone once said to me, "You can know who the birth mother is, but the biological father is only known by what the mother tells you." Just because something appears on an official document doesn't make it a fact.

Why do many marriage records not show the parents of the couple?

You should consider it a bonus when they do! In most state and local jurisdictions, the marriage was recorded in a legal document as a binding contract between two people. It was not created for genealogists, just as a legal document. The identities of the parents of the parties were irrelevant to the purpose of the record. The same marriage record found in a church, especially for some religions, may contain this information since the family unit was crucial to the church. Remember that these documents were created for purposes other than our research. You must also consider that the state or local record may be the marriage *license* record and a marriage might not have even taken place! If the marriage record was recorded by a clergyman (some records list this fact) or a justice of the peace, it would be considered a marriage record since in most cases clergymen could only perform marriages, not issue licenses. In some states and time frames, licenses were not required, but the churches might have had rules governing posting of the banns, or notices of the intent to marry. Some religions do not recognize a civil marriage, only those performed by their own clergy. Because of this, you might find two separate records of the event.

How can I be sure I am getting all the information that appears on the original when I have to request it by mail?

One of the most important things to keep in mind is the type of forms that are currently in use by town or county clerks. Most agencies have a short form or a long form of any record, and the price usually varies for each. The short form has a small amount of information included and is usually intended to be kept in a wallet or used for identification. **Genealogical researchers should always ask for a photocopy of the original, if possible, or of the long form of the record.** Be careful when evaluating the data on a long form, as additional information on the original may not have been transcribed to the form. Consider how you fill out an application or form: You fill in the answers to the questions asked. You do not provide any information that is not specifically asked for. Since most clerks use a standard form to transcribe data, they will not include information that is not asked for on the form. I have never encountered a clerk who added information that wasn't requested.

Important

The importance of this fact hit home when I obtained a death record for an individual and the information did not fit what I already knew about her. Her parents' names, her age, her place of birth, etc., were different than those I had from other records. I looked on this "official" certified death record I obtained to see who the informant—the person providing the information to the clerk—was. This piece of information was not on the transcribed form but was in the original; it answered my questions. The informant was a rooming house resident who only knew the deceased casually, not a family member. I would not expect her to have known all of the personal information about the deceased, but I wish she wouldn't have guessed instead of saying, "I don't know."

Always keep in mind that any transcription can contain not only errors but also misinterpretation of the original handwritten document. How careful was the clerk in interpreting the handwriting? I have had documents where closer inspection or comparison to the original showed that the clerk copied information from two adjacent records and mixed the information together. This occurs most often when the original is in a ledger book and a record is written across the page, all on one or two lines. When the clerk reads past the bound spine of the book, it is easy to jump up or down a line. Some books are not even lined or have lines that are not numbered to assure accuracy. A clerk might not necessarily be as careful as you would be.

I have also received certified record copies that include misinterpreted information or typographical errors, errors that completely threw off my research. One such record was a death record from the state of Maine. The subject of the record was listed with a birthplace of Canton, Maine, when in fact she was born in Canton, Massachusetts. The clerk transcribing the record in Maine was familiar with the Canton in that state and inadvertently changed the state! Since the acceptable or common state abbreviations have changed many times, this is a common error. Many old records use the *Ms.* abbreviation for *Massachusetts* and a present-day clerk might misinterpret it as *Mississippi*. If something doesn't look right about the record, question it. Do so in a polite and nonaccusatory manner as most people do not like to have their mistakes brought to light. (The clerk in the Maine case tried to make me pay for a corrected certificate!) Imagine the confusion that might have been caused by a certified copy of a record with incorrect information.

Another reason to try to obtain a photocopy of the original record is that in many cases side margin notes pertaining to the record may have been made. Such notes often occur in church and some civil records. Italian civil records of birth contain many side notes indicating when and to whom the individual later married. Since a clerk looked up the birth record at the time of the marriage, the clerk jotted the marriage information down on the birth record.

Tip

The same practice occurs in some church records, such as Catholic marriage records. Birth records might have margin notes regarding marriage or death dates of the individual—you never know until you look. Clerks rarely copy these side margin notes when transcribing a birth record; after all, you did request a birth record, not the marriage record. Sometimes we have to be creative when we ask for information. When I write to a facility to get a copy of a record, I specify that I would also like any side margin notes or data not included on the standard form. Many times this has resulted in my receiving a photocopy, even after a clerk has told me they don't photocopy records. I can only assume that the clerk decided it was easier to photocopy the record than to try to type all the information on the form. The reason doesn't matter since my goal was to get all of the available information.

How can I compare the transcribed record to the original without going to the repository?

One of the many wonderful inventions that helps genealogists is the microfilm machine. Many of the original books of earlier vital records have been microfilmed and may be available to you through the Family History Centers, microfilm rental companies, state or county libraries, or interlibrary loan. I always try these options before I spend money on a certificate filled in by a clerk. I decided a long time ago that a certified form is not always worth the price of the paper it is printed on. I would rather pay for rental of a microfilm of the original records, where I might find other relatives as well, than someone else's interpretation of the document. I often think about wallpapering my bathroom with all the useless certificates I accumulated early in my research!

If microfilm copies of the originals are not available, you can use statewide indexes to make a list of all the documents you need to look at—then you have an excuse to travel to look at them. After all, purchasing certificates might cost as much as going to the repository—it works for me! You can also ask someone living in that area to obtain the information for you. Another family genealogist will probably be more careful than a clerk who has no personal interest in your search.

How do I locate such an individual?

To locate individuals to do research in distant states and counties, look online at the USGenWeb site (see chapter seven) and find the page for your county of research interest. Many of the sites linked to USGenWeb list people willing to look up information for you, free or for a small fee. You can also post on the county or town site a query asking for an interested researcher who might be able to get the record for you. Since I live near an NARA facility, I have often exchanged research in the National Archives for research of vital records in other states. **Barter for your research!** This is a great way for other researchers to get information in exchange for helping you out. I have also found that researchers who live in an area often have a good working relationship with the clerks and can get a photocopy rather than a transcription of a record. Because the clerks may be a researcher's relatives or friends, she might have an easier time than you in getting the information.

Money Saver

Another way to find researchers in another geographic area is to join a genealogical or historical society there. By doing this, I have met many wonderful individuals who have provided me with an abundance of knowledge as well as assistance with my research. Who knows an area, its history, and its records better than someone who lives there and uses the records on a regular basis? Historical or genealogical librarians are valuable people to talk to and get to know. Many of the records located in local and county libraries or historical societies are in one-of-a-kind manuscript form, and the librarians know the contents better than anyone else. If a librarian or society member helps you without asking for payment and you cannot swap research time, consider making a donation to the library or society to show your appreciation for her efforts.

CHURCH RECORDS

What information is usually contained in a church record?

This varies as much as religious denominations do. Depending on the beliefs of the religious group, the records can contain a great deal of family information or very little. For some religions you may find the names and marriage dates of the parents of a bride and groom, witnesses' names and relationships, baptismal information, birth information, etc. These records can also vary by locality and the church's ethnic identity, if any.

An example is records of an Italian Catholic church. Many of the records, especially from the late nineteenth and early twentieth centuries, list the actual place of birth within the foreign country and may contain copies of birth or baptism records received from the parish church in that locality. Consider these finds a bonus, since the priest probably spelled the surname and village of origin correctly! Since some religions include birth and baptism certificates as part of the marriage record, these church records can be a gold mine. Don't expect the same amount of information for your ancestor if the church and clergy were not of the same ethnicity as your ancestor. Many of these U.S. ethnic churches continued well into the twentieth century. Two such ethnic churches in Ipswich, Massachusetts, were not phased out until the 1990s, when the Polish and French Catholic churches in the United States were combined with another local church.

For some religions, such as Quaker, the records may contain a list of all persons who were in attendance at the ceremony and information pertaining to the family's previous residence. The Quaker records also contain certificates of removal for couples wishing to move from one area to another. These records can help you track the family's migration. If a member of the Quaker community married outside of the faith, the marriage record may not be included with the church records, but the record of disownment of that individual, perhaps with the date and place of marriage, might be. Records of women's and men's meetings can also be valuable to you along with the actual marriage records.

Specific religions also have unique records pertaining to their sacraments and beliefs. In the Catholic church you may find in addition to the birth, marriage, and death records those of first communion, confirmation, dispensations, etc. Some religions also have a form of census records to keep track of the members of any given parish. Tithing lists are one such record; these list all of the members who paid their required donation to the church and can provide many clues as to what families were members at any given time. Again, if you understand the religion, you have a better chance of obtaining all the possible records from them. Some records are kept in the church, a local church archive, or a national facility specific to that religion. Check genealogical reference books for the locations of these facilities.

How do I locate church records if the church no longer exists?

First check one of the many resource books that list different types of records state by state to determine if there is a repository for that denomination in a state. Books such as *Ancestry's Red Book* cover church records under each individual state listing.

Specific religious denominations may have records in archives in several states or just one national repository. The Catholic church has at least one diocesan jurisdiction in each of the fifty states as well as one each for the District of Columbia and military services. It has in some states as many as a dozen or even more (California has twelve; Texas, fourteen). The book *U.S. Catholic Sources*, compiled by Virginia Humling (Ancestry, Inc., 1995), lists all of these diocesan offices and their addresses and phone numbers, what areas they cover, what records or collections they hold, and specific instructions about obtaining records. Many records are still in the area churches; records from closed or defunct churches are most likely stored in a church archives or another church of the denomination.

The Work Projects Administration (WPA) created some inventories of church records from the early 1900s. Check your state archives to determine if the records for that state were inventoried and where the lists are currently kept. **Remember that the WPA lists include *not* names of individuals or records for them** but only an index or inventory to what churches had records and where the records were at the time of the inventory.

Reminder

How can I determine what might be included in church or synagogue records?
If you are dealing with a religion that is unfamiliar to you, it is imperative that you learn something about that religion or denomination. Every religion has unique records, and different denominations within the same religion will also have a variety of record types. One example of these differences is under the umbrella of Protestant records. Protestant religions include Baptist, Congregationalist, Episcopal, Lutheran, Methodist, Pentecostal, and Presbyterian, to name just a few major denominations. Variations also occur within the records of any one of these Protestant denominations.

Learning about the religion and denomination will provide you with many clues as to what records you might find, what they might contain, and where to locate them. There are books available that outline records pertaining to a specific religion. Avotaynu (155 North Washington Avenue, Bergenfield, New Jersey 07621; <http://www.avotaynu.com>) is a publishing company that produces many genealogies and research aids for Jewish research. Many ethnic genealogical societies will also be able to assist you with religious records, especially the idiosyncrasies of that ethnicity's approach to record keeping.

A wonderful article detailing religious records was published in the March/April 2001 issue (volume 19, number 2) of *Ancestry* magazine. The article covered Catholic, Jewish, Latter-day Saints, Protestant, and Quaker records. Each subarticle was written by a noted genealogical researcher knowledgeable in that particular religion. The article provides a good overview of what to expect. If you do your homework before tackling these records, you will be more successful (and a lot less stressed!). The article also contains a useful listing of other books or articles about each religion.

What other church sources might be valuable?
Some churches or religions may publish quarterly newsletters, periodicals, or church histories that can provide you with additional data. County and town histories often list the clergymen who were associated with a particular church. Histories written at key anniversary dates, such as the church's one hundreth anniversary, may also list members, deacons, clergymen, and any number of other details of interest.

Some churches and religions keep a census of sorts, consisting of member lists, perhaps tithing lists, or lists that were used to assess church fees or taxes or determine the number of communicants within a given parish or diocese.

Notes

If the church maintained a school, seminary, hospital, or cemetery, you might find additional records to search. Church-affiliated cemeteries may have listings of burials and information on such matters as family plots and plot ownership that will prove valuable to your research. Determine whether these facilities existed by looking at city directories or newspapers for the time period of interest. I located an orphanage for Italian children in Boston by reading a 1920 newspaper ad asking for donations. This particular orphanage was established in response to the influenza epidemic that decimated the population in the Italian North End of Boston in 1918 and 1919. This orphanage is still in operation today and accepts troubled children of all races and creeds. Their records may be valuable to the descendants of those early-1900s orphans.

Can I obtain copies of these records without going to the church or church archives?

While the staff or volunteers at some archives and churches will assist you in obtaining such records, they will not as a rule do the research for you. I have had good luck visiting churches and searching (sometimes with the assistance of a clerk) for records of interest. If you would like to visit the church or archives, you should first determine whether they have the records for the time period you are interested in. Many churches only hold recent records, while older records are sometimes stored at an archive, a religious library, or elsewhere.

Whenever you plan a visit to a facility, be it a church or an archive, you should make an appointment. This common courtesy might make the difference between research success and failure. Verify that the facility houses records for the time period in question and the records are open to you as a researcher. Also ask about the most convenient time to visit the facility. Sometimes people just show up at a church and find that, while the church does have the records, either they are not available at that location or no one is there to help. Ask about the ability to make photocopies of any pertinent records. Some records, usually more recent ones, are considered confidential, and you may be refused access to them.

I had a wonderful experience when I visited the church where my great-great-grandparents were married in Canada. I was visiting the area with my husband, who was there on business, and I wanted to search the church's records for my family. I had called ahead and was given a day and time to come to the rectory. There, I was greeted warmly and had the clerk all to myself. She not only photocopied records for me but translated the ones documented in French as well. She was excited to make copies of my family research pertaining to that church and had even arranged a tour of the church for me. I got to sit in the pews and stand at the altar in the church of my ancestors.

The church had been established in 1689, so in 1989 when I was there they were celebrating their 300th anniversary. I was given books on the history of the church and the early families, and I even had lunch with the parish priest! My ancestors were in the records all the way back to the establishment of the church, and I came away with a wonderful appreciation for the church and its records. I have since made several visits to the church, and always called in advance.

FURTHER READING

Ancestry's Red Book: American State, County & Town Sources, rev. ed., edited by Alice Eichholz, Ph.D. Salt Lake City, Utah: Ancestry, Inc., 1992.
The Genealogist's Handbook for New England Research, 4th ed., by Marcia D. Melnyk. Boston, Mass.: New England Historic Genealogical Society, 1999.

Sources

How to Get the Most out of Death Certificates, by Carolyn Earle Billingsley and Desmond Walls Allen. Conway, Ark.: Research Associates, 1991.

International Vital Records Handbook, 4th ed., by Thomas Jay Kemp. Baltimore, Md.: Genealogical Publishing Co., Inc., 2000.

Locating Lost Family Members & Friends, by Kathleen W. Hinckley. Cincinnati, Ohio: Betterway Books, 1999.

The Source: A Guidebook of American Genealogy, rev. ed., edited by Loretto Dennis Szucs and Sandra Hargreaves Luebking. Salt Lake City, Utah: Ancestry, Inc., 1997.

U.S. Catholic Sources: A Diocesan Research Guide, compiled by Virginia Humling. Salt Lake City, Utah: Ancestry, Inc., 1999.

Where to Write for Vital Records: Births, Deaths, Marriages, and Divorces, by National Center for Health Statistics. Washington, D.C.: NCHS, updated regularly. (Note: To obtain the latest edition, write to Superintendent of Documents, Government Printing Office, Washington, D.C., or go online at <http://www.cdc.gov/nchs/howto/w2w/w2welcom.htm>.)

FOUR

Census Records

CENSUS: an official counting or listing of people, goods, or industries within a certain governmental or political jurisdiction for determining such things as seats in the House of Representatives, taxes, membership, financial aid, etc.

The many different types of census schedules include federal, state, county, territorial, and church. Any listing of names, physical counting, and/or recording of individuals for any purpose can be considered a census of sorts.

Consider present-day telephone books and their precursor, the city directory. A telephone book is a listing of people within a specific jurisdiction who have telephones registered in their names. A city directory is a listing of adults living within a specific geographic area who are employed, enrolled in college or otherwise designated for inclusion within the list.

A membership roster is another type of census. This might be a list of church members, school attendees, or employees. A census gives you for a moment or period of time a snapshot that was created for governmental, business, or organizational use.

If you think of any list of individuals as a sort of "census," you will see the magnitude of records that are available to you. Understanding a particular census or list, the original purpose of the enumeration, and how it was used will make your research in those records much more productive.

When most researchers refer to the census, they are most likely referring to the U.S. federal census, which has been taken every ten years, beginning in 1790. The counting and listing of individuals by geographic location provides the federal government with the statistics they need to apportion the seats in the House of Representatives, thereby providing fair and equal representation to the population as well as fair distribution of federal money. In the early censuses, however, individ-

Idea Generator

uals were not created equal. Women, children, slaves, Indians, and some other groups were not permitted to vote and were not available for military service, so it was not deemed necessary to break them down into age brackets. This helps explain why early census records listed "free white males" in several age categories, while women were grouped together as one group under "free white females" regardless of their age. Blacks, both free and slaves, and Indians were not always counted as individuals and were counted without regard to their age or sex.

The most often used census is indeed the U.S. federal census. It is a valuable tool for the family history researcher as well as the academic scholar. It can provide a picture of a specific geographic area at a specific time, thus providing an overview of a social culture from an earlier time. Many different statistics can be gleaned from the lists to determine the ethnic makeup, occupations, monetary wealth, migration patterns, etc., in an area. This social history is important for understanding the lives of our ancestors.

The first federal enumeration of the population took place in 1790. The official day of the census was the first Monday in August. All census takers were instructed to list the household as it was on that date, disregarding any births or deaths that had occurred after that date, regardless of when the census taker actually visited the household. Any person living in that household on the given day was to be counted, according to the rules for that specific census, by the census taker. Some census takers followed the date rule to the letter, while others were not so careful. All information could be obtained from any member of that household, a neighbor, or whoever would provide it, so it is not always accurate, and the census records do not indicate who the informant was.

The census taker made several copies of his lists, and all the errors common in transcription could have occurred in the duplicate copies. **Keep all of this in mind when using the census; use every listed item as a clue, but not as a hard fact.** Viewing a family over their lifetimes—looking in many census records—will give you a truer picture of the family members, their ages, etc., than looking at just one.

Important

A number of schedules, or types of censuses, make up the U.S. federal census records. They are

- **population schedule:** list containing the names of heads of households (1790 to 1840) with a tally of all other individuals living in the household by age bracket; list of names of all individuals living within one family unit (1850 to 1930) indicating sex, age, place of birth, etc.
- **agricultural schedule:** list, including values, of goods produced, livestock owned, size and status of property, etc., on American farms. Available for 1850, 1860, 1870, and 1880.
- **industry and manufacturing schedule:** lists of industries manufacturing goods; include business statistics, production amounts and values, number of employees, type of power used in the manufacturing, etc. Available for 1820, 1850, 1860, and 1870.
- **mortality schedule:** list of persons who died within the year immediately before the official census date in 1850, 1860, 1870, and 1880, including information regarding age, sex, occupation, place of birth, cause of death, etc.

- **veteran's and widow's schedule:** lists of Union veterans, or their widows, who served in the Civil War and were still living in 1890. Give residence, age, service rendered, injuries or illnesses, and whether they received a pension. The 1840 census lists Revolutionary War pensioners or their widows on page two of each enumeration.
- **slave schedule:** lists the name of the slave owner and the number of slaves held. Shows slaves' sex and age only (does not include the name of the slave). Available for 1850 and 1860.
- **defective, dependent, and delinquent schedule:** lists of persons who were insane, blind, deaf, homeless, or generally dependent on the government or others for services. Taken in 1880 only.
- **social statistics schedule:** may include real estate values, government services (libraries, poor houses, etc.) as well average wages for some occupations within that geographic area. Taken in 1850 through 1880.

Some states or territories also took censuses, either on their own or with federal assistance. Each of these different schedules was meant to gather information pertaining to federal or local government needs. Using all available census records for your ancestors will give you a broad picture of your family and their lifetimes. If you understand that a census is merely the counting or recording of specific information as it applies to a specific population, you will utilize the records more productively.

How often and on what dates were the federal censuses taken?

The federal censuses have been taken every ten years and began in 1790 (1791 for Vermont). Due to privacy laws, only census records seventy-two years old and older are available for open research. **Each census has an "official date" that should always be noted**. The census taker, regardless of what day he recorded the information, was to list the occupants of any given household on the official date of that year's census. The official dates for each year up to 1930 are listed below:

Notes

1790	2 August (first Monday in August)
1800	4 August (first Monday in August)
1810	6 August (first Monday in August)
1820	7 August (first Monday in August)
1830 through 1880	1 June
1890	2 June (first Monday in June)
1900	1 June
1910	15 April
1920	1 January
1930	1 April

This means that a child born on 20 April 1910 should *not* be listed in the 1910 census. The enumerator was to list only those people living in the household on 15 April 1910. In some cases it took months for the enumerator to visit every household and record the data. In the early census years (1790 to 1840), the enumerators were allowed anywhere from nine to eighteen months to complete their task. In 1850, 1860, and 1870, they were allowed only five months to record all of the residents; from 1880 to 1920, only one month. Some enumerators followed the rules strictly, while others did not.

Example
The 1920 federal census for San Francisco, California, lists seventeen individuals, both male and female, with the notation that they are "bodies in the morgue" (E.D. #258; page 2 B; lines 84–100). Census taker Josephine M. Ertola visited the morgue on Merchant Street on 4 January and 5 January 1920, according to her notations. Since those "bodies" were alive on 1 January 1920, the official census date, she followed the rules and counted them in her enumeration.

Why is the U.S. federal census such an important record for genealogists and historians?
The U.S. federal censuses, begun in 1790 (except for Vermont, which was taken in 1791) and still taken every ten years, are snapshots of entire neighborhoods or towns on a given day in history. By looking at every census during a person's lifetime, you can have an overview of that person's entire life. The census records from 1790 through 1840 list only the head of the household and then a count of individuals by age and sex. While not every member of the household is listed in detail, you can still get a good picture of the household and its makeup. Federal census records through the 1920 census are available to researchers. (The 1930 census records will become available in April 2002 after the seventy-two-year privacy period has passed.) If you have an ancestor who was born before 1850 and died after 1920, you should be able to find him in a total of seven population census lists. If he was involved in agriculture (1850–1880 only) or manufacturing (information regarding the business, not the individuals employed there), you have additional schedules to review. If he was a soldier in the Civil War, you might also be able to find him in the 1890 veteran's and widow's schedule, making the total eight or more.

Where can the schedules for the federal census records be obtained?
All surviving population schedules of the decennial census records have been microfilmed and are available in all of the National Archives and Records Administration regional facilities as well as in Washington, DC, at the National Archives. Additionally, the Family History Library has copies of all the U.S. federal census records and many of the state censuses. Many local libraries and historical societies have in their collections copies of some federal census records for their geographic area.

Additionally, census images now appear on the Internet. Genealogy.com <http://www.genealogy.com> and Ancestry.com <http://www.ancestry.com> now have databases containing the actual images of the U.S. federal census records available online. These subscription databases can be a real convenience for researchers without easy access to the microfilm copies. CDs with images of specific census years and locations are also being produced.

U.S. AND SPECIAL CENSUS RECORDS—AVAILABILITY OF POPULATION SCHEDULES

State	1790	1800	1810	1820	1830	1840	1850	1860	1870	1880	1890	1900	1910	1920	1930
Alabama	—	—	—	NO	YES	YES	YES	YES	YES	YES	F	YES	YES	YES	YES
Alaska	—	—	—	—	—	—	—	—	—	—	NO	YES	YES	YES	YES
Arizona	—	—	—	—	—	—	YES	YES	YES	YES	NO	YES	YES	YES	YES
Arkansas	—	—	—	NO	YES	YES	YES	YES	YES	YES	NO	YES	YES	YES	YES
California	—	—	—	—	—	—	YES	YES	YES	YES	NO	YES	YES	YES	YES
Colorado	—	—	—	—	—	—	—	YES	YES	YES	NO	YES	YES	YES	YES
Connecticut	YES	YES	YES	YES	YES	YES	YES	YES	YES	YES	NO	YES	YES	YES	YES
Delaware	NO	YES	YES	YES	YES	YES	YES	YES	YES	YES	NO	YES	YES	YES	YES
Dist. of Col.	YES	YES	NO	YES	YES	YES	YES	YES	YES	YES	F V	YES	YES	YES	YES
Florida	—	—	—	—	YES	YES	YES	YES	YES	YES	NO	YES	YES	YES	YES
Georgia	NO	NO	NO	YES	YES	YES	YES	YES	YES	YES	F	YES	YES	YES	YES
Hawaii	—	—	—	—	—	—	—	—	—	—	—	YES	YES	YES	YES
Idaho	—	—	—	—	—	—	—	—	YES	YES	NO	YES	YES	YES	YES
Illinois	—	—	YES	YES	YES	YES	YES	YES	YES	YES	F	YES	YES	YES	YES
Indiana	—	NO	NO	YES	YES	YES	YES	YES	YES	YES	NO	YES	YES	YES	YES
Iowa	—	—	—	—	—	YES	YES	YES	YES	YES	NO	YES	YES	YES	YES
Kansas	—	—	—	—	—	—	—	YES	YES	YES	NO	YES	YES	YES	YES
Kentucky	NO	NO	YES	YES	YES	YES	YES	YES	YES	YES	V	YES	YES	YES	YES
Louisiana	—	—	YES	YES	YES	YES	YES	YES	YES	YES	V	YES	YES	YES	YES
Maine	YES	YES	YES	YES	YES	YES	YES	YES	YES	YES	V	YES	YES	YES	YES
Maryland	YES	YES	YES	YES	YES	YES	YES	YES	YES	YES	V	YES	YES	YES	YES
Massachusetts	YES	YES	YES	YES	YES	YES	YES	YES	YES	YES	V	YES	YES	YES	YES
Michigan	—	—	NO	YES	YES	YES	YES	YES	YES	YES	V	YES	YES	YES	YES
Minnesota	—	—	—	—	—	—	YES	YES	YES	YES	I V	YES	YES	YES	YES
Mississippi	—	NO	NO	YES	YES	YES	YES	YES	YES	YES	V	YES	YES	YES	YES
Missouri	—	—	NO	NO	YES	YES	YES	YES	YES	YES	V	YES	YES	YES	YES
Montana	—	—	—	—	—	—	—	YES	YES	YES	V	YES	YES	YES	YES
Nebraska	—	—	—	—	—	—	—	YES	YES	YES	V	YES	YES	YES	YES
Nevada	—	—	—	—	—	—	—	YES	YES	YES	V	YES	YES	YES	YES
New Hampshire	YES	YES	YES	YES	YES	YES	YES	YES	YES	YES	V	YES	YES	YES	YES
New Jersey	NO	NO	NO	NO	YES	YES	YES	YES	YES	YES	F V	YES	YES	YES	YES
New Mexico	—	—	—	—	—	—	YES	YES	YES	YES	V	YES	YES	YES	YES

continued

U.S. AND SPECIAL CENSUS RECORDS—AVAILABILITY OF POPULATION SCHEDULES, CONTINUED																
State	1790	1800	1810	1820	1830	1840	1850	1860	1870	1880	1890	1900	1910	1920	1930
New York	YES	YES	YES	YES	YES	YES	YES	YES	YES	YES	F V	YES	YES	YES	YES
North Carolina	YES	YES	YES	YES	YES	YES	YES	YES	YES	YES	F V	YES	YES	YES	YES
North Dakota	—	—	—	—	—	—	—	—	—	—	V	YES	YES	YES	YES
Ohio	—	NO	NO	YES	YES	YES	YES	YES	YES	YES	F V	YES	YES	YES	YES
Oklahoma	—	—	—	—	—	—	—	YES	NO	I	V	YES	YES	YES	YES
Oregon	—	—	—	—	—	—	YES	YES	YES	YES	V	YES	YES	YES	YES
Pennsylvania	YES	YES	YES	YES	YES	YES	YES	YES	YES	YES	V	YES	YES	YES	YES
Puerto Rico	—	—	—	—	—	—	—	—	—	—	—	—	YES	YES	YES
Rhode Island	YES	YES	YES	YES	YES	YES	YES	YES	YES	YES	V	YES	YES	YES	YES
South Carolina	YES	YES	YES	YES	YES	YES	YES	YES	YES	YES	F V	YES	YES	YES	YES
South Dakota	—	—	—	—	—	—	—	—	—	—	V	YES	YES	YES	YES
Tennessee	NO	NO	F	YES	YES	YES	YES	YES	YES	YES	V	YES	YES	YES	YES
Texas	—	—	—	—	—	—	YES	YES	YES	YES	F V	YES	YES	YES	YES
Utah	—	—	—	—	—	—	YES	YES	YES	YES	V	YES	YES	YES	YES
Vermont	YES	YES	YES	YES	YES	YES	YES	YES	YES	YES	V	YES	YES	YES	YES
Virginia	NO	NO	YES	YES	YES	YES	YES	YES	YES	YES	V	YES	YES	YES	YES
Washington	—	—	—	—	—	—	—	YES	YES	YES	V	YES	YES	YES	YES
West Virginia	—	—	—	—	—	—	—	—	YES	YES	V	YES	YES	YES	YES
Wisconsin	—	—	—	YES	YES	YES	YES	YES	YES	YES	V	YES	YES	YES	YES
Wyoming	—	—	—	—	—	—	—	YES	YES	YES	V	YES	YES	YES	YES

Codes:
- — = State or Territory did not exist, or census was not taken.
- NO = Census was taken, but schedules were destroyed.
- YES = Schedules are available for all, or nearly all, counties.
- F = Fragments of general schedule only.
- V = Special Schedules for Union Veterans and their widows are available.
- I = Special Schedules for Indian Reservations only.

Some information on this chart is from *Guide to Genealogical Research in the National Archives* (Washington, D.C.: National Archives and Records Service), pages 26–27

The Church of Jesus Christ of Latter-day Saints has produced the entire 1880 census on fifty-six CDs. This set is available for purchase through the FHL in Salt Lake City and online at <http://www.familysearch.org>.

Where can schedules for state or other censuses be obtained?
They may be found in many locations, depending on the type of census and the governmental division that took the census. State census records are most

often available at the state archives in that state. Some are transcribed and available online at the USGenWeb Internet site <http://www.usgenweb.com> under each individual state or county. To locate these census records, consult one of the genealogical resource books listing state holdings, or check *State Census Records* by Ann S. Lainhart to determine if a state took a census in any given year and where it is available. Not all states took their own censuses, and some have not survived, but these records are worth looking for. The states that did take censuses usually did so every ten years on the five-year mark (1855, 1865, etc.), so these censuses can fill in the ten-year time gaps of the federal censuses.

Some of the state censuses provide valuable information. The New York state censuses were taken every ten years and began in 1825. The amount of information contained increases with each census, just as it does in the federal censuses. The 1845 New York state census asked if an individual was born in New York, New England, other states, Latin America, the British Empire, France, Germany, or other nations in Europe. The 1845 New York census also includes nine Iroquois tribes living on eighteen reservations in New York. Censuses were taken in 1855, 1865, 1875,1892, 1905, 1915, and 1925. These years include a listing for every member of the household and varying amounts of information, including what county in New York or what state the individual was born in. There are also questions regarding naturalization status, when and where citizens were naturalized, number of times married, occupations, and usual place of employment. See *State Census Records* for information on New York and other states that took censuses.

Why was the first U.S. federal census taken in 1790?

The U.S. Constitution established the counting of the population of "free individuals" in order to apportion the seats in the House of Representatives and to apportion taxes on that population. The Constitution also states that the first census must be taken "within three years after the first meeting of the Congress of the United States, and within every subsequent ten years, in such a manner as they shall by law direct." The early census enumerations counted only "free persons" on an individual basis, excluded Indians who lived on treaty land and were therefore not taxed or allowed to vote, and counted "all others" including slaves as three-fifths of a person for determining the representation in Congress. To offset the relatively small white population in the southern states, the South wanted to count each slave as one person. The northern states objected to this, and the famous three-fifths compromise was the result. It satisfied the southern states' desire and need for more representation and at the same time satisfied (to a degree) the northern states' demand that the slave population not be counted.

Why are some of the earliest lists sometimes in alphabetical order and sometimes not?

The census takers made several copies of their lists, and some census takers alphabetized the subsequent lists. Some of the earliest census records have been transcribed into book format, and in some books the records were put in alphabetical order, thereby ruining the neighborhood picture that is so valuable. Since a microfilmed copy may be that of a second, third, or later copy of the original census, it may show entries in alphabetical order. Our ancestors were not born and did not live in alphabetical order, and it is unfortunate that the census records that survived do not include all the nonalphabetic ones.

Definitions

What is an enumeration district?

An enumeration district is the specific geographic area assigned to the individual census taker (enumerator) with the instructions to count and record the population living within those boundaries following a set of criteria. In simpler terms, an enumeration district is a specific neighborhood assigned to one census taker to count. Some microfilms and books that list the enumeration boundaries include the names of the boundary streets (but not all streets included within). These boundary streets may be divided down the middle with the even-numbered side in one enumeration district and the odd-numbered side in another. In census years when you cannot locate an individual or family in the index or there is no index, but you know they should be there, these enumeration district descriptions become an important tool, especially for larger city locations, to locate your ancestor.

Why were names only of the heads of household listed in the first six census enumerations?

The original intent of the census was to count free persons and indicate those who were in the age bracket to vote or serve in the military. The names of all of the individuals were not important to that count. In the earliest enumeration (1790), only males are broken down into age groups. Since women were not allowed to vote or subject to military service, their ages were irrelevant. In 1790 the enumerator had to count only five categories. They were (1) free white males sixteen years and older, (2) free white males fifteen years and under, (3) free white females of all ages, (4) all slaves, and (5) other free persons.

The breakdowns become more specific over the next five census enumerations (1800 to 1840). By 1840 there were thirteen age categories for free white males; thirteen age categories for free white females; twelve categories for free colored persons (broken down by sex and age); three age categories (no indication of sex) for deaf and dumb individuals; and one category each for blind or alien (foreigners not naturalized) individuals, the number of persons collecting military pensions, and the number of persons attending school. Additional information listed slave owners by name and the numbers of male and female slaves owned, detailed by age, sex, and color.

Since the counting of the population helped determine representation in Congress, only the total of free persons and slaves (counted as three-fifths each) was really needed. All of the columns for information in 1840 indicates the government's interest in the status of colored and alien individuals living within its boundaries.

What questions were asked in each census year?

U.S. CENSUS OVERVIEW						
1790–1840	1790	1800	1810	1820	1830	1840
Name of head of family & number of free white males (within specified age groups) & free white females (age groups unspecified) in each household	YES	YES	YES	YES	YES	YES
Number of free white females, within specified age groups, in each household	NO	YES	YES	YES	YES	YES
Name of slaveowner & number of slaves owned	YES	YES	YES	YES	YES	YES
Number of male & female slaves, within specified age groups, owned by each owner	NO	NO	NO	YES	YES	YES
Number of foreigners, in each household, not naturalized	NO	NO	NO	YES	YES	NO
Number of deaf, dumb, & blind persons, within specified categories, in each household	NO	NO	NO	NO	YES	YES
Name & age of each person receiving federal pension	NO	NO	NO	NO	NO	YES
Number of persons in each household attending specified classes at school	NO	NO	NO	NO	NO	YES
1890 UNION CIVIL WAR VETERANS INFORMATION						
This census includes the following information on veterans or widows of veterans *ONLY*: 1. Name of veteran 2. Name of widow, if appropriate 3. Veteran's rank, company, regiment, or vessel 4. Post Office address 5. Dates of enlistment & discharge & length of service in years, months, & days 6. Nature of disability 7. Remarks						

Why can't I locate a federal census or index for a
state in every census year from 1790 to 1930?

For several reasons there may not be a census schedule for any given location or year. Not all states existed at the time of the first census (1790), so there may not be a schedule covering that geographic area. One important fact is the date the state you are interested in actually became a state or territory. Many states' earliest census schedules are listed as territorial censuses rather than by the state name.

Another reason that some schedules no longer exist is the destruction of the originals by fire, water damage, or loss over the years. For all practical purposes the 1890 population schedules were lost in a fire; other censuses were rendered unreadable due to water damage from floods, fires, etc.

Indexes for some states were created by private enterprise, while the Soundex and Miracode indexes were compiled by government divisions (e.g., Social Security Administration, WPA, etc.) for their own use. More and more, indexing is being done in the private sector, making previously unindexed censuses more useable by researchers.

U.S. CENSUS OVERVIEW

1850–1930	1850	1860	1870	1880	1885*	1900	1910	1920	1930
Name & age	YES	YES	YES	YES	YES	YES	YES	YES	YES
Name of street & number of house	NO	NO	NO	YES	YES	YES	YES	YES	YES
Relationship to head of family	NO	NO	NO	YES	YES	YES	YES	YES	YES
Month of birth, if born within year	NO	NO	YES	YES	YES	YES	NO	NO	NO
Sex, color, birthplace, & occupation	YES	YES	YES	YES	YES	YES	YES	YES	YES
Whether naturalized or papers taken out	NO	NO	NO	NO	NO	YES	YES	YES	YES
Year of naturalization	NO	NO	NO	NO	NO	NO	NO	YES	NO
Number of years in U.S.	NO	NO	NO	NO	NO	YES	YES	NO	NO
Year of immigration to U.S.	NO	NO	NO	NO	NO	NO	NO	YES	YES
Value of personal estate	NO	YES	YES	NO	NO	NO	NO	NO	NO
Value of real estate	YES	YES	YES	NO	NO	NO	NO	NO	YES
Whether home/farm free of mortgage	NO	NO	NO	NO	NO	YES	YES	YES	YES
Marital status	NO	NO	NO	YES	YES	YES	YES	YES	YES
Age at first marriage	NO	NO	NO	NO	NO	NO	NO	NO	YES
Whether married within the year	YES	YES	YES	YES	YES	NO	NO	NO	NO
Month of marriage, if within year	NO	NO	YES	NO	NO	NO	NO	NO	NO
If temporarily or permanently disabled	NO	NO	NO	YES	YES	NO	NO	NO	NO
If crippled, maimed or deformed	NO	NO	NO	YES	YES	NO	NO	NO	NO
Time unemployed during census year	NO	NO	NO	YES	YES	YES	YES	NO	YES
Whether deaf, dumb, blind or insane	YES	YES	YES	YES	YES	NO	YES	NO	NO
Whether a pauper	YES	YES	NO	NO	NO	NO	NO	NO	NO
Whether a convict	YES	YES	NO	NO	NO	NO	NO	NO	NO
Whether able to speak English	NO	NO	NO	NO	NO	YES	YES	YES	YES
Whether able to read & write or attended school	YES	YES	YES	YES	YES	YES	YES	YES	YES
Birthplace of father & mother	NO	NO	NO	YES	YES	YES	YES	YES	YES
Whether father & mother of foreign birth	NO	NO	YES	YES	YES	YES	YES	YES	YES
Mother tongue of self & parents	NO	NO	NO	NO	NO	NO	YES	YES	YES
If veteran or widow of a veteran	NO	NO	NO	NO	NO	YES	YES	NO	YES
Number of years in present marriage	NO	NO	NO	NO	NO	YES	YES	NO	NO
Number of children born	NO	NO	NO	NO	NO	YES	YES	NO	NO

* Five states and territories (Colorado, Florida, Nebraska, New Mexico Territory, & Dakota Territory) chose to take an 1885 census with federal assistance.

Why is there no 1890 federal census?

A population enumeration was taken in 1890, but more than 99 percent of the records were destroyed by fire in January 1921 at the Commerce Building in Washington, DC. Only a little more than six thousand names were extracted from the surviving schedules.

The 1890 Union Veteran's Schedule was taken as well, and the records for all states alphabetically from Alabama through Kansas were totally destroyed along with approximately one-half of the Kentucky schedules. Records for states alphabetically from Louisiana through Wyoming survived the devastation. The surviving schedules list only Union soldiers or their widows and do not include Confederate soldiers or their widows. The schedule does not, however, list all members of the household; it lists only the soldier or his widow.

Why is the information provided on the census so irregular and unreliable?

The enumerators were instructed to gather the information from the individual households, if possible, or to gather the information from whoever could or would provide it. This means that **information could have been, and often was, provided by a child living in the household or even a neighbor, increasing the risk of inaccurate information.**

Reminder

Keep in mind also that in many cases the age of a person was unknown. Many assumptions were made about the ages of individuals, and many people only knew their ages based on what someone else—their parents perhaps—had told them. If a child was very big or small for her age, nonrelatives might incorrectly guess her age. Watch for listings where all of the ages are rounded off to the nearest ten, such as thirty, forty, fifty. These inaccuracies show up most in the 1790 to 1840 enumerations since there is no way to know the exact ages within the categories provided. There was already a wide range in each category. When every member of the household was listed (beginning in 1850), each person's age is specified. When you look at census listings for many years, the variation in any given person's listed age will show up clearly. Interestingly there are many times when the men appear to have aged more than ten years between each census and women appear to have aged less than ten years. By averaging a person's age through several censuses, you will have a better picture of the individual. Remember that no one had to prove any of the information given. Many individuals could not read or write, so they would not have known if the information provided to the census taker was recorded properly or accurately.

Why is it important to record the data from all of the columns on a census?

Many of the columns on an enumeration can provide clues to other records that you should look at. Some censuses asked if the individuals owned or rented their homes or farms. If a person owned property, there should be a land deed documenting the purchase of that property or there may be a land grant for military service. From 1880 forward, each individual was asked for his place of birth as well as the birthplaces of his father and mother. This can be valuable information when you track the migration of the family. The 1870 census has columns showing if an individual's parents were of foreign birth, if the person was born or married within the previous year, and the value of real estate owned. Since the 1870 listing does not specifically ask if they owned their residences, the column listing real estate value is important for determining if land records should be searched. Even though the question may not have been asked directly—"Do you own your home?"—the "value of real estate" column can provide clues.

Paying close attention to every column can also help you determine a possible migratory route for the family. Look at the children's ages and places of birth to get clues as to other localities you might want to search.

Should I transcribe the information to a form or photocopy the actual census page?

I always make a photocopy of the actual census page, including the heading, and do a transcription later. This serves two purposes:

1. You do not waste valuable time hand-copying information—possibly incorrectly—when you could be looking at additional records.
2. You will have information about your ancestors' neighbors, neighborhood makeup, or other family groups living in multiple-family houses.

Research Tip

Another habit that has paid off for me is photocopying the previous or following page in the census if my ancestor's family appears at the top or the bottom of a page. The number of times that I have found other relatives who lived nearby has convinced me that this one additional copy is a worthy expense. Remember that your ancestors did not live in a vacuum, but in a neighborhood comprised of relatives and possibly others from the same country or region as your ancestors. Squeeze every possible bit of information from every census record you look at.

What do all of the abbreviations included in the census represent?

Every census enumeration has its share of abbreviations for you to deal with. The columns were often small, and abbreviations were necessary to get all of the required information onto the form. While some standard abbreviations were used by many census takers, others seemed to have made up their own shorthand. (See page 68 for a list of abbreviations that I have encountered or read about over the years.)

One of the most often misinterpreted abbreviations on the census seems to be one in the citizenship columns of the 1900, 1910, and 1920 census schedules. A person listed as being foreign born was asked if he was a U.S. citizen, if he had taken out his first papers, or if he remained an alien. The three abbreviations that should appear in this column are "Al" (alien), "Pa" (first papers have been filed), or "Na" (naturalized citizen). Many researchers misread the "Na," interpreting it as "no" and thus incorrectly concluding that an ancestor was not naturalized.

Other overlooked abbreviations are in the home ownership and relationship columns of a census. The column might show if the individual owned or rented his property. "O" signifies ownership while "R" indicates rental. Some censuses asked if there was a mortgage on the property or if it was owned free and clear.

"F" indicates free and clear, and "M" means mortgaged. Some schedules also indicate if the residence was a house ("H") or a farm ("F"). All of these facts are important to you as you search when searching for additional records for your ancestors. If the individual owned property, you should look for land or property deeds and perhaps tax records.

In the column (from 1880 on) indicating the individual's relationship to the head of the household you might encounter some strange abbreviations. You should find out what they stand for, so you can get a thorough picture of the household and its occupants. The most common abbreviations that will appear are "W" for wife, "S" for son, and "D" for daughter. An individual with a different surname than the head of household may be listed as "Bo" (boarder), "B" (brother), "Fl" (father-in-law), "Gd" or "Gs" (granddaughter or grand-son), or any number of other relationships. One abbreviation that I came across completely changed my research strategy. The abbreviation for my great-grand-mother was "AdD," which indicated that she was an adopted daughter of the couple she was enumerated with. Abbreviations can provide important infor-mation that you should not overlook. Understanding every single notation that appears on a census schedule is imperative to successful research.

Why doesn't the census list full legal names of the individuals?

Again, the census takers listed for individuals age, sex, and other information that the government needed, which did not include exact names. Since most people did not have what we consider today to be a "legal name," they are usually listed by whatever name they were known by. This is especially true if children or neighbors provided the information. Most of my ancestors' names as listed in the censuses and in documents from their later years are not the same names as on the birth records. Some census takers listed individuals by initials only. People did not have copies of their birth or marriage records, except for listings in the family Bible, as it was not important to the day-to-day living of an individual before the time of Social Security and driver's licenses.

Why are so many people's names misspelled in the census lists?

The enumerator spelled most names phonetically as he heard them. Keep in mind that there was no standardized spelling until well into the twentieth century. Once Social Security numbers and driver's licenses became necessary, standardization came into practice. Another fact to remember is that many people in the general population could not read or write—at least not in English—so they would not necessarily have known if the census taker misspelled their names. Again, the census was needed for a head count of people in certain age and sex brackets, and the spelling of names was not crucial to the gathering of that data.

Important

How accurate are the printed or online indexes for the census records?

Some printed indexes for the U.S. federal censuses have an estimated 20 percent error rate. This includes omissions as well as transcription errors. Since this figure represents a one-in-five error rate, you must use the indexes carefully. Just because you cannot find an individual in an index does not mean the person is not in the census. The person may actually be in the index, but not where you would expect her to be alphabetically. Because the indexes were created by individuals reading a handwritten document, the interpretation of the written name could have caused additional spelling errors above and beyond the census taker's misspellings. An individual may also appear in the index but not on the cited page. Utilize the indexes, but don't take inclusion or exclusion of an individual as the final word. Look for additional information that will allow you to search the census by locality.

Since most of the online indexes are actually the same lists that were printed in book form, all inherent errors are alive and well in the electronic versions. Add to that any data entry or transcription errors made while converting the original data into electronic format, then into books, and then back to the current electronic format, and you see many additional chances for errors.

If you don't find an individual in the available indexes, you may find it worthwhile to go through the census of that community line by line. If an individual lived in a city, you may have to do some advance research to determine which ward he resided in, but it is often worth the effort.

Research Tip

What is a Soundex or Miracode index?

Soundex (Miracode for 1910) is an indexing format that was devised to index a surname by the way it sounds rather than by the spelling. This was achieved by coding only the consonant sounds and disregarding the vowels and the consonants that act as vowels. In the coding guide below, you will see that like-sounding consonants are grouped together. All Soundex codes consist of a letter and three numbers (e.g., C253).

Code	Letter(s)
1	B P F V
2	C S K G J Q X Z
3	D T
4	L
5	M N
6	R

Disregard vowels (*A, E, I, O, U*) and the consonants *W, H,* and *Y,* which are often silent and may sound and act as vowels.

To determine the Soundex code for a surname, start by writing down the surname and all known or possible spelling variations. Next cross off all vowels and the letters *W, H,* and *Y.* (Note: If the surname begins with one of these disregarded letters, do not cross out that initial letter.) Then write the initial consonant followed by the numbers from the chart that corresponds to the next three consonants.

For example, WATSON would look like W~~A~~TS~~O~~N. The code would begin with the *W.* The next letter not crossed out is a *T.* Consult the chart. The *T* is coded as a 3, so you have W3. Continue coding the *S* and the *N,* and you get W325. This is the Soundex code for the surname Watson.

Several other rules also apply.

- A Soundex code is always one letter and three numbers. If there are not enough letters to code, fill in the code with zeros. For instance, HALE = H400 since only the *L* gets coded. The name JOY would be J000. If the name has more than three codable letters, disregard the extra letters. For WASHINGTON, the code starts with *W* since it is the first letter of the surname. Cross out the *A*, *H*, *I*, and *O* leaving five more consonants. Code the *S*, *N*, and *G*, and the Soundex code is W252. Disregard all remaining letters once you have the letter and three numbers for the code.

- If two letters that are side by side have the same code (double letters or "mn," "ck," "sc," etc.), use that code only once. (Note also that the letters *W* and *H* are completely disregarded when not an initial letter and do not act as separators for like-coded letters, a discovery made by Tony Burroughs.) To illustrate, for JACKSON the *C*, *K*, and *S* would all code as 2. Therefore, disregard the *K* and *S*. This would result in the Soundex code J250. Another example is HENNESSEY. In this name, cross out one letter in each double-letter occurrence as well as the vowels and the *Y*, leaving HNS. The resulting Soundex code is H520.

- If the double letters or like-coded letters begin the name, use only the first letter. For example, in SCHNEIDER, the *S* and *C* both code as 2, so disregard one of them. You cannot eliminate the first letter of the surname, as that begins the code, so disregard the *C*. The resulting Soundex code is S536. Using Schneider to illustrate why Soundex works, consider some variant spellings of this name: SHNYDER, SNIDER, SCHNIDER.

S̶C̶H̶N̶E̶I̶D̶E̶R̶	(leaving SNDR)	= S536
S̶H̶N̶Y̶D̶E̶R̶	(leaving SNDR)	= S536
S̶N̶I̶D̶E̶R̶	(leaving SNDR)	= S536
S̶C̶H̶N̶I̶D̶E̶R̶	(leaving SNDR)	= S536

As you can see, all these variant spellings result in the same code.

- If the surname begins with a prefix (e.g., Mc, Mac, O', Di, Van, etc.), you must code it both with and without the prefix. These prefixes were often overlooked by the transcribers when the Soundex cards were created, and names may appear as, for example, Hooten rather than Van Hooten or Donald rather than McDonald.

So many names were misspelled when recorded, but using such an index groups like sounding names together. In most cases, especially when you deal with immigrant names, this is a valuable trait. Occasionally it is more work. Using the many spellings you may have for a given surname, try coding the name using the Soundex guide. In most cases the spellings will code the same unless the first letter of the variant spellings is different. An example of this is

CZARNICKI = C652   ZARNICKY = Z652   SARNICKI = S652

Warning

As you can see, the numerical portion of each code is the same, while the first letter changes each code.

Another problem to watch out for is names containing a silent _G_ or _D_, such as WEIGHT, LIGHT, HOUGHTON, HODGES, RODGERS, etc. Since the letters _D_ and _G_ are coded letters, some spellings of the surname will result in a variety of codes.

Examples:

ROGERS = R262	RODGERS = R326	
WEIGHT = W230	WAIT = W300	WACHT = W230
LIGHT = L230	LITE = L300	
HOUGHTON = H235	HOOTEN = H350	

Always code the variant spellings to see if the code remains the same.

The Miracode system follows the same rules as Soundex, but the microfilmed cards look different than the Soundex cards. The Soundex cards provide you with a volume number, enumeration district number, sheet (page) number, and line number, while the Miracode cards indicate the enumeration district and the family number (instead of a page number). The 1910 index includes only twenty-one states: Alabama, Arkansas, California, Florida, Georgia, Illinois, Kansas, Kentucky, Louisiana, Michigan, Mississippi, Missouri, North Carolina, Ohio, Oklahoma, Pennsylvania, South Carolina, Tennessee, Texas, Virginia, and West Virginia. While fourteen of these states were indexed using only the Miracode system, six were indexed using only the traditional Soundex system. Louisiana was indexed with both the Soundex and Miracode systems. All other states currently have no name index available, although some states may be creating indexes for their geographic region.

When you look at the Miracode index cards, the information will appear as follows:

Sample Miracode Card

Bradford Co.	Monroe	101 0136 0678 Penn
R240 ROCKWELL	Zerah	W 65 Penn
	Mary	W 63 NY

Top line indicates:

county	town	volume ED family # state

Soundex cards look like this:

Sample Soundex Card—Family

| R240 | Penn | 1920 | | vol. _____ E.D. _____ |
| | | | | sheet _____ line _____ |

ROCKWELL, Zerah
W   Sept 1857 63   Penn   (citizenship)

Huntingdon Co.
Monroe   Main St.   210

NAME	*Relationship*	*Age*	*Birthplace*	*Citizenship*
ROCKWELL, Addie	Wife	60	Penn	
ROCKWELL, Howard	son	35	Penn	
ROCKWELL, Edith	d-I-l	32	NY	
WILLEY, Edward	f-I-l	83	Penn	
SMITH, Joseph	boarder	25	Canada	Na

There should be a separate index card for any individual living in a household listed as a boarder or whose surname is different from that of the head of the household. For the above Soundex card example, you should find a card that indexes Edward Willey and a card for Joseph Smith. The individual card looks like the following:

Sample Soundex Card—Individual

| W400 | Penn | | vol. _____ E.D. _____ |
| | | | sheet _____ line _____ |

WILLEY, Edward
W   83   Penn   (citizenship)

Huntingdon Co.
Monroe   Main St.   210

Enumerated with ROCKWELL, Zerah

Relationship to above father-in-law

Remarks _____
_____
_____

Why can't I find my ancestor in the Soundex, Miracode, or book indexes?
While these indexes make finding many individuals much easier, many errors lead to "missing" persons. First make sure that you know all possible spellings and Soundex codes for the surname in question. When you look at the cards within

Reminder

a specific code does the surname you are searching for show up? If not, you might be looking in the wrong code. Many computer programs, as well as the computers at the regional National Archives facilities, will code the name for you. At the National Archives Internet site, you can type in your surname and have it automatically coded for you (go to <http://www.nara.gov/genealogy/soundex/soundex.html>). Double-check your code. If the code is correct, be careful to look for possible nicknames instead of the "legal" first name of your research subject. Remember that anyone could provide the information to the census taker, even a neighbor. I could not find my great-grandfather Spencer Rounds in the index, so I looked at all of the cards bearing the surname Rounds. Since I knew his wife's name—Malona—and the names and ages of all his children, I was able to determine that the card listing "Tink" Rounds, a nickname I was unaware of, was for the correct family. I also noticed that the surname Rounds (R532) was often spelled Round (R530), which yielded a different Soundex code to search.

If you still cannot locate the individual in the index, look at the beginning of each given name alphabetical list (e.g., R532, A. Rounds) in case the enumerator only listed the individuals by first initial. Perhaps your individual is listed under his middle name. Also, try looking under the wife's first name in case she lived alone or was widowed.

Another reason you may not be able to locate your ancestor in the index is that she was not the head of the household. Most indexes, both in book format, on CDs, and in Soundex or Miracode have entries for only the head of the household. An exception to this is when an individual living within a household has a different surname than the head of the household. If your ancestor lived with her parents, a sibling, or grandparents with the same surname, she will not appear in the index. All individuals living within the household will be listed on the head of household's Soundex or Miracode card. This includes all individuals with a different surname as well. They may only be listed as "and 3 boarders" rather than by name, but they should be indexed separately as well. Most book indexes only list the head of household and do not include all individuals living within the household.

If you are still unsuccessful, try to find a city directory for the area in question. Look at city directories or street listings for several years prior to and after the census year. If the individual is in these directories, you can then determine what ward or enumeration district the address is in (see page 179). Then you will have to look through the town, ward, or enumeration district to see if the person appears. I have found many individuals this way that should have been indexed but were not.

Also keep in mind that some people were simply missed by the census taker, either intentionally or by mistake. Many individuals didn't trust anyone asking so many questions and avoided giving the information. Others might have moved during the period of time that the census taker was given to enumerate his district. I have also found individuals in the actual census whose last names are incorrect. An elderly couple living with a married child might inadvertently be listed under the surname of the son-in-law rather than under the proper surname. For example, Nelson Braman and his wife, Addie Braman, lived with their daughter and her husband on the 1920 census date.

The household was listed as

Hileman, Joseph	head	40y
Hileman, Elizabeth	wife	36y
Hileman, Sidney	son	10y
Hileman, Braman	father	75y
Hileman, Addie	mother	69y

These are just some of the many reasons that your ancestor might not be in the index. It is always worth it to look through the geographic location if you have other evidence that they were indeed living there during the census year. Many people are right where they are supposed to be, but they were either recorded or indexed incorrectly or not indexed at all.

Which states have indexes of any type?

While there is no complete listing of all census indexes that have been compiled, some general lists should help you locate many indexes for certain time frames.

1790 to 1850	Most states have printed index books available, and some CDs are also available.
1860, 1870	Some states have printed index books and CDs available.
1880	Soundex index for families with children ten years old and younger. Some book and CD indexes are also available.
1900	Soundex indexes for all states are available.
1910	Soundex or Miracode indexes are available for twenty-one states.
1920	Soundex indexes for all states are available.
1930	Soundex indexes are available for Alabama, Arkansas, Florida, Georgia, Kentucky**, Louisiana, Mississippi, North Carolina, South Carolina, Tennessee, Virginia, and West Virginia** only.

*Note: Only seven counties in these states are included in the index.

You should also look to see if any state organizations have published indexes to their own counties or states for specific years. One good place to check for these publications is the USGenWeb at <http://www.usgenweb.com> on the Internet. Many local and county organizations have either published or posted the indexes on their Web sites. A query posted on a state or county Web site asking if an index exists can't hurt either.

Warning

How inclusive are the indexes in CD format and on the Web?
The major problem in answering this question is that many different companies are publishing indexes in databases and CD formats. Some are well done and easy to use while others are difficult to navigate. Many of the indexes on the market (both CD and database formats) contain the same indexes that were originally printed in book format and are no more inclusive than the original book. Estimates of the accuracy of the original book indexes suggest that 25 percent to 40 percent of individuals are either not listed at all, misspelled, or otherwise incorrectly indexed.

An entire book on the problems with the census indexes is *A Practical Guide to the "Misteaks" Made in Census Indexes*, edited by Richard H. Saldana. Saldana points out the myriad of problems that might have caused your ancestor to be missed or incorrectly listed in the index. This book also has an appendix called "Possible Mistakes Chart" which can be used as a checklist to see if you have looked for all possible causes for not finding an individual. Saldana also includes a listing of common names and their abbreviated form as they might appear in the index as well as a listing of the most common spelling errors that occur. Using these lists to do a complete and thorough search in a digital index will result in more successful searches.

Some of the CDs state that they contain, for example, the 1860 index for "selected counties" within several states. Look for the documentation that lists the counties included when determining if your ancestors might appear in that index or not. Many of the online indexes list the states included for any given year but not what counties within that state are included or omitted. This is an important step if you don't know that the individuals should or should not appear in the index. Just because you don't find them in the index does not mean that they are not there; they are just not in that version of the index.

To help you determine if the county you are interested in is included in the index you can search for an individual that you know lived in that county in that census year. You can also set your search criteria for a common name such as Smith, Miller, or Jones to see what counties are represented in the index. If the database or CD allows you to search by location in a specific year you can search for the county without listing a surname. This can be tedious if a state has many counties and you do not know if or where your ancestor lived within the state.

Why are only households with children ten years old and younger indexed in 1880?
In 1935 a Soundex index was created for the 1880 federal census. The index was compiled by clerical workers from the Works Progress Administration (later renamed the Work Projects Administration) for the Social Security Administration. Individuals who were ten years old or younger in 1880 would have been born between 1869 and 1880, making them fifty-five to sixty-five years of age in 1935. The WPA index was compiled to confirm a person's age after they applied for Social Security benefits in the mid to late 1930s.

Households with no children or with children eleven years or older and households of single individuals are not included in the index. Many researchers are surprised to find their ancestor's family indexed since the ancestor may have been elderly, widowed, or single. Extended families were quite common during these early census years, and grandparents, widowed parents, and grandchildren often lived together in the same household. Every household with a child in the ten-and-under age bracket was indexed regardless of the child's relationship to the head of the household. Even if that child was the child of a servant or other employee living with the family the entire family will appear in the index. **(See page 52 for information on the 1880 census on CD-ROM.)**

See Also

Why are only twenty-one states indexed for the 1910 census?

In the early 1960s the Soundex and Miracode indexes were compiled for twenty-one states by the census bureau. It has been stated, although not confirmed, that the states that were indexed were those states that did not have statewide birth registrations by the 1910 census date. Since many individuals did not have birth certificates in their possession, proving age would require obtaining a birth record from the state of birth or verifying age in a federal census.

The Miracode index was created by computer, and the cards are therefore typed. Soundex cards are handwritten and follow a similar format to the 1900 and 1920 cards. The states that were indexed are listed below with indication of whether each state's index is under the Miracode or Soundex system of indexing.

State	Index System	State	Index System
Alabama	Soundex	Missouri	Miracode
Arkansas	Miracode	North Carolina	Miracode
California	Miracode	Ohio	Miracode
Florida	Miracode	Oklahoma	Miracode
Georgia	Soundex	Pennsylvania	Miracode
Illinois	Miracode	South Carolina	Soundex
Kansas	Miracode	Tennessee	Soundex
Kentucky	Miracode	Texas	Soundex
Louisiana*	*see below*	Virginia	Miracode
Michigan	Miracode	West Virginia	Miracode
Mississippi	Soundex		

* Note that Louisiana has both a Miracode index and Soundex index covering different locations. New Orleans and Shreveport, Louisiana, were indexed with the Miracode system, and the remainder of the state was indexed under the Soundex system.

What abbreviations appear in the census schedule columns?

The following are some, but probably not all, of the abbreviations you might encounter when using census records. These have been compiled over many years by several individuals, but we keep finding new ones all the time. Remember that each census taker might have used his own versions of the "official" abbreviations.

Household Abbreviations

A = aunt
Ad = adopted
AdCl = adopted child
AdD = adopted daughter
AdGcl = adopted grandchild
AdM = adopted mother
AdS = adopted son
Al = aunt-in-law
Ap = apprentice
At = attendant
Asst = assistant

B = brother
B Boy = bound boy
B Girl = bound girl
Bar = bartender
Bl = brother-in-law
Bo = boarder
Boy = boy
Bu = butler

C = cousin
Cap = captain
Cha = chambermaid
Cil = cousin-in-law
Cl = child
Coa = coachman
Com = companion
Cook = cook

D = daughter
Dl = daughter-in-law
Dla = day laborer
Dom = domestic
Dw = dishwasher

Emp = employee
En = engineer

F = father
FaH = farm hand
FaL = farm laborer
FaW = farm worker
Fi = fireman
First C = first cousin

Fl = father-in-law
FoB = foster brother
FoS = foster son
FoSi = foster sister

Gcl = grandchild
Gd = granddaughter
Gf = grandfather
GGF = great-grandfather
GGM = great-grandmother
GGGF = great-great-grandfather
GGGM = great-great-grandmother
GM = grandmother
Gml = grandmother-in-law
Gn = great- or grandnephew
Gni = great- or grandniece
Go = governess
God Cl = godchild
Gs = grandson
Gsl = grandson-in-law
Gua = guardian

H Maid = housemaid
Hb = half brother
Hbl = half brother-in-law
He = herder
Help = helper
HGi = hired girl
HH = hired hand
Hk = housekeeper
Hlg = hireling
HSi = half sister
HSil = half sister-in-law
Husb = husband
Hw = house worker

L = lodger
La = laborer
Lau = laundry

M = mother
Maid = maid
Man = manager
Mat = matron
Ml = mother-in-law

N = nephew
Ni = niece
Nil = niece-in-law
Nl = nephew-in-law
NU = nurse

O = officer

P = patient
Pa = partner
Ph = physician
Por = porter
Pr = prisoner
Pri = principal
Prv = private
Pu = pupil

R = roomer

S = son
Sa = sailor
Sal = saleslady
Sb = stepbrother
Sbl = stepbrother-in-law
Scl = stepchild
Sd = stepdaughter
Sdl = stepdaughter-in-law
Se = servant
SeCl = servant's child
Sf = stepfather
Sfl = stepfather-in-law
Sgd = stepgranddaughter
Sgs = stepgrandson
Si = sister
Sil = sister-in-law
Sl = son-in-law
Sm = stepmother
Sml = stepmother-in-law
Ss = stepson

Ssi = stepsister
Ssil = stepsister-in-law
Ssl = stepson-in-law
Su = superintendent

Ten = tenant

U = uncle
Ul = uncle-in-law

Vi = visitor

W = wife
Wa = warden
Wai = waitress
Ward = ward
Wkm = workman
Wt = waiter

Soundex Abbreviations
(ones that are not listed above)

FB = foster brother
FF = foster father
FM = foster mother
FSi = foster sister

GA = great aunt
GU = great uncle
Hm = hired man

I = inmate

Citizenship Status Codes

Al = alien
Na = naturalized
Pa = first papers filed
NR = not recorded or not reported

Sources

FURTHER READING

The American Census Handbook, by Thomas Jay Kemp. Wilmington, Del.: Scholarly Resources, 2001.

Ancestry's Red Book: American State, County & Town Sources, rev. ed., edited by Alice Eichholz, Ph.D. Salt Lake City, Utah: Ancestry, Inc., 1992.

Internet Source

The census catalogs of the National Archives microfilms are available online at <http://www.nara.gov/publications/microfilm/census/census.html>.

The Census Book: A Genealogist's Guide to Federal Census Facts, Schedules, and Indexes, by William Dollarhide. Bountiful, Utah: Heritage Quest, Inc., 2000.

1850, 1860, 1870 United States Census Key, compiled by Col. Leonard H. Smith Jr. American Genealogical Lending Library, 1997.

Guide to Genealogical Research in the National Archives of the United States, by National Archives and Trust Fund Board. Washington, D.C.: NARA, 2000.

Map Guide to the U.S. Federal Censuses, 1790–1920, by William Thorndale and William Dollarhide. Baltimore, Md.: Genealogical Publishing Co., Inc., 1987.

1900 Federal Population Census, by National Archives Trust Fund Board. Washington, D.C.: NARA, 1978.

1910 Federal Population Census, by National Archives Trust Fund Board. Washington, D.C.: NARA, 1982.

1920 Federal Population Census, by National Archives Trust Fund Board. Washington, D.C.: NARA, 1991.

A Practical Guide to the "Misteaks" Made in Census Indexes, edited by Richard H. Saldana. Salt Lake City, Utah: Saldana & Co., 1987.

A Research Aid for the Massachusetts 1910 Federal Census, by Mary Lou Craver Mariner and Patricia Roughan Bellows. Sudbury, Mass.: The authors, 1988.

A Research Guide for the New York 1910 Federal Census, compiled and edited by Ann Hunt. Pittsfield, Mass.: Friends of the Silvio O. Conte National Archives, 1999.

The 1790–1890 Federal Population Censuses: Catalog of National Archives Microfilm, by National Archives Trust Fund Board. NARA, 1997.

State Census Records, by Ann S. Lainhart. Baltimore, Md.: Genealogical Publishing Co., Inc., 1992.

200 Years of U.S. Census Taking: Population and Housing Questions, 1790–1990, by the U.S. Department of Commerce, Bureau of the Census. Washington, D.C.: USDC, 1989. Reprinted by Heritage Quest, Inc., 1992.

Your Guide to the Federal Census, by Kathleen W. Hinckley. Cincinnati, Ohio: Betterway Books, 2002.

FIVE

Military Records

Military records may not be the first thing to come to mind when you research your ancestors, unless you have heard some family stories about an illustrious ancestor's military career, capture, etc. They are, however, helpful and enlightening documents that can add dimension and facts to your family history. Many will provide you with detailed information on an individual and his family.

Finding these records involves a bit of advance research to determine if your ancestor was in the military in any capacity, and, if so, whether it was with the local, state, or federal government. There are many different levels of military service, just as in any other type of record. Determining what, if any, wars, skirmishes, or military engagements occurred during your ancestor's lifetime is only the first step in learning whether he served the country in a military capacity.

Entire books detail both specific and general military records. James C. Neagles's *U.S. Military Records* is just one such book. The author explains in depth the types of records created during and after military service, including veterans' pension and burial records. He goes into great detail regarding the content of the different types of documents. He also outlines the different levels of government where records might be accessed and includes locations of these valuable resources to aid you in making the most of them.

How can I determine if my ancestor served in the military?

First you must know what time frame he lived in and what battles or wars took place during his lifetime and where he lived. The following is a list of wars involving North Americans from 1622 through 1975. Obviously military engagements have occurred after the time period covered in this list, but this will get you started. Some of these military engagements were state events, while others were territorial or federal in nature. I bet you didn't realize how many battles or wars involved our ancestors, did you?

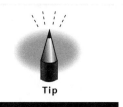

Tip

Look for town or county histories, bicentennial histories, or anniversary editions of town histories, church foundings, etc., to find names of local residents credited with military service.

Dates	Conflict and Location
1622–1644	Jamestown Conflict—In Virginia, between Powhatan Indians and English settlers.
1636–1638	Pequot War—Between Pequot Indians and Puritan settlers in Connecticut.
1675–1676	King Philip's War—Wampanoag Indian uprising led by a son (who had the Christian name Philip) of Massasoit against Connecticut, Massachusetts, and Rhode Island militia.
1676	Bacon's Rebellion—Indian war and civil conflict against Virginia government.
1689–1697	King William's War—French against English in America, mostly in New England and New York.
1702–1713	Queen Anne's War (War of Spanish Succession in Europe—In America, English fought French in Massachusetts, South Carolina, Florida, and Canada. English gained much of Canada.
1715–1716	Yamasee War—In South Carolina and Georgia, between Yamasee Indians and white settlers.
1739–1742	War of Jenkin's Ear—Between England and Spain in America (Georgia and Florida).
1740–1748	King George's War (War of Austrian Succession in Europe)—English fought French and their Indian allies in northern New England, New York, and Canada.
1754–1763	French and Indian War (Seven Years' War in Europe)—In America, British and colonists fought French and Indians. France lost all territory in Canada and east of the Mississippi. Involved mostly northern colonies and Canada.
1760–1761	Cherokee Uprising—Cherokee Indians against settlers in the Carolinas.
1763–1764	Pontiac's Rebellion—Indians led by Chief Pontiac against English in Michigan, New York, and Pennsylvania.
1771	War of the Regulators—Civil conflict in North Carolina.
1774	Lord Dunsmore's War—Indians against forces led by royal governor of Virginia in Virginia, Pennsylvania, and Ohio.
1775–1783	Revolutionary War (19 April 1775–11 April 1783)—American colonies against England.
1786–1787	Shay's Rebellion—Civil conflict in western Massachusetts.
1794	Whiskey Rebellion—Civil conflict against excise tax on whiskey in western Pennsylvania.
1798–1800	War With France—French harassment of American ships on Atlantic coast and in West Indies.
1801–1805	Barbary Wars—United States against Tripoli in North Africa. Extortion for allowing trade in the Mediterranean and piracy were the issues.

1812–1815	War of 1812—U.S. war with Great Britain. Capturing of Washington, DC. The British burned the Capitol, the Library of Congress, and the White House.
1813–1814	Creek Indian (War 27 July 1813–9 August 1814)—In Alabama and Georgia.
1817–1819	Florida or Seminole War—Tennessee, Georgia, and Kentucky militias aided U.S. Regular Army.
1831–1832	Black Hawk War—Between Sauk and Fox Indians, led by Black Hawk, and U.S. troops. Illinois and Michigan militias involved.
1835–1842	Second Seminole War—Sixty thousand militias and the Army, with 41 percent casualties. In the end, the Army removed Indians to Oklahoma. Militias from Missouri, Alabama, and Georgia.
1835	War of Texas Independence—Texas territory fought Mexico. Remember the Alamo!
1837–1838	Patriot's War—Between British and Canadian troops and American and Canadian patriots. Along U.S./Canadian border. Final battle in Ontario.
1838–1850	Cherokee Disturbances and Removal—From North Carolina, Tennessee, Alabama, and Georgia to Oklahoma.
1839	Aroostook War—Maine/Canada boundary dispute. Army and Maine militia took part.
1841–1842	Dorr Rebellion—Rhode Island conflict over voting restrictions. Rhode Island militia involved Navaho Wars—Army fought the Navaho in New Mexico and Arizona.
1846–1848	Mexican War (13 May 1846–2 February 1848)—United States gained California, New Mexico, and Rio Grande River as Texas border. Army and National Guard sent from several states, even Vermont.
1848–1858	Third Seminole War—Continuing skirmish in the Everglades of Florida.
1855–1858	Yakima Wars—Army volunteers fought Indians in Washington, Oregon, and Idaho.
1857–1858	Utah War—Army occupation of Salt Lake City after conflicts with Mormon settlers.
1861–1866	Civil War, War Between the States, or War of the Rebellion (19 April 1861–20 August 1866)—Union States: Maine, Vermont, New Hampshire, Massachusetts, Connecticut, Rhode Island, New York, Pennsylvania, Ohio, Indiana, New Jersey, Michigan, Illinois, Iowa, Wisconsin, Minnesota, Oregon, California, and Kansas; Confederate States: Virginia, North Carolina, South Carolina, Georgia, Florida, Tennessee, Alabama, Mississippi, Arkansas, Louisiana, Texas. Border states not seceding: Delaware, Maryland, Missouri, and Kentucky. West Virginia separated from Virginia in 1861

	and was admitted to the Union in 1863.
1865–1900	Indian Wars—Army protecting western settlers against the Sioux and Cheyenne in the Dakotas and Montana (1866–1890); the Apache in Arizona, New Mexico, and Mexico (1870–1886); the Modoc in California (1872–1873); and the Nez Perce in Idaho and Montana (1877).
1898	Spanish American War (20 April 1898–12 August 1898)—In Cuba and the Philippines. Philippine Insurrection—Most troops were National Guard from several states.
1899	Boxer Rebellion—An attempt by the Boxers to expel foreigners from China.
1916–1917	Mexican Punitive Expedition—National Guard sent after Pancho Villa. Recalled January 1917.
1917–1918	World War I, or First World War (6 April 1917–11 November 1918)—United States against Germany.
1941–1945	World War II, or Second World War—United States against Japan (8 December 1941–14 August 1945). Against Germany (8 November 1942–7 May 1945).
1950–1953	Korean War—United Nations Peace Action. Treaty signed 26 July 1953.
1954–1975	Vietnam War—U.S. withdrawal completed 29 April 1975. 58,000 Americans died.

Do any census records list military service?

The Union veteran's census schedule of 1890 enumerated living Union veterans or their widows. It indicates branch and unit of service, dates of enlistment and discharge, post office address, and whether a veteran was a pensioner or wounded in the war. The surviving census records cover the states alphabetically from Kentucky (where only half of the census records survived) through Wyoming, including the District of Columbia. The remaining states—Alabama through Kansas plus half of the Kentucky schedule—were destroyed by fire, as were the schedules for the 1890 population census records for nearly the entire country. Some Confederate veterans are actually listed on this census; these entries are crossed out, but most are still readable.

The 1840 federal census also lists Revolutionary War pensioners or their widows on the second page of each enumeration.

You should also check for state and territorial census records that might indicate military service in your specific states of interest. Ann S. Lainhart's book *State Census Records* details these records and what can be found in them. Also check James C. Neagles's military records book for specific states to determine what, if any, state or territorial censuses or lists of pensioners might exist.

What other resources might indicate military service?

Organizations such as the Daughters of the American Revolution and the Sons of the American Revolution (DAR and SAR) maintain records of descendants who have applied for membership in the organization based on Revolutionary War soldiers' service. Applicants must provide many documents to prove the ancestors' service, and their descent from the ancestor. These documents can be of great value to you. The DAR lineage books are published, with comprehensive indexes, and available on the Internet and in many libraries. Ancestry .com has some DAR databases.

Using these books to determine if your ancestor, or one of his relatives, is included can save you many hours of research by providing you access to one or more files with information already documented. Remember, though, that you should always verify facts from others' research.

Many DAR records have been published, including Bible records, burial records, family records, and lineages that have been accepted for membership in the DAR. Check what's available online at <http://www.dar.org/library/onlin lib.html>.

What is included in the DAR burial records for Revolutionary War soldiers? Many of these records are basic, while some are amazing! You will never know until you look. **If you do not find your soldier listed in one of the many printed DAR burial records, do not give up.** I was looking for information regarding an Isaac Case, recorded in Patricia Law Hatcher's *Abstract of Graves of Revolutionary Patriots* as being buried in the Little Valley Cemetery in Cattaraugus County, New York. The cemetery had no birth or death information, and a stone was not found. I was trying to determine his death date and age at death to possibly link him to a William Case living in Cattaraugus County in the early 1800s. Several Isaac Cases were listed in the DAR lineage books, but none of the lines came down through a William and Sophia Case. Using the Internet and Ancestry.com, I located a record for an Isaac Case listing him as being a Revolutionary patriot buried in the Little Valley Cemetery. The record appeared as follows:

Reminder

Name	Cemetery	Location	Reference
CASE, Isaac	Little Valley Cem	Little Valley NY 58	*Abstract of Graves of Revolutionary Patriots*, Vol. 1, p.—Serial: 12259; Vol. 4

Having no idea what this reference was, I looked for an explanation—this is always a good idea. At the bottom of the page listing the record, I saw the link "More information about this database." Clicking the link took me to a three-page explanation of the Serial Set records. It states:

> This collection of abstracts of grave sites contains information originally published in the Senate documents of the National Society, Daughters of the American Revolution, as well as the Society magazine. Veterans and patriots of the Revolutionary War whose graves were found between 1900 and 1987 are included in this first volume. Included in each entry is the name of the patriot, the cemetery in which the headstone is found, and occasionally others who are located nearby or opposite the grave.

See Also

Also see Patricia Law Hatcher's *Abstract of Graves of Revolutionary War Patriots*, four volumes (Dallas, Tex.: Pioneer Heritage Press, 1987), and the CD-ROM set, *The SAR Revolutionary War Graves Register* (Buffalo, N.Y.: Progeny, 2000).

Now I knew what the source document was, but not where to I locate it. First I tried without luck the NARA regional facility in Massachusetts, and then I contacted the Boston Public Library—the largest public library in the state. In the microtext room they indeed had the Serial Set records. Using the citation from the Ancestry.com Web site I was able to access the information. It included the following: "Isaac Case, born RI 1739, died 20 Aug 1821, served in Captain Perry Sherman's Company, Colonel John Hathaway's Regiment, buried Little Valley Cemetery, Cattaraugus County, New York."

While this is not definitive proof of a father and son relationship between Isaac and William Case, it makes a strong case for at least some familial relationship since the two men are buried in the same cemetery. William and Sophia Case named their first son Isaac Reuben Case and their second son William Henry Case (William being Sophia's father's name). Without at least an approximate date of birth and death for Isaac Case I could not have placed Isaac in a previous generation of William's family. I still need to prove that Isaac is William's father or grandfather, but locating this burial information has provided additional clues to follow up on.

How do I locate military records?

Records regarding military service are held at many different levels of government and at libraries. Utilizing books like *U.S. Military Records*, by James C. Neagles, you can get an overview of where to start looking in both the state and federal document centers. Most researchers begin looking for that Civil War or Revolutionary War soldier that they heard about in family stories. The majority of records for these wars are housed in the National Archives, but some may be in state or regional archives and libraries.

What records does NARA have for the Revolutionary and Civil Wars?

The most-used records pertaining to these two wars are the pension records generated when a soldier or his widow, applied for a government pension. Proof of service—and in the case of a widow's application, her marriage to the soldier—had to be established. Documentation can consist of affidavits, from other individuals such as clergymen or family members, and even in some cases family Bible pages and samplers. There is almost no end to the amazing items found within the pension files.

While the Revolutionary War pension records have been microfilmed, the Civil War pension files have not. The index to the Civil War pension records is available at all NARA branches, but the original papers are all stored in the Washington, DC, NARA facility. These records can be accessed in person or through a mail request.

Civil War pensions were not available to Confederate soldiers, and you must look to the state the soldier served for any resulting pension or remuneration for service. Some of these records are now held at the NARA branches and in Washington.

Are there indexes for Civil War and Revolutionary War pension records?

There are index cards on microfilm for the Civil War (Union veterans only) pension files held in Washington, DC. The cards list the state the soldier served, the date of his or his widow's application, and file numbers to access the files.

NAME OF SOLDIER:	Rogers, Homer				(3-H-3)
NAME OF DEPENDENT:	Widow, Rogers, Ellen E.				
	Minor,				
SERVICE:	I^d 45" Mass. Inf				
DATE OF FILING.	CLASS.	APPLICATION NO.	CERTIFICATE NO.	STATE FROM WHICH FILED.	
1906 Dec	Invalid,	1354.781	1129523	Mass	
1908 Aug	Widow,	901.745	660.792	Mass.	
	Minor,				
ATTORNEY					

Figure 5-1
Civil War Pension index card for Homer Rogers. NARA record group T288, General Index to the Pension Files, 1861–1934.

The Revolutionary War pension files are in alphabetical order, so no index is needed. A soldier's entire pension file follows the card indicating his name and state of service.

A series of books entitled *Genealogical Abstracts of Revolutionary War Pension Files* (three volumes) by Virgil D. White contains abstracts of the pension files. Utilizing these volumes you can determine if your ancestor or his widow applied for or received a pension for Revolutionary War service. This book lists the soldiers in alphabetical order and includes for each the dates of service, date of application, spouse's name, date of marriage, residency, date of death, and other important information gleaned from the original file.

Once you have determined that your ancestor had a pension, you can look at the actual pension file on microfilm at any of the NARA facilities. The file is divided into two parts; selected and nonselected records. The first section includes documents that the pension office determined to be of importance to the pension application. The second section holds documents that were perhaps not necessary to the decision as to whether or not the pension would be granted. Look at all of the documents as some of the nonselected records have wonderful family information as well as affidavits by friends and associates attesting to an individual's character and eligibility for the pension.

What if my ancestor is not listed in the index or abstract books?

Whether or not your ancestor applied for a pension you can get valuable information from these files. I always look at the files for other individuals with the same surname whose service or residency matches my ancestors'. I have found

Printed Source

affidavits by my ancestors included in the files of brothers, uncles, and nephews. You won't know what you will find until you look. You can also take this one step further and look at the pension records for the surname of a soldier's spouse. Your ancestor might have provided an affidavit or other proof that the applicant did indeed serve his country. Many familial relationships are documented in these affidavits.

What information might be included in the Revolutionary War pension files? This example of one such file for a rejected pension demonstrates the valuable information that can be included.

Case Study

Case Study of Revolutionary War pension application

I looked for a pension record for Samuel Rogers, who served out of Connecticut or Vermont. His wife's name was Mehitable, and he died in 1811 in Thetford, Vermont. First I looked in the abstract books and found a Samuel Rogers whose wife's name was Mehitable and who served in the Connecticut and Vermont lines as well as privateer service.

The abstract reads

> ROGERS, Samuel, Mehitable, CT & VT Lines also Privateer Srv., R8954, sol m Mehitable Hubbard 16 Jun 1774 at Middletown CT & in Aug 1779 they moved to Thedford VT where sol d 25 Mar 1811, wid appl 8 Jun 1837 at Eaton in Orleans Co VT & was living with a son-in-law William Comings or Cummings.

Warning

Make sure that you know what all of the abbreviations included in an abstract mean so you will completely understand what you find. The above example indicates a file number R8954. This means that the file holds a rejected pension application.

This certainly looks like the person I was researching, so I moved on to the next step: accessing the microfilmed file. Included in the actual pension file were the following documents:

- affidavits from Jeduthan Loomis, Joseph Reed, Mehitable (Hubbard) Rogers, William Cummings, Samuel Farnsworth, Elizabeth Hubbard, John Boardman, Edward Johnson, and John Fisk (clerk of Middletown, Connecticut)
- a copy of the official commission document giving Samuel Rogers command of the ship *Hector* and signed by Governor Trumball of Connecticut
- a letter from John Crane stating that Samuel and Mehitable's marriage is listed in the First Ecclesiastical Society of Middletown records
- copies of four chits recording expenses for wine, cheese, and toddy and notations about a found purse and an attack on the ship *Hector*.

Several of the affidavits told the story of the Rogers family's life in Middletown and their subsequent migration to Thetford, Vermont, in 1779. Jeduthan Loomis's affidavit stated that "Mrs. Rogers wife of said Samuel was a lady of excellent mind and high respectability of character."

The widow, Mehitable Rogers, provided a firsthand account of a Revolutionary War event. She stated in her affidavit:

> After we removed to Thetford my husband was not out in the war except on occasional alarms one of which was when Royalton was burnt at that time after my husband had gone to Royalton the neighborhood where we lived was so alarmed that we left our dwellings in the night and went through the woods with little or no road about three miles to the Connecticut River and I had four little children the youngest of which was but about three weeks old.

Later in this same document she stated, "My husband at the commencement of the War was worth a handsome property but by his having his property shifted into Continental money (which he had full belief would become good) it became of little or no value so that by the fall of paper money we lost nearly all of our property." This document bore the signature of the then eighty-five-year-old widow.

Since the chits were written on the back of the commission document, I assume that they are likely to have been written by Samuel Rogers, captain of the vessel and my fourth great-grandfather. Pretty great stuff for the file on a rejected pension!

With all of this documentation, why was the pension rejected? It took me a while to find the answer to that question. I finally found a book titled *Rejected or Suspended Applications for Revolutionary War Pensions* that provided the answer. It seems that the pension was rejected because Samuel Rogers's service was "on a letter-of-marque," meaning that he was considered a privateer and thereby not entitled to a pension.

What is a Hessian or a Hessian soldier?

These soldiers, who fought for the British during the American Revolution, were from the Hesse-Cassel and Hesse-Hanau regions of Germany. Many of these soldiers were paid by their local principalities in Germany for their service to the British Crown. It is estimated that approximately 40–50 percent of these soldiers remained in the United States after the war, and many more returned in later years to permanently settle in the United States. There were also nearly thirty thousand soldiers from the Anhalt-Zerbst, Anspach-Bayreuth, Brunswick, and Waldeck areas of Germany.

What if my ancestor was a loyalist?

Loyalists, those loyal to Great Britain during the Revolutionary War, have been the subject of many books and much research. Many loyalists who fled to and then settled in Canada applied to the British government for repayment of monetary losses caused by their support of Great Britain. Several books detailing these claims are available (see book list at end of chapter). Several books list known loyalists as well as a research guide for loyalist ancestry.

Are Civil War pension records as informative as the Revolutionary War pension records?

In many cases the Civil War pension records are even more extensive. They may contain items such as enlistment and discharge papers; muster sheets or cards showing attendance, expenses, and salary paid; and medical and family information to name just a few. My great-grandfather's Civil War pension record has more than 130 pages of documents! These include his enlistment and discharge papers, a listing of the birth and death dates for all of his fifteen children, drawings showing where on his body he was wounded, and bills submitted for his funeral.

Reminder

What other pension or veteran's claims are available?

Additional records are available for Revolutionary War and War of 1812 soldiers who received bounty land in exchange for their military service. **It is important to remember that bounty land was issued by not only the federal government but individual states as well.** Both the federal government and the individual states provided benefits for military service to many veterans. Consult James C. Neagles's book on military records for lists of specific records held by each individual state.

What records are available in addition to pension records?

Many additional records, often overlooked in research, can be of value to you. These include compiled service records for both the American Revolution and the Civil War. Compiled service records may include muster rolls, military engagements, correspondence, lists of persons found on pension rolls, copies of commissions, enlistment papers, etc. Note that the Civil War records are divided into records for the Union and Confederate armies.

These compiled service records include the records of
- Revolutionary War soldiers
- naval personnel during the Revolutionary War
- volunteer soldiers who served from 1784 until 1811
- volunteer soldiers who served in the War of 1812
- volunteer soldiers who served during the Indian Wars and disturbances
- volunteer soldiers who served during the Cherokee disturbances and removals
- volunteer soldiers who served during the Creek War
- volunteer soldiers who served during the Florida Wars
- volunteer soldiers who served during the War of 1837–1838
- volunteer soldiers who served during the Patriot's War of 1837–1838
- volunteer soldiers who served during the Mexican War
- volunteer Union soldiers who served during the Civil War
- the movements and activities of volunteer Union organizations*
- Confederate soldiers who served during the Civil War
- Confederate movements and activities*
- volunteer soldiers who served in the War With Spain
- volunteer soldiers who served during the Philippine Insurrection

- service in the U.S. Army, U.S. Navy, and U.S. Marine Corps.*
- U.S. Military Academy cadets and U.S. Naval Academy midshipmen
- black servicemen*

All of the above record groups except for those followed by an asterisk also contain indexes. Keep in mind that not all indexes are keyed by individual surname; some are by regiments or by date. Some actually contain cross-references to variant spellings of a name to make searching easier. See the NARA publication *Military Service Records* (in print or available online at <http://www .nara.gov/publications/microfilm/military/service.html>) for more detail on record group numbers and indexes.

What about service in World Wars I and II?

Service records were created and maintained by all military service branches in both of the World Wars. Unfortunately, about 80 percent of the records of individuals discharged from the Army between November 1912 and January 1960 and about 75 percent of those for individuals discharged from the Air Force between September 1947 and January 1964, alphabetically through Hubbard, James E., were destroyed in a fire at the National Personnel Records Center in St. Louis, Missouri, in 1973. These destroyed records were all one of a kind and had not been microfilmed or duplicated prior to the fire.

Valuable records that exist for World War I and World War II (fourth registration for the draft only) are open and available for research. The draft cards for World War I are filed first by state, then by county or city, then by draft board number, and then alphabetically by surname within the draft board of registry. You must know where an individual lived, locate the nearest draft board, and then search by surname. Most rural areas had only one draft board, making research easier than in larger cities, which could have had one hundred or more draft boards.

How can I determine which of the many draft boards within a city would most likely hold my ancestor's registration card?

Since many of the large cities had multiple draft registration boards it is important to determine where in the city your ancestor lived in the registration years 1917 and 1918. Using a city directory you should be able to determine what ward the individual resided in and then narrow down the registration boards (see page 179). Microfilms of maps showing the draft board districts are available in NARA's Washington, DC, facility and through the Family History Library and its Family History Centers.

Some draft registration cards have been indexed by name and are available to those who pay the subscriber's fee at the Ancestry.com Web site. Not all states are included, but the indexing project is still underway.

What will the draft registration cards tell me?

While the cards vary depending on the draft number, their information can be helpful to your research. There were three actual drafts for World War I, and

Research Tip

When researching immigrants' names, be sure to look alphabetically under both the surname and the given name since many of these uncommon names were recorded incorrectly. The spellings of names also vary as in any other record, so you must be diligent and look up all possible spellings.

World War II had seven drafts. Each of these drafts targeted specific age groups, and the registration forms changed slightly from one draft to the next. The information contained in the World War I draft cards might include, depending on which draft the person registered in, name, birth date and place, occupation, dependents, nearest relative, and country of allegiance of an alien.

One interesting fact to note is that the first draft for World War I required all males born between 6 June 1886 and 5 June 1896 to register. This included men of foreign birth whether or not they had already filed their intention to become U.S. citizens. The second draft was the only one in which the registrant was asked for his father's birthplace.

Where are the World War I draft registrations available?

The original draft registration cards are housed in the NARA regional facility in East Point, Georgia, and microfilm copies are available at the NARA regional facility covering the state in which registrations took place. All registration cards are available on microfilm from the Family History Library in Salt Lake City, Utah, or through rental at its Family History Centers worldwide. Check the NARA facilities list in chapter one for the location that covers your state of interest.

Why are registration records for only the fourth draft available for World War II?

The fourth of the seven drafts in World War II is the only registration open to the public due to privacy issues. Since the registrants in this fourth of seven drafts were born between 28 April 1877 and 16 February 1897, they all would have been between forty-five and sixty-five years of age at the time of the draft. Due to their ages at the time of registration, they are presumed to be deceased and their records therefore do not fall under the privacy act.

For additional information regarding the many draft registrations in both World War I and World War II consult Kathleen W. Hinckley's *Locating Lost Family Members & Friends*, chapter nine (see book list at end of chapter).

What if my ancestor's military service was not under the federal government?

To locate nonfederal military records you must first look to individual state and military archives. *U.S. Military Records* by James C. Neagles provides a comprehensive listing of records held in various state and local archives.

Example

Listed under the state of Iowa is the State Historical Society of Iowa and the records held there. Included in these record types are general records (persons subject to military duty, 1861 to ca. 1916; clothing books: records of clothing and equipment issued and charged to soldiers; etc.), Mexican War (1861–65) records, Civil War (1861–65) records, Spanish American War (1898–99) records, and World War I (1917–18) records. Next is a listing of published sources for Iowa for further research.

The resource books (see book list at end of chapter) available regarding military, state, and historical records disclose many avenues to research. Many facilities, including NARA, publish books or finding aids on their collections. For additional resources within a state of interest, check the Internet using the USGenWeb <http://www.usgenweb.com>. For information regarding specific military records or time periods, go to Cyndi's List at <http://www.cyndislist.com>.

What additional military records should I be aware of?

One type of record that is often overlooked is military hospital records. Both federal and state homes existed for veterans who served their country and needed medical care due to injury or old age.

The federal government has maintained veterans' homes since just after the Civil War. While current records are not available due to privacy laws, many of the records for Civil War soldiers are available through the NARA facilities. The following are national homes for disabled volunteer soldiers:

Notes

Name	Location	Date Founded
Eastern Branch	Togus, Maine	1866
Central Branch	Dayton, Ohio	1867
Northwestern Branch	Wood, Wisconsin	1867
Southern Branch	Kecoughtan, Virginia	1870
Western Branch	Leavenworth, Kansas	1885
Pacific Branch	Sawtelle, California	1888
Marion Branch	Marion, Indiana	1888
Roseburg Branch (successor to Oregon State Home at Roseburg)	Roseburg, Oregon	1894
Danville Branch	Danville, Illinois	1898
Mountain Branch	near Johnson City, Tennessee	1903
Battle Mt. Sanitarium	Hot Springs, South Dakota	1907
Bath Branch (successor to New York State Home at Bath)	Bath, New York	1929
St. Petersburg Home	St. Petersburg, Florida*	1930
Biloxi Home	Biloxi, Mississippi*	1930
Tuskegee Home (formerly a hospital)	Tuskegee, Alabama*	1933

The National Archives does not have records for this home.

Records of the homes are dated 1866–1938 and are part of the Records of the Veterans Administration (Record Group number fifteen). The records that hold the most genealogical importance are the historical registers of residents. Each page is divided into four sections consisting of the following:

Military History	time and place of each enlistment
	rank, company, and regiment
	time and place of discharge
	reason for discharge
	nature of disabilities when admitted
Domestic History	birthplace, age
	height, physical features
	religion, occupation
	marital status
	name and address of nearest relative
Home History	rate of pension
	date of admission to home
	conditions of readmission
	date of discharge from home
	cause of discharge
	date and cause of death and place of burial
General Remarks	information about papers about veteran
	admission papers
	army discharge certificate
	pension certificate
	information about money and personal effects if soldier died in home

Other types of records are

Registers of deaths—The only surviving registers are for the former New York State Home at Bath (1897–1937) and the former Oregon State Home at Roseburg (1894–1937).

Funeral records—Only records for the former New York State Home at Bath (1918–1921) are available.

Burial registers—Only registers for the Eastern Branch in Togus, Maine, (1892–1932 and 1935–1938) are available.

Hospital registers—Only registers for the Eastern Branch in Togus, Maine, (1873–1883) are available.

Did any homes predate the Civil War?

The U.S. Soldiers' and Airmen's Home (originally called the United States Military Asylum) had the following locations for the years indicated:

Greenwood's Island at East Pascagoula, Mississippi	operational from 1851 to 1855
New Orleans Asylum at New Orleans, Louisiana	operational from 1851 to 1852
Washington Asylum at Washington, DC	operational from 1851 to the present
Western Military Asylum at Harrodsburg, Kentucky	operational from 1853 to 1858

Records for these facilities include muster rolls, hospital registers, and death records covering various time periods.

Note that the Washington Asylum was renamed the U.S. Soldiers' Home in 1859, again renamed U.S. Soldiers' and Airmen's Home in 1972. It began admitting disabled and retired U.S. Air Force members in 1942.

What about state homes for soldiers?

Many states operated soldiers' homes at various times in U.S. history. Some have been consolidated with federal homes while others remain in operation as state facilities. In 1920, when a list of state homes was compiled, state-run soldiers' homes were in California, Colorado, Connecticut, Idaho, Illinois, Indiana, Iowa, Kansas, Massachusetts, Michigan, Minnesota, Missouri, Montana, Nebraska, New Hampshire, New Jersey, New York, North Dakota, Ohio, Oklahoma, Oregon, Pennsylvania, Rhode Island, South Dakota, Vermont, Washington, Wisconsin, Wyoming, and the District of Columbia. Many additional soldiers' homes have been established since that list was compiled, and the state veterans' association should be able to tell you the locations of such homes and hospitals.

What information can I obtain from a state veterans' hospital or home?

Obtaining information on deceased veterans can be well worth the effort but keep in mind privacy issues and restrictions. I had extremely good luck obtaining military service records for my husband's grandfather who died in a soldiers' hospital in Massachusetts in 1978. When I contacted the hospital I got the soldier's enlistment and discharge dates, birth and death dates, division of military services, location of service, and next of kin. Since an individual wishing to be admitted into such a home or hospital must prove that he is entitled to this benefit, his service information needs to be provided before admission. How long these records are maintained by the hospital varies by state and facility.

Reminder

What less obvious records are available for veterans?

While service, hospital, and pension records are some of the obvious records to search, you can also consult other records to determine if, when, and where an individual served in the military. Burial records are available from a number of sources both state and federal jurisdictions. Burials of military personnel took place overseas, in prisoner of war camps, and on military posts as well as in soldiers' homes. Most of these locations and facilities have at least some records that vary in content.

Records for burials in national cemeteries, of which Arlington National Cemetery in Washington, DC is the most widely known, are available through the Department of Veterans Affairs in Washington, DC. The records there cover all national cemeteries except for Arlington, which maintains its own set of records. Again checking with a state's veterans association will help you locate national cemeteries located in that state.

Records are also available for Confederate soldiers who died in federal prisons and hospitals in the North. These records are part of NARA record group

M918, Register of Confederate Soldiers and Citizens Who Died in Federal Prisons and Military Hospitals.

The National Archives also has a listing of Union soldiers who were buried at the U.S. Soldiers' Home from 1861 through 1918. Some indexes exist for these burials in national cemeteries for the states of Connecticut, Delaware, Iowa, Maine, Maryland, Massachusetts, Michigan, New Hampshire, New Jersey, Pennsylvania, Rhode Island, Vermont, Wisconsin, and the District of Columbia. Check for additional indexes compiled by historical societies and other organizations.

By utilizing the many resources available, both in libraries and on the Internet, you may find additional sources and information regarding military service and veterans records in local, county, or state libraries. Some records are in published format, while others may be held in manuscript collections. Remember to look for both federal and local military service for an individual.

Sources

FURTHER READING
General

All of the books listed in this category are either about military records specifically or they have chapters detailing records specific to the book's subject matter. Always be on the lookout in any book specific to ethnicities, immigrants, religions, or regions for information regarding military records, as well as subjects, such as land records, to see what might be addressed within the scope of that book.

A Genealogist's Guide to Discovering Your Female Ancestors, by Sharon DeBartolo Carmack. Cincinnati, Ohio: Betterway Books, 1998.

A Genealogist's Guide to Discovering Your Immigrant & Ethnic Ancestors, by Sharon DeBartolo Carmack. Cincinnati, Ohio: Betterway Books, 2000.

Guide to Genealogical Research in the National Archives of the United States, 3d ed., by the National Archives Trust Fund Board. Washington, D.C.: NARA, 2000.

How to Locate Anyone Who Is or Has Been in the Military, 4th ed., by Richard S. Johnson and Debra Johnson Knox. Military Information Enterprises, 1999.

Land & Property Research in the United States, by E. Wade Hone. Salt Lake City, Utah: Ancestry, Inc., 1997.

Locating Lost Family Members and Friends, by Kathleen W. Hinckley. Cincinnati, Ohio: Betterway Books, 1999.

Long-Distance Genealogy, by Christine Crawford-Oppenheimer. Cincinnati, Ohio: Betterway Books, 2000.

Military Service Records: A Select Catalog of Microfilms, by National Archives Trust Fund Board. Washington, D.C.: NARA, 1985.

The Sleuth Book for Genealogists: Strategies for More Successful Family History Research, by Emily Anne Croom. Cincinnati, Ohio: Betterway Books, 2000.

U.S. Military Records, by James C. Neagles. Salt Lake City, Utah: Ancestry, Inc., 1994. (Note: Chapter nine details hundreds of books regarding military records and history. These books are grouped by time period or specific war.)

Your Guide to Cemetery Research, by Sharon DeBartolo Carmack. Cincinnati, Ohio: Betterway Books, 2002.

Revolutionary War and the War of 1812

Abstracts of Graves of Revolutionary Patriots, 4 vols., by Patricia L. Hatcher. Pioneer Heritage Press, 1987–88.

American Women in the U.S. Armed Forces, by Charlotte P. Seeley and Robert Gruber. Revised by Purdy and Gruber. Washington, D.C.: NARA, 1992.

DAR Patriot Index, Daughters of the American Revolution. Washington, D.C.: 1994.

Genealogical Abstracts of Revolutionary War Pension Files, 4 vols., by Virgil D. White. Waynesboro, Tenn.: National Historic Publishing Co., 1990–92.

Guide to Genealogical Research in the National Archives of the United States, 3d ed., by NARA. Washington, D.C.: 2000.

A Guide to Pre-Federal Records in the National Archives, by Howard H. Wehmann. Revised by DeWhitt, National Archives Trust Fund Board. Washington, D.C.: NARA, 1989.

Hessians in the Revolutionary War, by Edward J. Lowell. Williamstown, Mass.: Corner House Publications, 1997.

Index of Revolutionary War Pension Applications in the National Archives, by National Genealogical Society. Washington, D.C., 1976.

Locating Your Revolutionary War Ancestor: A Guide to the Military Records, by James Neagles. Logan, Utah: Everton Publishers, 1983.

Military Service Records: A Select Catalog of National Archives Microfilm Publications, by National Archives Trust Fund Board. Washington, D.C.: NARA, 1985.

Rejected or Suspended Applications for Revolutionary War Pensions, with an Added Index to States, by U.S. Department of the Interior. Baltimore, Md.: Genealogical Publishing Co., Inc., 1969.

Resource Guide for the War of 1812, compiled by John C. Fredriksen. Westport, Conn.: Greenwood Press, 1985.

Ships and Seaman of the American Revolution, by Jack Coggins. Harrisburg, Pa.: Stackpole Books, 1975.

Soldiers and Patriots of the American Revolution, by Joseph Banvard. Boston, Mass.: D. Lothrop & Co., 1876.

Loyalists of the Revolutionary War

Bibliography of Loyalist Source Materials in the United States, Canada, and Great Britain, by Gregory Palmer. Westport, Conn.: Meckler Publishing Co., 1982.

Biographical Sketches of Loyalists of the American Revolution, by Gregory Palmer. Westport, Conn.: Meckler Publishing Co., 1982.

The New Loyalist Index, by Paul J. Bunnell. Bowie, Md.: Heritage Books, 1989.

The Old United Empire Loyalists Lists, by the United Empire Loyalist Centennial Commission. Baltimore, Md.: Genealogical Publishing Co., Inc., 1885; reprinted 1969.

Research Guide to Loyalist Ancestors: A Directory to Archives, Manuscripts, and Published Sources, by Paul J. Bunnell. Bowie, Md.: Heritage Books, 1990.

Civil War

Confederate Research Sources: A Guide to Archives Collections, by James C. Neagles. Salt Lake City, Utah: Ancestry, Inc., 1986.

Official Records of the Union and Confederate Armies in the War of the Rebellion, 128 vols., by U.S. War Department. Washington, D.C.: Govt. Printing Office, 1880–1900, Gettysburg, Pa.: National Historical Society, reprinted 1991.

Official Records of the Union and Confederate Navies in the War of the Rebellion, 31 vols., by U.S. War Department. Washington, D.C.: Govt. Printing Office, 1894–1927, Gettysburg, Pa.: National Historical Society, reprinted 1991.

Tracing Your Civil War Ancestors, rev. ed., by Bertram H. Groene. Winston-Salem, N.C.: Blair Publishers, 1980.

Where to Write for Confederate Pension Records, by Desmond Walls Allen. Bryant, Alaska: Research Associates, 1991.

World War I

Officers and Enlisted Men of the United States Who Lost Their Lives During the World War From April 6, 1917 to November 11, 1920. Washington, D.C. Govt. Printing Office, 1920.

Officers and Enlisted Men of the United States Navy Who Lost Their Lives During the World War From April 6, 1917 to November 11, 1920. Washington, D.C. Govt. Printing Office, 1920.

Soldiers of the Great War, 3 vols., by W.M. Haulsee, F.G. Howe, and A.C. Doyle. Washington, D.C.: Soldiers Record Publishing Association, 1920.

World War II

The Invisible Soldier: The Experience of the Black Soldiers, World War II, compiled by Mary P. Motley. Detroit, Mich.: Wayne State University Press, 1975.

SIX

Immigration and Naturalization Records

Most researchers have at least one immigrant ancestor in their family trees. Immigrant research is one of the fastest growing interests of today's genealogists. In most cases you must pinpoint the exact region or town within the old country before you can attempt research in the foreign records. Few countries have national indexes to birth, marriage, or death records. At best you might locate some regional records, but even for those you need more specifics than "they came from Poland." In many cases the only available records are in churches. Knowing a great deal about your research subject provides many clues to help you narrow down possible locations for records.

When you begin researching the immigrant generation, you must exhaust all records in the United States before trying to use foreign records. This means the records for not only your direct ancestral line but for all of the collateral lines as well. Most immigrants traveled from the old country with others from their village or region, and they often settled together in the same area. All of the people who interacted with your immigrant family probably had ties to the same village or region in the old country. People of the same ethnic group living together in one area shared the same cultural background, religion, cuisine, traditions, etc. Many small communities of immigrants opened family markets, thus providing others with the food they were accustomed to in the old country. Ethnic churches held religious services in the native tongue. Similar occupations were another tie that bound many immigrants together. Stone masons, fishermen, farmers, etc., would settle with others in the same occupations.

Two very effective research techniques that can aid you in your immigrant research are cluster genealogy and surname searches. With cluster genealogy you look at all of the people who lived in a geographic area and were of the same ethnic group (e.g., Italian, Irish). These are all of the people who married into your family, witnessed family documents, were sponsors or godparents for your ancestors, bought or sold property from or to your immigrant family,

Important

belonged to your family's church or fraternal groups, etc. The events and places for interaction are almost endless in number and important to consider.

Surname searches are effective when you isolate a specific surname in one town or county in a country. When researching my grandmother's family in Essex County, Massachusetts, I could not determine where in Italy they had originated. Only two members of the immediate family became U.S. citizens, and neither listed an identifiable place of birth. They had the common surname Bruno, which made a complete surname search overwhelming. I looked at the other surnames in the immediate family and found that my great-grandmother's maiden name was Zarrella, a less common name. I then looked at every naturalization record showing the surname Zarrella (or any variant spelling) in Essex County, Massachusetts. I concentrated on the period 1906 and later since most of the other southern Italians seem to have emigrated around the turn of the twentieth century. I located thirty-eight Zarrella naturalization records for Essex County.

Next I created a chart for the pertinent information for each individual. I listed name, date of birth, place of birth, date of entry to the United States, current residence, court of naturalization, and date of naturalization. When I entered this information in a standard format on a list I noticed that two prominent villages were named: Petruro Irpino and Torrioni. I managed to locate both of these villages in an Italian atlas and saw that they were small villages alongside each other in the hills around Avellino, Italy. I concentrated my search in these two villages and ordered microfilmed records from the Family History Library in Salt Lake City. I found the marriage record for my grandmother's sister in the Torrioni records! By looking at the Zarrella individuals who lived in the same geographic area as my Bruno family I was able to determine a village of origin.

After several years I have determined that all but one of the thirty-eight Zarrella individuals are related to my grandmother's family, which reinforced the theory that they immigrated to and settled together in this country.

NATURALIZATION RECORDS

How can I find naturalization records for my ancestors?

First determine when and where they settled upon arrival in this country. You can often accomplish this through birth, marriage, death, and census records as well as some family papers or stories. Remember to start with the present generation and work backward. By the time you get to the immigrant generation you will know quite a bit about the families—information that will be valuable to you later.

Once you have looked at all possible records for your ancestors you should be able to determine approximately when they arrived in the United States. Several of the later U.S. federal census records show the year of immigration and citizenship status. As early as 1870 the census takers asked if a person's parents were foreign born in addition to asking for each individual's place of

Technique

birth and citizenship status. By looking at the census records carefully you should be able to determine an immigration time frame.

If your research subject is listed as a citizen in the 1900 U.S. census, you need to locate her records in the state she resided in. Naturalizations that took place before 27 September 1906 were filed in the court of record. Prior to that date an individual could go to any court of record (federal, state, county, police, etc.) to apply for citizenship. The only copy of that naturalization record was kept in that specific court. The federal government took over the process upon the creation of the Bureau of Immigration and Naturalization (later to become the Immigration and Naturalization Service [INS]) in 1906. From that date forward the naturalization could take place in any court of record using the federally supplied forms but a copy of that record was forwarded to the bureau in Washington, DC, thereby creating a master file of all naturalizations. The federal government regulated the distribution of these forms and thereby controlled the number of courts that were able to naturalize individuals. This solved the problem of each state creating its own rules and forms. More consistent records were created.

The 1900, 1910, and 1920 census records indicate if an individual was a citizen or not. One of four designations appears: "Al" for alien, meaning he had not begun the process of becoming a citizen; "Pa" (this does not stand for Pennsylvania), meaning that he had filed his first papers, the declaration of intention to become a citizen, but was not yet a citizen; "Na," meaning that the naturalization process had been completed; or "NR," meaning that the citizenship information was not recorded by the census taker. Many researchers misread "Na" as "No" and incorrectly assume that the individual was not yet a citizen. Again, understanding the record you are using, in this case the census, is key to gaining accurate information.

If your research subject became naturalized after 27 September 1906, look for the record in the local (usually county) court first since these courts were close to the immigrant's place of residence. Next try the National Archives regional facility that covers the immigrant's state of residence. (See the NARA locations list in chapter one.)

Another record to check for information about the date and court of naturalization is the voter registration lists or cards that some town or county clerks maintained. When a foreign born person registered to vote, she would have presented her certificate of naturalization to the clerk to prove her citizenship. Many of these certificates are still among the family papers; my grandmother's was stamped on the back with the dates and towns where she registered to vote. One of the town halls had maintained the original registration cards. From hers I learned on what date she was naturalized and in which court, which led me to find her complete file of naturalization documents. The same technique worked for locating her older brother's papers.

Some naturalization records have alphabetical indexes, while others are indexed by the Soundex system. (See chapter four for an explanation of the Soundex coding system.) Once you determine where the index for the geographic region of interest is located, check the index for your ancestor, keeping in mind the spelling variations that may occur for the surname. The index card or book usually gives the name of the individual, the court of record, the date of admission (or granting of citizenship), and perhaps other information such as date and place of birth. These indexes are not created equally, and many variations in format occur. Be patient and persistent when searching these indexes.

Why are there no naturalization records for my grandmother and her children, all of whom were born in the old country?

If the husband and father of a household became a citizen before 22 September 1922, his wife and minor children received derivative citizenship through him. Since the laws changed many times, the time frame is important to decide what rules applied. Prior to 22 September 1922, a married woman carried the citizenship status of her husband. This applied to women born abroad or in the United States. If a woman born in the United States married an alien, she lost her U.S. citizenship. When the law was changed, she had to apply to regain her citizenship as the new law did not reverse the effects of the original law.

When using the federal census records, look for females whose naturalization status is recorded as alien but whose birthplace is in the United States. Many researchers who are unaware of the old citizenship law take this to be an error in recording.

Before 22 September 1922 a married woman could not become a citizen in her own right. A single, divorced, or widowed woman could apply for citizenship, but married women held whatever status their husbands did. After 22 September 1922 a woman married to a U.S. citizen could apply for her own citizenship without filing the declaration of intention, or first papers, and no period of residency was required. A married woman did not, however, automatically become a citizen by virtue of her husband's citizenship. When checking for the husband's papers, also look for a naturalization record for the wife. If he filed after 22 September 1922, you may find a petition for the wife to regain her lost citizenship. See the certificates on pages 94 and 95.

Reminder

Another reason why naturalization papers might not exist is the practice of granting group naturalization to an entire territory when it became part of the United States. Congress granted citizenship to all residents of Hawaii in 1900, Puerto Rico in 1917, and the Virgin Islands in 1927. Other territories that were granted citizenship enmasse were Alabama, Alaska, Florida, Louisiana, Mississippi, and Texas.

What else might have resulted in the loss of citizenship?

Any individual who was a U.S. citizen, either by birth or through the naturalization process, could lose his citizenship status by serving in a foreign army or voting in an election in a foreign country. Enlistment of any U.S. citizen in the military service of an allied country (England, Canada, Italy, etc.) prior to the United States's involvement in World War I resulted in the loss of his U.S. citizenship. This citizenship status could be regained by filing an Application to Take the Oath of Renunciation and Allegiance. These documents can be very informative, sometimes listing the original court of naturalization. One such application was found in the U.S. District Court at Boston NARA records listing that the individual, who enlisted in the Italian army in 1915, had become a citizen by virtue of his father's naturalization in the Superior Court in Sacramento, California. He reapplied and was granted citizenship in the U.S. District Court at Boston on 14 November 1921. See the example on page 96.

What laws applied to the children of aliens?

Some of the laws applying to alien children were

- 1795 to the present: An alien child becomes a citizen when one of his parents is naturalized, provided he lives in the United States.
- 2 March 1907–23 May 1934: An alien child became a citizen when she began her permanent residence in the United States.
- 24 May 1934 to the present: An alien minor child becomes a citizen five years after beginning his U.S. residency.
- 26 March 1804–26 September 1906: An alien child could become a citizen if her father had filed the declaration of intention but died before completing the naturalization process by taking an oath of allegiance.

It is important to know what rules applied to women and children at the time that an event would have taken place.

Could my ancestor purchase land without first becoming a citizen?

As a general rule the answer to this is yes. One exception to that statement is in the state of Indiana. From 14 January 1818 until the law was repealed on 13 January 1846, an immigrant wishing to purchase land in Indiana had to have filed his declaration of intention or "made an oath of affirmation in writing . . . to be recorded, that he is a resident of this state." This law was incorporated into the Homestead Act of 1862. This act encouraged naturalization by granting a U.S. citizen title to 160 acres of land, providing it was tilled for five consecutive years. Immigrants who had filed their declaration of intention to become a citizen were also eligible for this land grant. In order to secure ownership at the end of five years, they had to provide their declaration of intention and petition for naturalization. Copies of these papers can often be found in the homestead files.

The Alien Land Act passed in California in 1913 specified that aliens who were ineligible for U.S. citizenship could not own agricultural land but could retain any land they already owned as of that date. In 1913 Asians were considered ineligible to obtain U.S. citizenship, so they were prohibited from purchasing land in the state of California. (See *A Genealogist's Guide to Discovering Your Immigrant & Ethnic Ancestors*, by Sharon DeBartolo Carmack.)

Why did so many immigrants never bother to become citizens?

The common misconception among researchers is that the immigrants to the United States wanted to become citizens. This belief usually prevails when the researcher does not understand the social history aspects of the emigration

ORIGINAL
(To be retained by Clerk of Court)

UNITED STATES OF AMERICA

No. **10**

APPLICATION TO TAKE THE OATH OF RENUNCIATION AND ALLEGIANCE AND FORM OF SUCH OATH (Form No. N–408)

(Filed under Section 317 (b) of the Nationality Act of 1940, 54 Stat. 1146–1147)

Commonwealth of Massachusetts } ss:
County of Succolk

In the _____ District _____ Court
of _____ the United States at Boston, Massachuset·

This application to take the oath of renunciation and allegiance, hereby made and filed, respectfully shows:

(1) My full, true, and correct name is _____ Isabelle LaPierre _____
(Full true, name, without abbreviation, and any other name which has been used, must appear here)

(2) My present place of residence is _____ 43 Essex Street, Lowell, Mass (3) My occupation is _____ Housekeeper _____
(Number and street) (City or town) (County) (State)

(4) I am 62 years old. (5) I was born on May 9 1885 in _____ Lowell _____ Massachusetts _____ USA
(Month) (Day) (Year) (City or town) (County, district, province, or state) (Country)

(6) My personal description is as follows: Sex female ; color white ; complexion medium color of eyes brown; color of hair grey;

height 5 feet 2 inches; weight 138 pounds; visible distinctive marks _____ none _____

(7) I was married; the name of my husband is _____ Adrien LaPierre _____; we were married on Sept 9 1913
(Month) (Day) (Year)

at _____ Lowell Massachusetts; he was born at _____ Montreal, Quebec, Canada _____ on March 25 1891
(City or town) (State) (Country) (City or town) (County, district, province, or state) (Country) (Month) (Day) (Year)

and now resides at _____ deceased _____
(Number and street) (City or town) (State) (Country)

(8) I lost, or believe that I lost, United States citizenship solely by reason of my marriage on Sept 9 1913 to Adrien LaPierre
(Month) (Day) (Year)

then an alien, a citizen or subject of _____ Great Britain _____, and my marital status with such person was terminated on Jan 23 1945
(Name of country) (Month) (Day) (Year)

by _____ death _____
(State by what means marital status terminated)

(9) Wherefore, I pray that I may be permitted to take the oath of renunciation and allegiance to the United States as prescribed in Section 335 (b) of the Nationality Act of 1940.

I, aforesaid applicant, do swear (affirm) that I know the contents of this application subscribed by me, that the same are true to the best of my own knowledge, except as to matters therein stated to be alleged upon information and belief, and that as to those matters I believe them to be true, and that this application is signed by me with my full, true name: SO HELP ME GOD.

Isabelle La Pierre
(Full, true and correct signature of applicant, without abbreviation)

Subscribed and sworn to before me by the above named applicant, in the office of the Clerk of said Court at **Boston Mass.**

this **21st** day of **July**, Anno Domini 19 **47**

James S. Allen
Clerk.

By *Anna C Crowe*
Deputy Clerk. (SEAL)

OATH OF RENUNCIATION AND ALLEGIANCE

I hereby declare, on oath, that I absolutely and entirely renounce and abjure all allegiance and fidelity to any foreign prince, potentate, state, or sovereignty of whom or which I have heretofore been a subject or citizen; that I will support and defend the Constitution and laws of the United States of America against all enemies, foreign and domestic; that I will bear true faith and allegiance to the same; and that I take this obligation freely without any mental reservation or purpose of evasion: SO HELP ME GOD. In acknowledgment whereof I have hereunto affixed my signature.

Isabelle La Pierre
(Full, true and correct signature of applicant, without abbreviation)

The foregoing oath was administered to the applicant this **29th** day of **July**, 19 **47**

(SEAL) Judge.
(or)
James S. Allen
Clerk.
By _____
Deputy Clerk.

U. S. DEPARTMENT OF JUSTICE
IMMIGRATION AND NATURALIZATION SERVICE
(Edition of 1-13-41)

NOTE TO CLERK OF COURT.—No fee is to be collected in connection with the filing of this application.

16—19545   U. S. GOVERNMENT PRINTING OFFICE

Figure 6-1
Repatriation certificate for Isabelle LaPierre. NARA record group 21, U.S. District Court, Boston, Mass. Repatriation of Women Who Married Non-American Citizens Act of 25 June 1936.

Form 2234
U. S. DEPARTMENT OF LABOR
IMMIGRATION AND NATURALIZATION SERVICE

351
ORIGINAL
(To be retained as the court record)

APPLICATION TO TAKE OATH OF ALLEGIANCE TO THE UNITED STATES UNDER THE ACT OF JUNE 25, 1936, AND FORM OF SUCH OATH (PUBLIC—NO. 793—74th CONGRESS)

This form is for use under the Act of June 25, 1936 (Public—No. 793—74th Congress) by a woman residing within or under the jurisdiction of the United States, who was a native-born citizen of the United States and who has, or is believed to have, lost United States citizenship solely by reason of marriage prior to September 22, 1922, to an alien, and whose marital status with such alien has terminated. A woman, residing elsewhere, who is otherwise qualified should take up her case with an embassy, legation, or a consular officer of the United States. The oath of allegiance prescribed herein may be administered by any naturalization court in the United States to which this application is made. This form, which constitutes the court record of the transaction, should be executed in triplicate. The original should be retained as the record of the court. The duplicate, duly certified by the clerk of court, should be forwarded to the Commissioner of Immigration and Naturalization, Washington, D. C., through the proper District Director or Divisional Director of Immigration and Naturalization on the first day of the succeeding month. The clerk of court shall furnish to the applicant, upon her demand, at a cost not exceeding $1, a certified copy of the proceedings, under the seal of the court, including a copy of the oath administered. The triplicate copy of this form, which should be duly certified by the clerk, may be furnished to the applicant who makes such demand. If no such demand be made, the triplicate, uncertified, shall be forwarded with the duplicate as provided above.

In the ___U. S. District___ Court at ___Boston, Mass.___

Before ___George C. Sweeney___, J., presiding.

I, ___Marion Louise Savage —nee Metcalf___, was born at ___Quincy, Massachusetts___
367 Somerville Ave., Somerville, Mass.
on ___May 19, 1892___, and was married on ___July 10th, 1912___ to

___Timothy Savage___ then an alien, a citizen or subject of ___Great Britain___
I lost, or believe that I lost, United States citizenship solely by reason of such marriage. My marital status with such alien terminated on ___October 1, 1931___ by ___divorce which became absolute that date.___
The following available documents which support the foregoing facts are herewith exhibited by me: ___
Birth Certificate, showing birth at Quincy,Mass., May 19, 1892;
Marriage Certificate, showing I married Timothy Savage at Cambridge,Mass.,July 10, 1912 - and divorce decree showing divorce granted me at Middlesex Probate Court, on April 1, 1931, and which became absolute on October 1, 1931.___
I hereby apply to take the oath of allegiance as prescribed in section 4 of the Act of June 29, 1906 (34 Stat. 596; U. S. C., t. 8, sec. 106), to become repatriated and obtain the rights of a citizen of the United States.

Marion Louise Savage
(Signature of applicant)

Subscribed and sworn to before me this ___21st___ day of ___August___, 19__40__

[SEAL]
___James S. Allen___
Clerk.
By ___William Lyons___, Deputy.

Upon consideration of the foregoing, it is hereby ORDERED and DECREED that the above application be granted; that the applicant named therein be repatriated as a citizen of the United States, upon taking the oath of allegiance to the United States; and that the clerk of this court enter these proceedings of record.

Dated ___September 9th, 1940___. J. ___

OATH OF ALLEGIANCE

I hereby declare on oath, that I absolutely and entirely renounce and abjure all allegiance and fidelity to any foreign prince, potentate, state, or sovereignty, and particularly to ___ * * * * * * ___

of whom (which) I have or may have heretofore been a subject (or citizen); that I will support and defend the Constitution and laws of the United States of America against all enemies, foreign and domestic; that I will bear true faith and allegiance to the same; and that I take this obligation freely without any mental reservation or purpose of evasion; SO HELP ME GOD. In acknowledgment whereof I have hereunto affixed my signature.

Marion Louise Savage
(Signature of applicant)

The foregoing oath was administered to the applicant in open court this ___9th___ day of ___September___, 19__40__

[SEAL]
___James S. Allen___
Clerk.
By ___, Deputy.

U.S. GOVERNMENT PRINTING OFFICE   14—3373

Figure 6-2
Repatriation certificate for Marion Louise Savage. NARA record group 21, U.S. District Court, Boston, Mass. Repatriation of Women Who Married Non-American Citizens Act of 25 June 1936.

59 Summer St Natick

Form 136.

OATH OF ALLEGIANCE TO THE UNITED STATES, PREPARED IN CONFORMITY WITH SUBDIVISION TWELFTH OF SECTION 4 OF THE ACT OF JUNE 29, 1906, AS AMENDED BY THE ACT APPROVED MAY 9, 1918, PUBLIC NO. 144, SIXTY-FIFTH CONGRESS, AND REGULATIONS MADE THEREFOR.

U. S. DEPARTMENT OF LABOR
BUREAU OF NATURALIZATION

This form has been prepared and adopted by the Bureau of Naturalization, Department of Labor, for use in carrying into effect the provisions of subdivision twelfth of section 4, of the act of June 29, 1906, as amended by the act approved May 9, 1918, Public No. 144, Sixty-fifth Congress, by which any American citizen who is deemed to have expatriated himself by taking an oath of allegiance to enter the military or naval service of a country "at war with a country with which the United States is now at war" may resume his American citizenship. This oath of allegiance should be taken on this form, in triplicate, before any court authorized to naturalize aliens. One copy should be retained for the court record and two copies should be forwarded to the Bureau of Naturalization, whence one will be transmitted to the Department of State, as a compliance with the requirements of the law. Formal evidence to the individual is not required by law.

NOTE.—No American could expatriate himself "when this country is at war," or after April 5, 1917.

I, _____ Vincenzo Di Giacomoantonio _____, a citizen of the United States,
(Give full name.)

born at _____ Teramo, Italy _____ on _____ August 11, 1887 _____
(City or town.)   (State or foreign country.)   (Month, day, and year.)

father, Carmine, naturalized Oct. 7, 1901 at U.S.Circuit Ct., Boston,
(If naturalized citizen, give court, city or town and State, and date of naturalization.)

entered the { military / ~~naval~~ } service of _____ Italy _____ on _____ April 16 _____, 191 6.
(Name of country.)   (Month and day.)

and thereupon took the prescribed oath or obligation necessary to enter that service, and have never done any other act by which I could be held to have expatriated myself. It is my desire to freely take and subscribe to, without mental reservation or purpose of evasion, the following oath of allegiance to the United States for the purpose of being restored to the status of an American citizen, as provided by subdivision twelfth, section 4, of the act of June 29, 1906, as amended by the act approved May 9, 1918, Public No. 144, Sixty-fifth Congress:

    I hereby declare, on oath, that I absolutely and entirely renounce and abjure all allegiance and fidelity to any foreign prince, potentate, state, or sovereignty; that I will support and defend the Constitution and laws of the United States of America against all enemies, foreign and domestic; and that I will bear true faith and allegiance to the same.

Vincenzo Digiacomantonio
(Sign here full name exactly as given above.)

Subscribed and sworn to before me this _____ 22nd _____ day of _____ October _____, 19 23.

[SEAL.]   *Joseph J. Sullivan*
Deputy Clerk.

In the _____ District _____ Court of _____ the United States _____

_____ Massachusetts District _____ at _____ Boston, Mass. _____

Upon consideration of the foregoing, and the applicant having taken the above oath of allegiance in open court, it is hereby ORDERED AND DECREED, That the clerk of this court enter of record in the minutes of the court that the above oath of allegiance has been taken by the applicant herein named, and that he forward two copies of this affidavit and order to the Bureau of Naturalization, United States Department of Labor, Washington, D. C.

Dated _____ October 22, 1923. _____   *James A. Lowell*

PERSONAL DESCRIPTION OF THE CITIZEN.

Height _5_ feet _6_ inches; color _____ white _____; complexion _____ dark _____; color of eyes

_____ brown _____; color of hair _____ black _____; visible distinguishing marks _____ none. _____

14—1645

Figure 6-3
Application to Take the Oath of Renunciation and Allegiance. NARA record group 21, U.S. District Court, Boston, Mass. Repatriation of Soldiers Act of 9 May 1918.

and immigration process. **Many immigrants left their old country for America not because they wanted to live here but because they could not survive in the old country.** Many immigrant groups, such as the Irish and the southern Italians, left because of severe poverty and the risk of starvation. Widespread famines, wars, religious persecutions, and poverty caused many individuals to pack up their few worldly goods and travel halfway around the world looking for a better life. Many fled to save their lives from invading armies and religious persecution and to avoid being forced into military service.

Once an immigrant arrived in his new country his time was consumed with finding a job and providing for his family. Many immigrants had no need or desire to become citizens. Whether they were citizens or not made little difference in their day-to-day lives. Unless there was some other motivation or gain for the individual, why would he take time off and lose wages from a low-paying job, travel to a courthouse, and provide a foreign government with all of his personal information to gain only the right to vote? Unless he was active in local politics, like some Irishmen in larger cities, he might not have participated in or even understood the political process. For some immigrant groups, especially the Irish, voting was a major tool for political power. Many encouraged others to become citizens and become eligible to vote in exchange for help in hard times or obtaining and keeping a job. For many immigrants the act of voting in itself was a strong statement that for the first time they could actually have a say in their own government.

Many immigrants led productive lives and contributed greatly to the social and economic culture in this country without the benefit of U.S. citizenship. Many foreign born men became citizens after serving in a military capacity in the United States. From 17 July 1862 until 8 May 1918 any honorably discharged veteran could gain citizenship without filing a declaration of intention, one year's residency, and with no waiting period enforced.

What is a collective naturalization?

A collective naturalization occurs when the government, by treaty, acquires the whole or part of a territory from another nation and grants citizenship privileges to a group of people. All residents living within the said territory are considered citizens with no papers or records filed. When the United States accepts a territory as a new state, as it did Hawaii, all residents are granted citizenship through the collective naturalization process.

How do military naturalizations differ from regular ones?

Military naturalization records for several reasons are usually less complete than the average post-1906 records. An immigrant could become a citizen upon honorable discharge from the military beginning 1 August 1862. The original law of 1862 allowed for honorably discharged army veterans to become naturalized without having to file a declaration and with only a one-year residency requirement. This statute covered many soldiers from the Civil War.

On 9 May 1918 a law that still applies today went into effect for military personnel. During World War I any alien who served in the U.S. armed forces was not required to file a declaration or have a certificate of arrival to become a citizen, and he only had to meet a one-year residency requirement. These naturalizations took place at military camps, bases, or area courts. These records therefore can be troublesome to locate. The NARA facility in Washington, DC, has an index (RG85) to these military naturalization records. Also try to use the voter registration cards in the person's town or city of residence to see if the military base of record is noted. You can also try the NARA regional facility covering that geographic region, then the state archives for the state the military base was in. Some records are still held in the court of record, while some are part of the military record for an individual.

The military naturalization records from World War I that I have researched provided little reliable information. With no certificate of arrival you have no guarantee that the immigrant arrived at the port named on the date stated or even on the boat named. Since no documentation was required for any of these items, the data may be inaccurate but serve as clues to follow up on.

The military naturalization laws were extended many times and also include World War II and later military actions. In 1894 an act was passed that required any peacetime enlistee either to be a U.S. citizen or to have filed his declaration.

Definitions

What papers did the immigrants have to submit to become a U.S. citizens?
To become a U.S. citizen after 1906, the immigrant was required first to file a declaration of intention, also referred to as the "first papers," which represented his request for citizenship. After the required waiting period, the length of which changed several times, the immigrant filed his petition for naturalization, or "final papers." The petition documents the name and place of the court where the declaration was filed and the date of that filing. The declaration was usually filed with the petition in one permanent file. The petition number is the finding aid, along with the court name and location. The immigrant was then given a certificate showing court; date; petition number; immigrant's name, address, and age; and certificate number. This certificate number has no bearing on the location of the record. The certificates were consecutively numbered on a pad and issued in numerical order. Look on the certificate for the petition number and the court location to locate the entire record.

For all arrivals after 29 June 1906 a certificate of arrival was required as part of the naturalization process. If a petitioner listed a date and ship of arrival, the passenger list was searched, the information was verified, and a certificate of arrival was issued. In some cases the immigrant did not know her exact date of arrival or the ship name, especially if she arrived as a child.

Notes

What information will I find on these papers?
While no one list of information will match every document, the following is information you might find on post-1906 records:

Declaration of Intention (First Papers)
- name of individual
- address of individual

- occupation
- birthplace or nationality
- country from which emigrated
- birth date or age
- personal description, including marks of identification
- marital status
- last foreign residence
- port of entry
- name of ship
- date of entry
- date of document
- photograph of the individual

Petition for Naturalization (Final Papers)

- name of individual
- address of individual
- occupation
- date emigrated
- country from which emigration occurred
- birthplace
- date and place of the declaration of intention
- birth date or age
- name and age of spouse
- birthplace of spouse
- date and place of marriage
- address of spouse (where spouse resides or if deceased)
- names, ages, birthplaces, and residences of children
- last foreign residence
- port and mode of entry (by ship, plane, train, etc.)
- name of ship
- date of entry into the United States
- name used at the time of entry
- names, addresses, and occupations of witnesses (who must be citizens themselves)
- date of the document
- personal description, including any identifying marks (scars, missing fingers, etc.)

Certificate of Naturalization

- name and address
- birthplace or nationality
- country of origin
- birth date or age
- personal description (including sex; height; weight; and hair, eye, and complexion color)
- marital status

- name and location of court granting the naturalization
- petition number
- date of naturalization
- signature of the individual
- picture of the individual

Certificate of Arrival
- individual's name
- port of entry
- date of arrival in that port
- manner of arrival (name of ship, train, plane, etc.)

What happened to the declaration of intention if the
immigrant did not complete the naturalization process?
After 22 September 1906, two copies were made in addition to the original declaration of intention. The original was kept by the court of record, one copy was given to the person applying for citizenship, and the second copy was sent to Immigration and Naturalization in Washington, DC. If the declarant (person applying for citizenship) never completed the process by filing a petition for naturalization, the Immigration and Naturalization copy was eventually destroyed (the declaration of intention was valid only for a seven-year period), the applicant's copy remained with his papers, but the original was retained by the court of record. The declarations for which naturalization was never completed were bound in volumes in numerical order. To obtain a copy of the declaration of intention, first determine the court in which it was filed. Again, start by checking the records of the county court, and then check the NARA for the federal courts. If the immigrant filed the declaration in one state, moved to another, and then died, the declaration may be difficult to locate. This is why all of the background work on the family in census records and vital records is so important. Knowing all of the places that the immigrant might have lived after arriving in the United States gives you a selection of locations where you can start the search.

What is the certificate of arrival?
This document is sometimes included with the naturalization papers for an individual. Beginning 29 June 1906, immigrants filing their declaration of intention listed their arrival date, the ship name, and their port of arrival. This information was forwarded to the appropriate ports of entry, and the ship manifests were checked. If the information was verified, the INS issued a certificate of arrival and sent it back to the court of naturalization. Following this process and marking the actual manifest when a certificate of arrival was issued helped to prevent naturalization fraud since multiple individuals could not use the same arrival record to apply for citizenship. This certificate is on file with the naturalization papers in the court of record. Some certificates of arrival list the arrival date and port but not the manner of arrival. I have several that list manner of arrival as "SS Unknown," meaning that the

INS could not locate a record for the date stated by the subject but accepted his word regarding the information.

Where are the records created before 1906 held?

Some records created prior to 1906 are housed in the regional National Archives facilities, while others are in the state archives or local or county courts. Consult one of the many books on locating naturalization records from that earlier period to determine specific locations (see book list at end of chapter).

Some of the pre-1906 records are included with the regular court documents and papers, not filed or indexed separately as naturalization records.

What information appears on the pre-1906 records?

This varies from state to state since no federal standards were set for what to include. Most states had basic forms that list only the immigrant's name, country of origin, approximate arrival date, and port of arrival, and some courts never asked for even this basic information. Some handwritten documents include additional information, but again, it depends on the state laws in effect at the time of the document's creation.

Why did my ancestor wait until the 1930s or 1940s, more than thirty years after arriving in the United States, to become a citizen?

Again, if the right to vote was the only motivation for or benefit to becoming a citizen, many immigrants didn't bother to go through the process. This changed drastically as World War II was approaching. When tensions were building toward the start of World War II, many immigrants found themselves in a precarious position. If an immigrant's native country was not an ally of the United States and Britain, she worried what would happen to her during and after the war. Would the United States deport her? Would she be persecuted? Many immigrants had been U.S. residents for thirty years or more, and their children and grandchildren born in the United States were citizens. Going back to the old country was no longer an option for them. This motivated many immigrants to become citizens in the 1930s and 1940s. However, by this time some of the requirements for citizenship had become more stringent, and gaining it had become impossible for some immigrants.

Many immigrants from non-Allied countries (e.g., Japan, Italy, Germany) were labeled "enemy aliens" and placed in detention camps or had restrictions placed on their movements. San Francisco was one of the cities that placed severe restrictions on these individuals by not allowing them to be within a certain distance of the port, by confiscating their flashlights and radios, and by otherwise treating them with suspicion.

What restrictions might have prevented an individual from applying for citizenship?

During the early to mid 1900s it became required that the applicant have the ability to read and write in English. This affected particularly the older immigrants who might not have been able to read or write in their native tongue let alone in English. Many "enemy aliens" during World War II (Italians, Japanese, Germans) could not become citizens due to either the literacy requirement or outright exclusion. After the institution of the Naturalization Act of 1870, Asians (usually meaning Chinese, Filipinos, Japanese, or Koreans, but including those from Burma, India, Indochina, India, Indonesia, Pacific Islands, Persia, and Turkey) were ineligible for U.S. citizenship until the restriction was lifted in 1943.

The Chinese Exclusion Act of 1882, which later included other Asians, restricted immigration as well as citizenship. Those already in the United States could not have their families join them, and if they left the United States they were barred from reentry. For more details on these acts and how they affected specific ethnic groups and for additional details regarding laws and acts that addressed and affected the naturalization process, see *A Genealogist's Guide to Discovering Your Immigrant & Ethnic Ancestors*, by Sharon DeBartolo Carmack, *They Became Americans: Finding Naturalization Records and Ethnic Origins*, by Loretto Dennis Szucs, and *American Naturalization Records, 1790–1990: What They Are and How to Use Them*, by John J. Newman.

Important

Why are these records so important to my research?
Naturalization records and the associated passenger lists may be the most important tools in determining where in the old country your ancestor originated. Since the United States and many other countries have no national index to vital records or other records created about their citizens, you must place an individual in a certain area, county, or province in order to take your research back to the old country. To research in Italy and Ireland, for example, you must know the actual town (parish, comune, or village) an ancestor lived in before you can access any records. Many of the early records are church records and therefore are not under civil government authority at all.

Seek out any and all records to help you determine the origins of your ancestor before you try to "jump the pond" and do research in the old country. Since naturalization and immigration records (from the late 1800s and into the 1900s) are most likely to provide specific places of foreign birth or residency, you should always investigate them. Some very early records (especially prior to 22 September 1922 and the creation of the INS) have little information, depending on where and when the individual arrived or became a citizen. You won't know what you will find until you look!

IMMIGRANT PASSENGER LISTS

For what years do passenger lists or manifests exist?
On 2 March 1819, Congress passed the first law regulating the transportation of passengers to the United States. A high mortality rate had resulted from passengers being crowded onto cargo ships without thought to sanitation and provisions for those passengers. As a result of this law, a ship was restricted to a limit of two passengers for each five tons listed on the ship's registry. Listing not only cargo but also passengers traveling on the ship became necessary.

These lists are referred to as customs passenger lists. The original lists were maintained and kept under the authority of the customs collectors at the port of entry. Most of these lists are now held by the National Archives on microfilm (record group number thirty-six, records of the U.S. Customs Service) although a few are also held in the state archives of individual states. More detailed information regarding the individual ports and time periods is available in Michael Tepper's *American Passenger Arrival Records* and John Philip Colletta's *They Came in Ships*, 2nd edition.

Immigrant passenger lists as we know them now were instituted in the late 1880s and early 1890s. The actual starting date varied for different ports; Philadelphia started earliest, in 1883. Laws and regulations restricted the number of passengers, again by freight tonnage and deck space, and set the requirements for recording each passenger's information. The laws changed many times over the years and required even more information to be on the lists.

What were the major ports of arrival?

The five major ports of arrival in the nineteenth century were New York (receiving nearly three-quarters of the immigrants prior to 1880), Philadelphia, Boston, Baltimore, and New Orleans. During the eighteenth century the port of Philadelphia received the most immigrants. Certain immigrant groups tended to use certain ports of entry; for example, Asians arrived at the port of San Francisco. **Knowing the time frame of immigration and understanding the immigrant group and the laws governing exclusion for certain periods of time will help you determine the most likely port.** Not all immigrants followed the same pattern, but many people from the same areas of the world tended to use the same port of arrival due to the shipping lines that were available to them. (See *A Genealogist's Guide to Discovering Your Immigrant & Ethnic Ancestors*, by Sharon DeBartolo Carmack for additional information pertaining to your specific ethnic group.)

Research Tip

During the late nineteenth and early twentieth centuries about ninety-six U.S. ports of entry were in use including the Gulf coast and the Great Lakes in addition to the more well-known Pacific and Atlantic ports. Inspection stations did not exist until Castle Garden in New York opened in 1855. In 1892 Ellis Island took over the Castle Garden inspection station. San Francisco's Angel Island began operation in 1910.

For what years are passenger lists indexed?

Indexes exist for some ports for certain time periods. The major ports of New York, Philadelphia, Baltimore, Boston, and New Orleans have the following indexes:

Baltimore	1820–1897, 1897–1952
Boston	1848–1891, 1902–1906, 1906–1920
New Orleans	1853–1899, 1900–1952
New York	1820–1846, 1897–1902, 1902–1943, 1944–1948
Philadelphia	1800–1906, 1883–1948

Indexes for other miscellaneous ports cover the period of 1820 to 1873.

Tip

TIPS FOR LOCATING IMMIGRANTS IN INDEXES

- Look up the individual under all possible spellings, especially phonetically

- If surname has a prefix (*Mc, Van, Di,* etc.), look it up both with and without the prefix

- Look up the individual under the given name (in case the given and surname are transposed)

- Look up the foreign name under a literal translation (e.g., LeBlanc as White, Bruno as Brown)

While these are the time periods for the official indexes, organizations have also created indexes for specific ethnicities, ports, and time periods that may cover additional years. Several book series contain additional years of coverage. These include *Germans to America* and *Italians to America*.

How are the indexes arranged within these time periods?

While indexes for each port vary, the port of New York has alphabetical indexes for the time period of 1897 to 1902. Keep in mind that the surname might be misspelled or the card might be filed out of order because it was misread or misplaced.

The port of New York has the cards from 1902 to 1943 separated into two sections. Surnames beginning with the letters *A* through *D* are arranged by the Soundex code (see chapter four for an explanation of Soundex). Within a Soundex code they are alphabetized by the first letter or first two letters of the given name, then ordered by date of arrival or volume number. Surnames beginning with *D* through *Z* are also arranged by Soundex code and then alphabetically by given name, followed by those whose age was not given (for the years 1903–1910), then by age at arrival. (See *A Genealogist's Guide to Discovering Your Immigrant & Ethnic Ancestors*, by Sharon DeBartolo Carmack.)

The Ellis Island American Family Immigration History Center has more than 22 million indexed passenger records from 1892 through 1924 available online at <http://www.EllisIslandRecords.org>. You can search for an individual by his name (you may have to be creative with spellings), by his year of arrival, or by ship name. The site was launched in April 2001 and has become a powerful resource for immigrant research.

For a more detailed listing of the ports, the dates of passenger lists, and accompanying indexes see *Immigrant and Passenger Arrivals: A Select Catalog of National Archives Microfilm Publications* and the *National Archives Microfilm Publications in the Regional Archives System*, published by the National Archives and Records Administration. These are available at NARA regional facilities and at the main facility in Washington, DC.

What if I cannot find my immigrant ancestor in these card indexes?

Some ports also have book indexes that are arranged by date of arrival. The port of Boston has book indexes from 1 April 1899 through 14 September 1940. Since these are grouped by the ship's arrival date and then by specific ship you need to be fairly certain of the date or time period of arrival. The port of New York has book indexes for arrivals from 1906 through 1942. These lists are grouped by shipping line and then arranged chronologically by the date of arrival. The passengers are then indexed alphabetically for each ship within that shipping line (for example, the Red Star, Holland America, White Star, and American shipping lines). Most microfilmed copies of the book indexes cover a two- to six-month time period, so having a good idea of the date of arrival is important.

Why doesn't my immigrant ancestor appear in the passenger list indexes?

If you cannot find your ancestor on any passenger list for the time period of his arrival, consider that he may have been a crew member rather than a paying passenger. Crew lists exist for many ports for many different time frames. It is especially important to check these lists if the immigrant was a single male or a married man traveling by himself. Unfortunately, few, if any, of the crew lists are indexed.

A port of arrival that is often overlooked is St. Albans, Vermont. Any immigrant who crossed the Canadian/U.S. border from 1895 to 1952, regardless of whether she crossed in Vermont or Washington state, should be listed in these records. *The Saint Alban's Canadian Border Entries* divide the records into two time periods (1895–1924, 1924–1952) and has a Soundex index to each group. An additional record group, called *Canadian Border Entries Through Small Ports in Vermont*, covers the years 1895 to 1924. These indexes are alphabetical and grouped by the exact port of entry. They include permanent and temporary admissions on *Records of Registry*, card manifests, or *Primary Inspection Memoranda*, and some even have a photograph of the alien.

Idea Generator

How do I determine the date and port of arrival for my ancestor?

The item you should look for after researching your family in census records and vital records is the naturalization papers. If these papers list a date, port, and ship of arrival, first verify that a ship of that name arrived at that port on that date. You can consult two books to verify several of these facts. The first is *Morton Allen Directory of European Passenger Steamship Arrivals*, which covers the port of New York for the years 1890 to 1930 and the ports of New York, Philadelphia, Boston, and Baltimore for the years 1904 to 1926. This book is divided first by arrival year and then by shipping line (in alphabetical order). Listed under the shipping line name is the route the line traveled (e.g., Glasgow to New York, Spanish ports to New York). Below that is a list of dates and the ships that arrived on each date. (See the sample on page 106.) Several lines may have run the same route, so be sure to check them all. You may find the correct ship name but the date will not match, or you may find the date with a different ship listed. Using the ship name as the better of the two facts, try the date closest to the arrival date mentioned in the naturalization records.

Prince Line Arrivals, 1899, Mediterranean—New York

Arrival Date	Ship Name
Jan. 6	Roman Prince
Jan. 6	Trojan Prince
Jan. 21	Kaffir Prince
Feb. 2	Spartan Prince
Feb. 23	Tartar Prince
Mar. 11	Trojan Prince
Mar. 21	Roman Prince
Apr. 5	Kaffir Prince
Apr. 6	Spartan Prince
May 8	Tartar Prince
May 18	Trojan Prince

Look at the lists carefully to determine the approximate length of the voyage. Calculate how many days passed between arrivals for one specific ship. In the above example, the *Trojan Prince* arrived on 6 January, 11 March, and 18 May 1899. The shortest round trips took more than two months, meaning the transAtlantic trip was approximately three weeks or a month long. The time needed for the crossing was determined by the ship's power, the weather, and other outside influences that might have caused delays.

If you are unable to find a particular ship listed for a year of arrival, you should consult the book *Passenger Ships of the World, Past and Present*, by Eugene W. Smith. This book alphabetizes the ships within distinct shipping routes. There is a section on transatlantic, transpacific, Latin American, African, and Eastern oceans, and the California-Hawaii shipping lines. Within each of these categories is an alphabetical list of ships. The ship's name, shipping line, date of launch, maiden voyage, tonnage, size, engine type, sister ships' names, and other names that the ship bore are included, along with the date a ship was removed from service, was scrapped, or sunk. (See sample entry below.) This is an informative reference that can save you many hours of looking for a particular ship. I have had several instances when a ship is listed on a naturalization record as arriving at New York on a specific date, and then I learned that the ship was not even launched until several years after that date. This means that either the date or the ship name is incorrect on the naturalization and needs to be corroborated using other sources.

Sample entry from *Passenger Ships of the World, Past and Present*, by Eugene W. Smith:

Transatlantic Passenger Ships
Ancona (1908), Italia Line.
    Built by Workman, Clark & Co., Ltd., Belfast, Ireland. Tonnage: 8,210; increased to 8,885. Dimensions: 482' × 58'. Twin-screw, 16 knots. Triple

expansion engines. Two masts and one funnel. Launched: September 19, 1907. Maiden voyage: Genoa-Naples-Palermo-New York, April 23, 1908. Torpedoed and sunk by Austrian submarine in Mediterranean, November 7, 1915, with the loss of 206 lives.

Sister ships: *Taormina* and *Verona*.

How do I find a passenger list if the information on the naturalization record proves to be inaccurate?

Indexes that cover specific ports during certain time periods are available at the National Archives. Not all time periods are indexed, although many organizations are creating more indexes. Like in the census records, many individuals are missing from the card indexes. Consult the many books on passenger records to find additional resources (see book list at end of chapter).

If your ancestor either is not included in the indexes or arrived during a time period not indexed, you will have to narrow down the arrival time period before you can proceed. Since the U.S. censuses in the years 1900, 1910, and 1920 asked for immigrants' dates of arrival, years in the United States, and/or naturalization status, you should obtain and compare information from every available census. This is especially helpful if you need to use the book indexes, which are arranged by date of arrival.

Technique

From each of the available censuses (1850–1920) that list place of birth for an individual look at the immigration information, the ages and birthplaces of any children, and individuals who had the same birthplace as and lived near your ancestor. Since many immigrants to the United States traveled with others from the same area of the old country, determining when these others arrived can provide clues to narrow down the dates. I have used this technique in my research.

Example

After looking with no success for immigration dates for my great-grandparents, I went back to the census records and looked at entries for their neighbors. Most were listed as having been born in Italy, so I decided to look at their naturalization records to see if they were from the same village or province in Italy as my ancestors. Several had the surname that was my great-grandmother's maiden name. When I discovered that they were from the same town, I looked for them in the indexes and on passenger lists. Two of these individuals stated that they were coming to live with their cousin—my great-grandfather! Not only did I find reference to these individuals coming to live with my great-grandparents, I also found my great-grandfather on one of the lists. He was right there on the same list with another relative, but I did not find him in the index.

When looking for women on passenger lists and in the accompanying indexes, remember that they may be listed under either their married or maiden names. For example, Italian women are most often found listed under their maiden names rather than their married ones. In the Italian cultures, as well as the French Canadian, some women maintain their maiden names all of their lives. Italian women's death certificates in the old country are under the maiden name and indicate the name of their spouse (as shown on page 109).

What if my ancestor came through Canada before settling in the United States?

Many European and English immigrants traveled to Canada before arriving in the United States. This was due to several factors. During some time periods, such as 1891, restrictions were placed on the number of immigrants who could arrive from another country. For many of the English and the Irish, traveling to Canada was easy since it was part of the British Empire. The fares at any given time also led immigrants to purchase a less expensive passage and then travel by land to their final destination. Many Canadian steamship and railway companies offered lower fares than those for passage directly to New York or Boston, thereby increasing the number of arrivals into Canada of those who were bound for the United States. Estimates say that as many as 40 percent of all passengers to Canada were intent on getting to the United States. If an immigrant worried that he would be excluded upon arrival in the United States due to illness, mental health, or other reasons, he might try going to Canada instead. This was particularly true when an entire family emigrated from home together and any of the family members had serious health problems. If the family had arrived at Ellis Island or another port, some members of the family might have been granted entry while others would have been sent back to the old country. Some immigrants did not want to risk this, so they traveled to Canada, where restrictions were not as stringent. The English and the Irish headed to Canada were not, technically, traveling to a foreign country but to another British Territory.

The records of entry into the United States from Canada from 1895 to 1952 are called the Canadian Border Entries through the St. Albans, Vermont, District. These records include border crossings in Vermont and as far west as Washington. From 1895 to 1924 the entire border between the United States and Canada was included. In 1924 the border was divided into the Canadian Pacific and Atlantic ports with the records maintaining the St. Albans District title, as that was the official record location for these entries.

Where can I get the St. Albans border entry records?

The St. Albans records are available in the National Archives in Washington, DC, and in some of the NARA regional facilities. The majority of these records are contained within five record groups (see *Immigrant and Passenger Arrivals: A Select Catalog of National Archives Microfilm Publications* online at <http://www.nara.gov/publications/microfilm/immigrant/immpass.html> for a complete list of these records). They are

- M1461: Soundex Index to Canadian Border Entries Through the St. Albans, Vermont, District, 1895–1924
- M1462: Alphabetical Index to Canadian Border Entries Through Small Ports in Vermont
- M1463: Soundex Index to Entries Into the St. Albans, Vermont, District Through Canadian Pacific and Atlantic Ports, 1924–1952

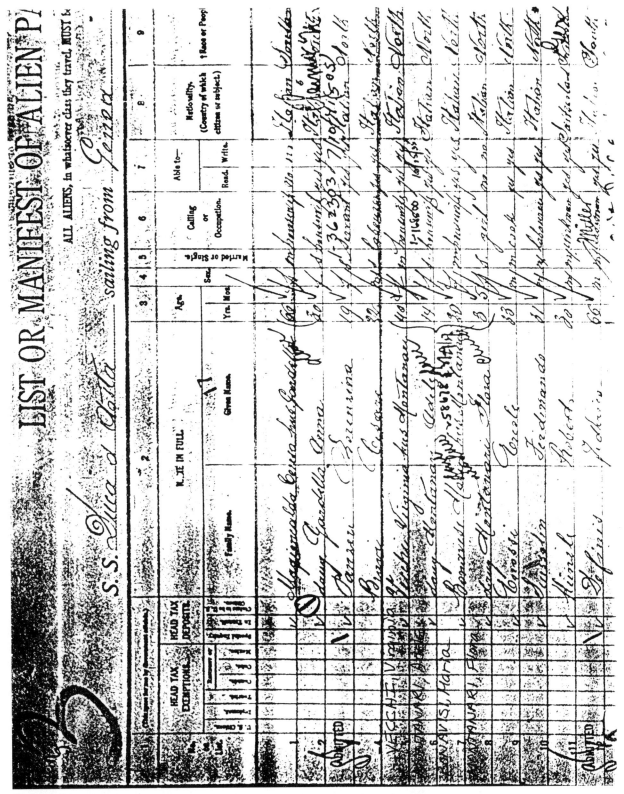

Figure 6-4
Passenger arrival record for Virginia (Vecchi) Montanari and her children from passenger manifest of the SS Duca d'Aosta, Navigazione General Italiana. Arrived in New York on 21 June 1915 (NARA Series T715; roll number 2418; 21 June 1915).

- M1464: Manifests of Passengers Arriving in the St. Albans, Vermont, District Through Canadian Pacific and Atlantic Ports, 1895–1954
- M1465: Manifests of Passengers Arriving in the St. Albans, Vermont, District Through Canadian Pacific Ports, 1929—1949

What about immigrants who arrived before the 1895 institution of the St. Albans lists?

If you are sure that they came through Canada, try looking at records for Boston, Portland, Maine, and any Pacific ports that had service between Canada and the United States. There were many coastal steamers in operation during the 1800s, and they may appear on one of these lists. It is still a good idea to check the indexes for St. Albans as well. I have found that many of the immigrants had relatives who stayed in Canada for one reason or another. Many of the immigrants that continued on to the United States went to and from Canada to visit and may appear on these lists in a later time period than you would expect. As long as the individual was not a United States citizen he should be recorded in these lists; once immigrants became citizens, they were no longer recorded. Canadian and U.S. citizens were able to cross the border as they do today, without being considered immigrants.

Important

Were names actually changed by immigration officials at Ellis Island?

No documented case proves that any immigrant's name was changed by Ellis Island officials. The passenger lists were prepared at the port of departure, using the papers the emigrant provided. The blank lists were provided to the shipping lines by the United States and were to be filled in as the passengers boarded the ship. Names were copied from the documents carried by the emigrants. On board the ship the officials were required to document any births or deaths that occurred during the passage. Once the ship arrived in New York harbor, the first-class and cabin passengers disembarked at a pier, and the steerage passengers were transported by ferry to Ellis Island (or Castle Garden, depending on the time frame) for processing. Numerous pictures of immigrants who had slips of paper bearing numbers attached to their clothing appear in the many books on immigration. These numbers corresponded to the list number that the immigrant appeared on. Officials asked the same questions that were asked when the passengers boarded the ship. The officials were instructed merely to verify the answers and had no need to write any names down—they were already recorded on the list.

If an immigrant appeared to be ill or of questionable character, was a woman traveling alone, or perhaps gave different answers than what was recorded on the list, she might have been detained. Her name would have been transcribed onto the list of detained passengers, usually at the end of the passenger list (for New York records only), and a record of all inquiries regarding that individual was maintained. A woman traveling alone was detained until a male relative showed up to get her. Many times the detained passenger list states the name and relationship of that male relative; in such instances you will have even more information.

Does the passenger list show who an individual's parents were?

In most cases it does not—at least not directly. However, if the parents and children traveled together, you should find that information (if the family is indicated as such). In some cases a man emigrated first, and his wife and children followed. For some later (late/1800s) passenger lists, passengers were asked, "Whom are you going to see?" The answer was many times "my father," with his name and address. Beginning in mid 1907, some passengers were also asked for the name and address of the nearest relative in the old country. This can be valuable information to help you bridge the ocean as you will have a specific street and town. The passenger list might also show (beginning in September 1903) where the immigrant was born and beginning in the 1890s his last permanent residence before emigration. Like naturalization records, passenger lists vary by time period. Most from the late 1800s and into the 1900s are quite informative when all the data is used. Again, know what questions the passengers were asked in the record, and utilize all of the information.

Once I have a copy of the passenger list, what else should I look for?

If you have requested from Washington, DC, and obtained just the page listing your ancestor, you are limited to that one page of information. But you can order the passenger list on microfilm from several different sources and review the entire ship's list. Since detained passengers are listed—only in the New York records and usually at the end of the list—you should review these pages. If your ancestor was detained an additional record may be available at the Immigration and Naturalization Service in Washington, DC. Many records were kept regarding the detained passengers, the reason for detaining them, the meals and medical services that were provided, and the final disposition of the individual's case, which might have included deportation or return to the country of origin.

You should also read the entire list to see what other passengers were from the same village as your ancestor. This can be a valuable clue in tracking your immigrant ancestor. Remember that many immigrants traveled in groups, settled with similar people, and interacted with them throughout their lifetimes. Knowing the names of the others from the same locale gives you additional names to search in the future. Check to see where these others were going and what relatives they listed as already being in that location. I found some relatives that I knew nothing about because I looked carefully at their entries. They were listed with the same birthplace as my grandfather and traveled on the same ship as some of his children. My grandfather was already in the United States, and his children indicated that they were going to live with their father, Bruno Iannizzi, 5 North Square, Boston, Massachusetts. Upon a closer look at the other individuals on that ship and from the same town, I saw that two others had stated that they were going to live with their uncle Bruno Iannizzi, 5 North Square. Always look for these little gems of information in passenger lists, censuses, and other records. Be thorough and gather all possible clues. On just one page of the passenger list for my grandfather's ship I found twenty-one individuals who also were from the village of Grotteria. Of these twenty-one people I have connected all but one to my family as relatives of my grandfather.

Can I obtain a picture of the ship my ancestors traveled on?
An item worth looking for is a photograph of the ship. The book *Ships of Our Ancestors*, by Michael J. Anuta provides pictures or drawings of nearly nine hundred of the passenger ships in operation from the mid 1800s to the mid 1900s. For each photograph the name of the ship, the beginning date of operation, the shipping line name, and the name of the museum or organization that supplied the picture are noted. In most cases you can contact the organization or museum and, for a fee, obtain a black-and-white print of the ship. Look for additional books in maritime museums, libraries, and educational libraries, as many are now out of print.

Sources

FURTHER READING
General Immigration and Naturalization Research

American Naturalization Records, 1790–1990: What They Are and How to Use Them, by John J. Newman. Heritage Quest, 1998.

American Passenger Arrival Records, A Guide to the Records of Immigrants Arriving at American Ports by Sail or Steam, by Michael Tepper. Baltimore, Md.: Genealogical Publishing Company, Inc., 1993.

Documents of Our Ancestors, by Michael J. Meshenberg. Teaneck, N.J.: Avotaynu, Inc., 1996.

A Genealogist's Guide to Discovering Your Immigrant & Ethnic Ancestors, by Sharon DeBartolo Carmack. Cincinnati, Ohio: Betterway Books, 2000.

Guide to Genealogical Research in the National Archives of the United States, 3d ed., by National Archives Trust Fund Board. Washington, D.C.: NARA, 2001.

Immigrant & Passenger Arrivals: A Select Catalog of National Archives Publications, by the National Archives Trust Fund Board. Washington, D.C.: NARA, 1983.

Morton Allen Directory of European Passenger Steamship Arrivals. Baltimore, Md.: Genealogical Publishing Co., Inc., 1979 (reprinted from 1931).

Passenger Ships of the World Past and Present, 2d ed., by Eugene W. Smith. Boston, Mass.: George H. Dean Co., 1978.

Ships of Our Ancestors, by Michael J. Anuta. Baltimore, Md.: Genealogical Publishing Co., Inc., 1983.

They Became Americans: Finding Naturalization Records and Ethnic Origins, by Loretto Dennis Szucs. Salt Lake City, Utah: Ancestry, Inc., 1998

They Came in Ships: A Guide to Finding Your Immigrant Ancestor's Arrival Record, by John P. Colletta, Ph.D. Salt Lake City, Utah: Ancestry, Inc., 1989, 1993.

Ethnic or Religious Groups
African-American

African American Genealogical Sourcebook, edited by Paula K. Byers. New York: Gale Research Inc., 1995.

Black Genealogy, by Charles H. Blockson with Ron Fry. Baltimore, Md.: Black Classic Press, 1991.

Black Roots: A Beginners Guide to Tracing the African American Family Tree, by Tony Burroughs. New York: Simon & Schuster, 2001.

Finding a Place Called Home: A Guide to African-American Genealogy and Historical Identity, revised and expanded, by Dee Palmer Woodtor, Ph.D. New York: Random House, 2000.

Slave Genealogy: A Research Guide With Case Studies, by David H. Streets. Bowie, Md.: Heritage Books, 1986.

Canadian

Atlantic Canadian Research, by Terrence M. Punch, CG (Canada) with George F. Sanborn Jr. FASG 2d ed. Boston, Mass.: NEHGS, 1997.

Books You Need to Do Genealogy in Ontario: An Annotated Bibliography, 2d ed., by Ryan Taylor. Fort Wayne, Ind.: Round Tower Books, 2000.

The French-Canadian Heritage in New England, by Gerard J. Brault. Hanover, N.H.: University Press of New England, 1986.

Genealogist's Handbook for Atlantic Canadian Research, 2d ed., by Terrance Punch with George F. Sanborn Jr. Boston, Mass.: New England Historic Genealogical Society, 1997.

Genealogy in Ontario: Searching the Records, 3d ed., by Brenda Dougall Merriman. Toronto, Ont.: Ontario Genealogical Society, 1996.

Here Be Dragons! Navigate the Hazards Found in Canadian Family Research: A Guide for Genealogists, by Althea Douglas. Toronto, Ont.: Ontario Genealogical Society, 1996.

In Search of Your Canadian Roots, 3d ed., by Angus Baxter. Baltimore, Md.: Genealogical Publishing Co., 2000.

Links to Your Canadian Past, by Peter Gagne. (Vol. 1 Acadia and the Maritime Provinces, Vol. 2 Quebec, Vol. 3 Ontario and the Canadian West). Pawtucket, RI: Quintin Pub., 1999.

Our French-Canadian Ancestors, Vol. I, by Thomas J. Laforest. Palm Harbor, Fla.: Lisi Press, 1983.

Our French-Canadian Ancestors, Vol. II, by Thomas J. Laforest and Gerald Lebel. Palm Harbor, Fla.: Lisi Press, 1984.

Our French-Canadian Ancestors, Vol. III, Roll of the Church in New France, by Thomas J. Laforest and Gerald Lebel. Palm Harbor. Fla.: Lisi Press, 1984.

Our French-Canadian Ancestors, Vol. IV, by Jacques Saintonge and Thomas J. Laforest. Palm Harbor, Fla.: Lisi Press, 1986.

The True Story of the Acadians, by Dudley J. LeBlanc. Pawtucket, R.I.: Quintin Pub., 1998.

English and Irish

Ancestral Trails: The Complete Guide to British Genealogy and Family History, by Mark D. Herber. Baltimore, Md.: Genealogical Publishing Co., Inc., 1998.

A Genealogist's Guide to Discovering Your English Ancestors, by Paul Milner and Linda Jonas. Cincinnati, Ohio: Betterway Books, 2000.

A Genealogist's Guide to Discovering Your Irish Ancestors, by Dwight A. Radford and Kyle Betit. Cincinnati, Ohio: Betterway Books, 2001.

General Alphabetical Index to the Townlands and Towns, Parishes and Baronies of Ireland, Based on the Census of Ireland for the Year 1851. Baltimore, Md.: Reissued by Genealogical Publishing Co., Inc., 1997.

In Search of Your British & Irish Roots: A Complete Guide to Tracing Your English, Welsh, Scottish, and Irish Ancestors, 4th ed., by Angus Baxter. Baltimore, Md.: Genealogical Publishing Co., Inc., 1999.

Irish Records: Sources for Family and Local History, 2d ed., by James G. Ryan, Ph.D. Salt Lake City, Utah: Ancestry, Inc., 1997.

Irish Relatives and Friends From "Information Wanted" Ads in the Irish-American, 1850–1871, by Laura Murphy DeGrazia and Diane Fitspatrick Haberstroh. Baltimore, Md.: Genealogical Publishing Co., Inc., 2001.

Researching Your Armagh Ancestors: A Practical Guide for the Family and Local Historian, by Ulster Historical Foundation, 2000.

Richard Griffith and His Valuations of Ireland, by James E. Reilly. Baltimore, Md.: Clearfield Co., 2000.

The Stones Speak: Irish Place Names From Inscriptions in Boston's Mount Calvary Cemetery, by Richard Andrew Pierce. Boston, Mass.: New England Historic Genealogical Society, 2000.

Tracing Your Irish Ancestors, 2d ed., by John Grenham. Baltimore, Md.: Genealogical Publishing Co., Inc., 2000.

Ulster Libraries: Archives, Museums & Ancestral Heritage Center, by Robert K. O'Neill. Belfast, Northern Ireland: Ulster Historical Foundation, 1997.

Your English Ancestry: A Guide for North Americans, rev. ed., by Sherry Irvine. Salt Lake City, Utah: Ancestry, Inc., 1998.

European

In Search of Your European Roots: A Complete Guide to Tracing Your Ancestors in Every Country in Europe, 3d ed., by Angus Baxter. Baltimore, Md.: Genealogical Publishing Co., Inc., 2001.

Finnish

Finnish Genealogical Research, by Timothy Laitila Vincent and Rick Tapio. New Brighton, Minn.: Family Sleuths for Finnish and Swedish Genealogical Research, 1994.

French (see also Canadian)

Beginning Franco-American Genealogy, by Rev. Dennis M. Boudreau. American French Genealogical Society, 1986.

The Foreign French: Nineteenth-Century French Immigration into Louisiana, 1840–1848, by Carl A. Brasseaux. University of Louisiana at Lafayette, 1992.

General or Multiethnic

Following the Paper Trail: A Multilingual Translation Guide, by Jonathan D. Shea and William F. Hoffman. Teaneck, N.Y.: Avotaynu, Inc., 1994.

A Genealogist's Guide to Discovering Your Immigrant & Ethnic Ancestors, by Sharon DeBartolo Carmack. Cincinnati, Ohio: Betterway Books, 2000.

U.S. Catholic Sources: A Diocesan Research Guide, by Virginia Humling. Salt Lake City, Utah: Ancestry, Inc., 1995.

Germany

Finding Your German Ancestors: A Beginner's Guide, by Kevan Hansen. Salt Lake City, Utah: Ancestry, Inc., 1999.

A Genealogist's Guide to Discovering Your Germanic Ancestors, by S. Chris Anderson and Ernest Thode. Cincinnati, Ohio: Betterway Books, 2000.

The German Research Companion, 2d ed., by Shirley J. Riemer. Sacramento, Calif.: Lorelei Press, 2000.

Germanic Genealogy: A Guide to Worldwide Sources and Migration Patterns, 2d ed., by Brandt, Bellingham, Cutkomp, Frye and Lowe. St. Paul, Minn.: Germanic Genealogical Society, 1997.

Germans to America: Lists of Passengers Arriving at U.S. Ports, 1850–1855, by Ira A. Glazier and P. William Filby. Multivolume. Wilmington, Del.: Scholarly Resources, 1988–.

In Search of Your German Roots: A Complete Guide to Tracing Your Ancestors in the Germanic Area of Europe, 4th ed., by Angus Baxter. Baltimore, Md.: Genealogical Publishing Co., Inc., 2001.

Lands of the German Empire and Before, by Wendy K. Uncapher. Janesville, Wis.: Origins, 2000.

Greek

Tracing Your Greek Ancestry, by Antonia S. Mattheou. Huntington, N.Y.: The author, 1992.

Hispanic

A Beginner's Guide to Hispanic Genealogy, by Norma P. Flores and Patsy Ludwig. San Mateo, Calif.: Western Book Journal Press, 1993.

Census Records for Latin America and the Hispanic United States, by Lyman D. Platt. Baltimore, Md.: Genealogical Publishing Co., Inc., 1998.

Finding Your Hispanic Roots, by George R. Ryskamp. Baltimore, Md.: Genealogical Publishing Co., Inc., 1997.

Hispanic American Genealogy Sourcebook (Genealogy Sourcebook Series) by Paula K. Byers. New York: Gale Group, 1994.

Hispanic Surnames and Family History, by Lyman De Platt. Baltimore, Md.: Genealogical Publishing Co., Inc., 1996.

A Student's Guide to Mexican American Genealogy (Oryz American Family Tree Series), by George R. Ryskamp and Peggy Ryskamp. Phoenix, Ariz.: Oryx Press, 1996.

Italian

Ethnics and Enclaves, Boston's Italian North End, by William M. De Marco. Ann Arbor, Mich.: UMI Research Press, 1980.

Finding Italian Roots—A Complete Guide for Americans, by John P. Colletta. Baltimore, Md.: Genealogical Publishing Co., Inc., 1993.

A Genealogist's Guide to Discovering Your Italian Ancestors, by Lynn Nelson. Cincinnati, Ohio: Betterway Books, 1997.

The Golden Door, Italian and Jewish Immigrant Mobility in New York City 1880—1915, by Thomas Kessner. New York: Oxford University Press, 1977.

Italian Genealogical Records, by Trafford Cole. Salt Lake City, Utah: Ancestry, Inc., 1995.

Italian-American Family History: A Guide to Researching and Writing About Your Heritage, by Sharon DeBartolo Carmack. Wilmington, Del.: Genealogical Publishing Co., Inc., 1997.

Italians to America: Lists of Passengers Arriving at U.S. Ports, 1880–1899. 12 vols. projected. Wilmington, Del.: Scholarly Resources, 1992–.

Jewish

FAQ: Frequently Asked Questions About Jewish Genealogy, by Warren Blatt. Teaneck, N.Y.: Avotaynu, Inc., 1996

Finding Your Jewish Roots in Galacia: A Resource Guide, by Suzan F. Wynne. Teaneck, N.Y.: Avotaynu, Inc., 1998.

From Generation to Generation: How to Trace Your Jewish Genealogy and Family History, by Arthur Kurzweil. New York: HarperCollins, 1994.

Getting Started in Jewish Genealogy, by Gary Mokotoff and Warren Blatt. Teaneck, N.Y.: Avotaynu, Inc., 2000.

The Golden Door, Italian and Jewish Immigrant Mobility in New York City 1880–1915, by Thomas Kesner. New York: Oxford University Press, 1977.

Jewish Family Names and Their Origins: An Etymological Dictionary, by Heinrich W. and Eva Guggenheimer. Hoboken, N.J.: KTAV Publishing House, 1992.

Jewish Roots in Poland: Pages From the Past and Archival Inventories (The Jewish Genealogy Series), by Miriam Weiner. New York: Routes to Roots Foundation, 1998.

Jewish Roots in Ukraine and Moldava: Pages From the Past and Archival Inventories (The Jewish Genealogy Series), by Miriam Weiner. New York: Routes to Roots Foundation, 1999.

Library Resources for German-Jewish Genealogy (Avotaynu Monograph Series), by Angelika G. Ellmann-Kruger and Edward D. Luft. Teaneck, N.Y.: Avotaynu, Inc., 1998.

Resources for Jewish Genealogy in the Boston Area, by Warren Blatt. Boston, Mass.: Jewish Genealogical Society of Greater Boston, 1996.

Scattered Seeds: A Guide to Jewish Genealogy, by Mona Freedman-Morris. Boca Raton, Fla.: R.J. Press, 1998.

Sources in the United States and Canada (The Encyclopedia of Jewish Genealogy, vol. 1), by Miriam Weiner. Northvale, N.J.: Jason Aronson, 1997.

Polish

Directory of Polish Roman Catholic Parishes in the Territory of the Former Austrian Partition—Galicia, by Jonathan D. Shea. New Britain, Conn.: Published by author.

Polish Genealogy and Heraldry: An Introduction to Research, by Janina W. Hoskins. Hippocrene Books, 1990.

Polish Roots, by Rosemary A. Chorzempa. Baltimore, Md.: Genealogical Publishing Co., Inc., 1993.

Translation Guide to Nineteenth Century Polish Language Civil Registration Documents (Birth, Marriage, and Death Records), compiled and edited by Judith R. Frazin. Northbrook, Ill.: Jewish Genealogical Society of Illinois, 1989.

Scandinavian

Norwegian Research Guide, rev. ed., by Linda M. Herrick and Wendy K. Uncapher. Janesville, Wis.: Origins, 2000.

Swedish Genealogical Dictionary, 3d ed., by Phyllis J. Pladsen and Joseph C. Huber. White Bear Lake, Minn.: Pladsen Sveria Press, 1995.

Swedish Genealogical Resources, 2d ed., by The Swedish Genealogical Group/Minnesota Genealogical Society. St. Paul, Minn.: SWG and MGS, 1987.

Scottish

The Original Scots Colonists of Early America, 1612–1783, by David Dobson. Baltimore, Md.: Genealogical Publishing Co., Inc., 1995.

Original Scots Colonists to Early America, Supplement 1607–1707, by David Dobson. Baltimore, Md.: Genealogical Publishing Co., Inc., 1998.

Tracing Your Scottish Ancestry, by Kathleen B. Cory. Baltimore, Md.: Genealogical Publishing Co., Inc., 1995.

Your Scottish Ancestry: A Guide for North Americans, by Sherry Irvine. Salt Lake City, Utah: Ancestry, Inc., 1997.

Welsh (see also "English and Irish")

Second Stages in Researching Welsh Ancestry, edited by John and Sheila Rowlands. Baltimore, Md.: Genealogical Publishing Co., Inc., 1999.

Welsh Family History: A Guide to Research, 2d ed., edited by John Rowlands, et. al. Baltimore, Md.: Genealogical Publishing Co., Inc., 1999.

SEVEN

Computers, the Internet, Indexes, and Computer Databases

T he Internet, the World Wide Web, e-mail, computerized databases, and research CD-ROMs have changed genealogical research. Using these electronic tools can make locating relatives, both living and dead, as easy as clicking a mouse. However, just because the information appears on a computer does *not* make it true. As in printed genealogies and other books, many unproven "facts" and assumptions are flying around in cyberspace. Use the information gleaned from submitted family pedigrees, record extractions, indexes, etc., as it is—secondhand or secondary information that may or may not be correct.

With the explosion of the Internet over the last ten years has come a wealth of information. This information is now available in your own home at any hour of the day or at a library that offers Internet access. The Internet, like any modern convenience, comes complete with its own problems and pitfalls. Many of the same rules that apply to basic genealogical research also apply to Internet research, but many additional rules and cautions must be observed when using the Internet.

Warning

There is a widespread misconception that everyone's family's information is already compiled and out there somewhere on the Net or in a library. While a wealth of information is available, the chances that someone somewhere has already compiled a completely accurate genealogy of your family are slim to none. Some compilations might include portions of your family, but as a totally complete file, it is unlikely to exist. Most of the available databases and compiled genealogies are valuable tools when used to find clues, but you must use caution before taking anything to be fact.

If you look closely at the many types of databases containing compiled genealogies, you will see that most "facts" have little or no documentation as to where the compiler found the information. Without knowing where the information was obtained you have no direct way to judge its accuracy. Where an item comes from is just as important to you as the item itself. Would you trust a birth date recorded in official town records or one carved on a tombstone? Knowing how and when a record you examine was created will help you determine its accuracy. This is also true for computer databases.

All typeset books, indexes, and computerized information are *not* original source material. Someone has compiled listings from other sources and created typeset or digital versions of the original information. When an individual reads an original handwritten document and converts it to a database or list, she transcribes or abstracts the information as she sees and interprets it. Different individuals presented with the same document may view its contents in entirely different ways.

Definitions

SOURCE TERMINOLOGY

Transcription: a verbatim record or copy of a portion or all of some proceedings, writings, or words.

Abstract: to set forth pertinent portions of a writing or document; the act of selecting pertinent portions of a writing.

Source: *What Did They Mean By That? A Dictionary of Historical Terms for Genealogists* by Paul Drake

---

When dealing with indexes and electronic databases, you must understand how they were compiled before you can determine their completeness and accuracy. Determining the completeness of an index or database can be accomplished fairly easily. If an index is in book form, turn to any page in the book and select the name of an individual or a town, then see if it is listed in the index. Checking whether items within the text that may be pertinent to your search are included in the index will help you see how inclusive the index is. Many indexes are terribly incomplete, and you may miss information if you rely on them. The information you seek may not be included in the index for a book that holds that information.

With so many records and indexes being computerized do I have to know how to use a computer to do genealogy?

While not a necessity, a computer to use in your research is certainly a valuable tool in the overall picture. Many researchers are older individuals who did not grow up with computers in their lives—or did they? Consider the appliances and conveniences that we enjoy today. Many of these items are controlled much the same as computers are—by electronic means.

A friend of mine who is a computer whiz helped me overcome my fear of using computers with a down-to-earth approach. He asked me if I use a VCR at home; I answered that I do. His next question was if I understand how it works. My reply was no. He then asked, "Does that stop you from using it?" Again, my answer was no.

119

He went on to ask me if my parents had handed me the keys to the car when I turned sixteen so I could just hop in and drive off. "Of course not" was my reply. He explained that you don't have to understand all of the inner workings of a machine to use it and that you don't just "get behind the wheel" and operate the machine either. The fact that most of us don't understand how a combustion engine works doesn't stop us from driving our cars, nor should lack of knowledge stop us from using a computer. We have to learn how to use it just as we learned to drive, step-by-step. He also pointed out that learning to use the computer is far safer than learning to drive a car (although I think both cause gray hair).

The most important piece of advice I have received from "computer types" is that the computer user is the final authority. If the computer doesn't do what you want it to or causes you frustration, you can always turn it off! It really gives you a sense of power when you realize that you can unplug it or turn it off! So, learn to use it as you learned to use all the other conveniences in your life, and don't let fear of new things keep you from expanding your knowledge. The computer is only one of the many tools you can use to your advantage in genealogical research. You mastered the photocopier and the microfilm machine, didn't you?

How are computer databases compiled?

Computer databases are compiled in one of three ways:

1. **Data entry:** As the name implies, the databases are compiled by individuals who enter the data letter by letter, word by word, into a computer. This type of database becomes a text document and is usually every-word searchable. This means that you can locate any single word or phrase within the text.

2. **Image scanning:** This type of database is created with images, or pictures, taken of actual pages. The computer considers the data to be a picture regardless of whether there are words on the page. Because of this, the index to the database is no better than any index included in the original.

3. **Optical Character Recognition (OCR):** When pages are scanned, the computer uses OCR software to interpret the image and translate it into words, or into a text document. If this is done correctly, the database should be every-word searchable, like a data entry database. However, most OCR software is not 100 percent accurate, and many characters get misinterpreted. Accurate proofreading is imperative if the data is to be useful. If spelling errors are not caught and corrected, the value of the database's search capability will be lessened. Since the computer searches for *exactly* what you input, misspelled words in the database will only be found in your search if they match your query. Very few databases are equipped to search for words or names by pronunciation rather than spelling. One exception to this is the Family History Library's search. The search capabilities of the FHL databases group like-sounding names together in the results it presents to you.

Understanding the differences between types of databases will help you search them more effectively and successfully. Unfortunately most databases do not provide information as to how they were compiled. You have to find that out yourself. (See the tips for effective searching on page 126.)

Internet Source

WEB SITES FOR GENEALOGISTS

Cyndi's List   http://www.cyndislist.com

USGenWeb   http://www.usgenweb.com

RootsWeb   http://www.rootsweb.com

FamilySearch   http://www.familysearch.org

Helm's Genealogy Toolbox   http://www.genealogy.tbox.com

Family Tree Magazine   http://www.familytreemagazine.com

NARA   http://www.nara.gov

Ancestry   http://www.ancestry.com

Family Tree Maker   http://www.familytreemaker.com

Genealogy.com   http://www.genealogy.com

What Web sites should I start my genealogical search with?

Books about using the Internet for genealogical research abound (see books at the end of this chapter). Many contain URLs, or Internet addresses, for the many sites available. Keep in mind that URLs change frequently, so the books may contain outdated addresses. Addresses of many sites, however, remain fairly constant and have links (online forwarding addresses) to other specialty sites.

Web addresses that appear online in articles or as links from other sites are more likely to be current and correct than those in printed books. Even so, the books still provide valuable information about specialty Web sites that may be of interest to you. While hundreds of thousands of Web sites are available to family researchers, you should start with some free basic beginner Web sites. Some of these are

- **Cyndi's List,** <http://www.cyndislist.com>: This is a site with thousands of links to other sites of genealogical or historical interest. This list is alphabetical by subject matter, time period, geographic location, organization name, etc. This site is like one-stop shopping for beginning researchers or those who are not yet comfortable using the Internet. It is also a real time-saver for advanced researchers looking for specific information. This Web site is kept current; new links are added and old links are deleted daily. Cyndi Howells, the Webmaster of Cyndi's List, indicates the new and updated entries, which makes searching the site easy and logical.

- **USGenWeb,** <http://www.usgenweb.org>: This site has links to separate state, county, and local sites. There is a volunteer-staffed site in every county of the United States. The county sites vary greatly in content depending on the number and expertise of the volunteers. Some of the county sites also provide links to specific town sites. I have found many census records (both state and federal) transcribed on these pages along with cemetery transcriptions, tombstone photographs, county histories, biographies, maps, book lists, offers of free lookups in certain books, and a myriad of other valuable items. The state and county sites also list the research facilities within the area that you can consult in your research. Most sites also provide links to the state vital records information and forms for requesting these records. Local historical and genealogical societies are also highlighted, giving you yet another resource. The US-GenWeb also has regional mailing lists where you can post queries or information to share with other researchers interested in that geographic area.

- **RootsWeb,** <http://www.rootsweb.com>: This site features surname-based lists, links to other sites, and a weekly newsletter containing information and instruction. Many of the surname lists provide valuable contacts and information from other researchers with the same surnames. The surname mailing lists can help you network with others interested in a family name. This group has recently expanded into the international scope of research. The WorldGen-Web is growing at a fast pace. With more and more researchers interested in their foreign ancestry, it was inevitable that this would happen. Using this site to determine what researchers are doing, what surnames are of interest, and networking with them is a powerful research method.

- **FamilySearch,** <http://www.familysearch.org>: This site is maintained by the Church of Jesus Christ of Latter-day Saints in Salt Lake City, Utah. Available on this site are the International Genealogical Index (IGI), the Ancestral File (family pedigrees submitted by researchers), the Family History Library catalog (listing all of the millions of rolls of microfilmed records and books stored in Salt Lake City), locations of Family History Centers in the United States and around the world, as well as resource guides pertaining to specific records of interest to you. All of this is available free of charge, and the resource guides—one for every U.S. state and foreign country—can be printed from the site. These guides contain information specific to geographic locations, highlight the records that are microfilmed and available for loan, supply word lists for using foreign records, and have guides to specific types of records (e.g., immigrant research, Hamburg passenger lists).

- **Helm's Genealogy Toolbox,** <http:// www.genealogy.tbox.com>: This Web site offers searches for other Web sites by subject matter and provides links to those sites.

- **Family Tree Magazine,** <http://www.familytreemagazine.com>: This site has a "SuperSearch" feature that allows you to search by surname or subject matter. It has links for ethnic tool kits, a Soundex code generator, forms to download, a bookstore, and even a free electronic newsletter that is automatically sent to your e-mail address. The free newsletters available from many different sites can help you stay up to date on all the new happenings in the genealogical world.

What about the sites that charge a subscription fee?

Commercial sites are popping up faster than you can keep up with them. Many offer databases including indexes, military records, census information, the Social Security Death Index, and newspaper obituaries; the list is nearly endless. First determine what your research needs are. If you are doing colonial research in the United States, one site may be better for you than others. Even these subscription-based sites include many free features.

Before you pay a fee, visit the site, print out or review the list of databases it contains, and determine if it would be of use to you. Most of these sites contain millions of names, but a great many of these databases and compilations are submitted by other researchers and may or may not have any documentation attached. The resources are only as good as the habits of the person who submitted them.

Also keep in mind that any digital or computerized database includes secondhand information at best. With the exception of the recent posting of census record images, all this data is typed, transcribed, or copied from other sources. Any database that is in digital or computer format is the result of someone's interpretation of a handwritten document—with all the inherent mistakes and problems associated with interpretation.

Important

Some of the more popular subscription-based Web sites are

• **Ancestry.com,** <http://www.ancestry.com>: This site contains more than seven hundred databases to search (some for free, others for members only), a daily newsletter listing new databases, articles and news important to genealogists and historians, instructional articles, and information about other sites. This site is subscription based and offers a separate subscription for the census images that are being posted. A major portion of the site is the Ancestry World Tree, which has pedigrees submitted from researchers like you. Again, the quality and accuracy of these are to be questioned since sources are often absent. They do offer links to send messages to the submitters, but what are the odds that the e-mail addresses are still good?

• **FamilyTreeMaker.com,** <http://www.familytreemaker.com>: This site contains individuals' submitted pedigrees, instructional articles, and more. Most of the database searches on this site result in a list of Family Tree Maker CDs that can be purchased. If you have access to them in a genealogical library, you can use the site as an index to the CDs and then use the CDs in the library rather than purchase them. The Family Tree Maker site also provides an educational center with articles of interest and information about record types. There are many free features to try on this and many other subscription- or profit-based sites.

• **Genealogy.com,** <http://www.genealogy.com>: While this site offers some paid subscriptions, such as Genealogy Library, it also offers for free many how-to articles and instruction for any level of genealogist. When you go to the Genealogy.com home page, simply click on "Learning" to access many wonderful articles. The site has more than a dozen articles just on Internet research. It also has a glossary of terms you might encounter and a resource center to locate societies and organizations. You can even use the Genealogy Library portion of the site without paying for a subscription. Input a name at the search tool, and a list of books or records that that name appears in will be displayed. You cannot get the complete record for free, but using the search capabilities will give you titles of sources to look at in the library or elsewhere.

What about using a search engine?

A search engine can be useful for finding a specific geographic location or subject. Keep in mind that most search engines are not designed specifically for genealogical searches. Helm's Genealogy Toolbox at <http://www.genealogy.tbox.com> searches for genealogical content rather than just for a name or place match. For foreign locations, I have found that Google <http://www.google.com> works well, especially for locating town Web sites in foreign countries. When using search engines keep in mind that new ones are always coming online and they all produce different results. Use a variety of search engines to see what you find. Some search engines, such as Dogpile at <http://www.dogpile.com> and Lycos at <http://www .lycos.com>, list the other search engines that they search all at once and can save you time and effort by doing these multiple searches for you. Many search engines offer tips on how to do simple and advanced searches. Take the time to read these help pages and get the most out of the search engines.

Many libraries, local and national genealogical societies, archives, and states have their own Web sites which vary in content from basic information regarding the facility or organization to databases and research assistance. Be creative when you use search engines. Consider them to be "card catalogs" of the Internet; you have to look for things under various headings to be successful.

What do all of those abbreviations in a Web address mean?

A uniform resource locator (URL) is no more than an Internet address to get you to a specific site. First look at the extension, the part after the dot at the end of the address. For U.S.-based sites, *.com* means a commercial site, *.org* indicates a nonprofit organization, *.net* means a network, *.edu* means an educational facility, and *.gov* means a government site. Commercial sites contain a lot of database materials, but these profit-based operations often have memberships and advertising as well as data. The .org sites sometimes have sponsoring ads to help defray costs, but you do not need to pay to use them. Many of the .edu sites are for college or university libraries and sometimes include their card catalogs online so you can search them. The .gov sites are local or federal government Web sites such as the National Archives and Records Administration site.

What is a link?

A link is nothing more than a forwarding address. When you click on a link you go to another location within the same Web site or at another Web site. Some words in a Web site are underlined or a different color than the rest of the text or both; these may be links. Click on a link to go to another location with more information on a specified subject.

This new information might include additional links. You can easily get lost "surfing" with the many links and have no idea how you got to a site. This happens to all of us at one time or another. Most browsers—the software that enables you to use the Internet—have a "back" button or arrow you can use to retrace your steps. I liken this back function to the breadcrumbs that Hansel and Gretel left to find their way out of the forest. You can go step-by-step back through the Web pages to return to any previously visited page. This button or arrow may not be labeled "back," but look for an arrow pointing left for back or right for forward. The forward arrow is helpful if you go back too far. Think of each Web page as a page in a book and the forward and back buttons as how you turn the pages in either direction.

How else can I make these sites work to my advantage?

The Family Tree Maker and Ancestry sites can help keep you up-to-date on the new books and products available to genealogists. Many of those pertaining to general research and the Internet are not usually available in local bookstores. Keeping up with all the new products is easier with all the articles, advertising, and reviews that are on the Internet. **Most companies that deal in genealogical books and information have Web sites listing their products.** Search them out in genealogical publications such as *Everton's Genealogical Helper* magazine, F&W Publications's *Family Tree Magazine* <http://www.familytreemagazine.com>, *Family Chronicle* magazine <http://www.familychronicle.com/~magazine/>, *Heritage Quest* magazine <http://www.heritagequest.com>, and *Genealogical Computing* (an Ancestry publication), to name just a few. Appleton's Books & Genealogy <http://www.appletons.com> is a supplier of many books on research and computers, and offers many of the most popular genealogical software programs available. Advertisers list a URL (Web address) as well as a mailing address and toll-free phone number in ads in genealogical publications. Read the advertisements and articles dealing with the Internet to obtain even more leads to information.

Family Chronicle magazine and *Family Tree Magazine* are just two of the many genealogical magazines that review software, list Web sites and genealogical happenings all over the United States and Canada, and have wonderful articles on all types of records from all over the world.

Sources

What should I look for when using a new database online or on CD?

First look for some explanation of the contents of the database and where the information was obtained. Many contain information from previously published books and sources, and those databases should list these publications. These sources might be listed in the introduction or under a source information heading. If multiple books were used to create the database, you may need to determine which book any specific data came from.

How can I determine the specific source of the data?

First see how many books or sources were used to compile the database. Next search for a piece of information. Are the results shown with any indication as to which source provided that piece of information? If not, you will have to find and review the books or original record to determine the origin of the information. Remember that information without a source is a clue, not a fact.

How can I search a database efficiently and successfully?

You can follow many tips to make your search more productive, but you must take time to learn about and test each database to get the most out of it. Some databases, Web sites, and CDs have a file called "How to Search This Database" or "Search Tips" that you should read before jumping in. If you take a few extra minutes to read these instructions, you may save yourself hours of futile searching. **Many researchers incorrectly assume that the information they seek is not included in a database when in fact they just searched incorrectly for it.** Since many companies produce the databases and CDs, there are many ways to search them. The compilers of these databases are not all genealogists, and they don't necessarily understand our search needs or how we think.

Important

If a CD or Web site gives no search instructions, try a few searches to get an idea of how its search capabilities operate. First try to search for a name by inputting only a first initial and a common surname and check out the results the database produces. If you search for J. Smith are you presented with only entries that read J. Smith? The results might include all Smith entries with first names that begin with the letter *J*. These include not only all given names beginning with *J*, such as James, Janet, and Joseph, but also abbreviations, such as Jas., Jon., and Joe. Do the results include names that have middle initials? Does the middle initial affect the search? Try inputting "J.D. Smith" as search criteria. Does the database find all the Smith entries with first names that begin with *J*, or does it find only the ones with J.D.? This is important to know so you can get the most out of the database. By understanding how the database's search function responds, you will be better prepared to search the database. If it produces only results that exactly match your input you will have to do many searches to cover all possible variations of a name.

What if the search capabilities include a Soundex option?

The Soundex option can make searching for uncommon names much quicker. Soundex searches group like-sounding names together, but not as effectively as the FamilySearch site. Since it groups all surnames that have the same Soundex code (see chapter four for specifics), you may get more results than you can sort through. Try a search and then decide if looking through all of the results is worth your time. I often use the Soundex option as a way to find alternate spellings for a surname I am researching. All genealogists know that spelling is anything but consistent in the records. You may have three or more possible spellings to contend with for one name. Using the Soundex option may provide you with a few spelling variations that you had not considered, but it may lead you to believe that you have covered all spelling variations when, in fact, you have not. For example, with a Soundex search for the surname Wait most of the variant spellings will be found, but the variant spelling Weight will not.

What is meant by a "wild card" in the search criteria?

A wild card allows you to search a database using only the beginning or part of the name or subject you are looking for. You use a designated symbol to indicate the wild card. For example, if you want to search for the name Marlborough, you can enter "Marlb*" (where the asterisk is the wild card symbol) instead of the complete word. The search engine should provide you with all words in the database that begin with those five letters regardless of how the rest of the word is spelled, such as Marlboro or Marlborough.

If when you tested a database you determined that it will produce only results that exactly match your input (e.g., J. Smith), then you can use the wild card to search for all of the first names that begin with the letter *J* by entering "J* Smith" as your search criteria. When you get the results, check to see if first names beginning with *J* and having a middle initial are included. There is almost no limit to the various ways that you can search. You are limited only by your flexibility and imagination when searching.

What other steps can I take for more successful searching?

Some databases have the information you want and need included within the files, but a data entry error or a misspelling that you would never think of can keep you from finding it. One example of this is Ancestry.com's census index database. The database was compiled from the Accelerated Indexing Systems (AIS) books and maintained all the AIS errors and omissions. The Ancestry Web site produces a list of all of the census indexes that are included in your search. It does not, however, indicate if all counties or towns within any given year or state are included.

When searching for an individual in the 1860 census index for Pennsylvania I became frustrated. I had entered the name James Douglas and location Blair County, Pennsylvania, as my search criteria. The search result said there were no matches. After eliminating the given name and trying many spellings of Douglas, I was still unsuccessful. Since Douglas was a common surname in Blair County in the mid 1800s, I knew that there had to be some matches. I then dropped the surname altogether and simply searched for Blair County, Pennsylvania. No matches found! Although some Pennsylvania towns and counties are included in the index for 1860, Blair County is not among them. A search for just 1860 Pennsylvania shows that only a few counties are included in the database.

A similar problem I had demonstrated another drawback to these databases. I had for one of my ancestors a copy of a census record that I had found at the National Archives. He lived in Starksboro, Addison County, Vermont. The page number was not clearly visible on my copy, so I decided to search the indexes on Ancestry.com to get the complete page citation for my records. Imagine my surprise when the search of the index said that the family was not there. Remembering my search problems with Blair County, I searched for Addison County, Vermont. In the list of matching records were some Starksboro entries, so why had it not found my subject? When the database was converted to electronic format someone had inadvertently spelled Starksboro as St. Arksboro. After trying to search by every variation of that spelling (with and without

Case Study

the period and spaces) I was unsuccessful in bringing up even one record. Further testing showed that the town of Stamford, Connecticut, was also entered as St. Amford. Now I was on a roll. I checked to see if a town that really had a St. prefix had been entered as such. Imagine my surprise when several were not included in the search results. Apparently they had been entered based on how the name was written in the original record, and some are listed with St. while others are with Saint. The computer, which is literal, does not understand that St. and Saint represent the same thing.

With all of the problems evident with these databases, how can I use them to my advantage?

I certainly don't want you to think that electronic databases are useless; just know that they can be flawed. If you are knowledgeable about the drawbacks and problems, you will search more effectively and get better results for your efforts. If you take a few minutes to learn about a database you will get more from it. I use the databases, both on CD and online, almost every day, but I do not take them as the last word. If my research subject does not show up in a database search, that does not mean the subject is not in the original record or even in the database. It just means that the subject is not under anything I tried as my search criteria. This could be because the subject is not in the original index that was converted to electronic format or because a typographical error was made in the entry. Be realistic; not all individuals are listed in any index. The original AIS census indexes appear to have a 20 percent error and omission rate, so one in five individuals are either missing from or misspelled in the index.

Why are so many companies converting obviously flawed information to electronic format rather than creating new, original material?

The answer comes from basic economics. It takes thousands of hours to create an index to something such as a census. Using published or issued information that may now be out of copyright is an easy way to give the public what it wants—fast and convenient access to large amounts of information. While companies are generating hundreds of CDs with previously published data, some companies are creating indexes to data that may not have ever been indexed. By selling the prepublished data in a new format, they generate the funds needed to create new indexes. Many of the books that the data is extracted from may be out of print or unavailable to most researchers, thereby creating a need for better access to the information, no matter how flawed. It is no worse than using the originally published information in your research. Always keep in mind that typeset or electronic information is generally a secondary source at best!

Important

Once I determine where the information included in a database was obtained, what should I do?

Once you have found the original source of the database information, you should look at that source. It may be a previously published book or a manuscript. When the original source is a book, you must determine where the author got the information for the book. Does the original book list the sources of the information? Question the author's sources and evaluate how accurate the book might be. Somewhere in the history of that information should be an original source—perhaps a civil document, a family Bible, a census record. Your goal is to get back to the original source so you can evaluate the database's reliability.

Remember to verify the original source. Just because you obtained the information from a computer does not make it correct. The data is only as good as the original source's validity and the transcriber's accuracy. Unless the database includes original document images, such as microfilmed records, it is *not* a primary source. Many databases and Web sites may have additional information about the data included. Look for a link to this information on the Web site. Ancestry.com has a link that reads "More about this database" on the search results page. Click on that link and read about the database so you will be more informed about the records. Remember, you must understand the history of the original record before you can determine the database's reliability.

What can I learn from the many pedigrees that are on the Web and in databases?

The pedigrees or family records that comprise the majority of genealogical databases came from researchers like you who submitted their research for others to share. The information is only as good as the original research. Since most of these pedigrees do not list the sources you must establish the information as fact using other records. These pedigrees are a wonderful source of clues and have created a network of researchers working together on a common subject. Once you submit your information for inclusion on any of these Web sites, others may contact you to ask about your research and sources. Are you ready to answer these questions or do you have no sources for the data? Be careful about passing on information that is not proven as fact without indicating that clearly. Unfortunately most sites and databases have no place to put a cautionary note or explanation as to why you question facts within your pedigree or family information. Share and reproduce information with caution, and you will have fewer problems later on.

Should I submit my pedigree and family group sheet information to one of these Web sites?

That's a tough one to answer conclusively. As stated before, make sure you do not pass on erroneous or unproven information without indicating it as such. Since most of the Web sites that will post your information do not provide space for sources or notes, this is hard to do.

Also be aware that some sites offer you free Web space to create your own family Web site, but they then have the right to capture your information and include it on CDs that they sell for profit. I was very excited when I found one of my ancestors listed in the index for a Family Tree Maker CD. When I looked at that ancestor's information on the CD I discovered that it was, word for word, the exact same information I had shared with a cousin many years ago. She had sent it to one of the databases for inclusion without noting the original source—me! Since I did this research in the early stages of my genealogical education, some of it is incorrect. This is how research errors get passed along and repeated over and over until someone takes the information as fact. Remember the phrase "garbage in, garbage out" when using submitted data. It is only as good as the work of the researcher who submitted it.

Where else can I network with other researchers with common interests?

Many wonderful Internet sites provide you with the opportunity to post a query or question on any genealogical subject. As mentioned earlier in this chapter, you can use several types of criteria in your subject search. The USGenWeb is categorized by state and county locations. If you are researching a family that lived in Wayne County, Pennsylvania, you can post a question on the Wayne County Web site. Another researcher can just click on a link and respond to you. Most sites have a searchable archive that keeps all posted questions for at least a certain period of time. You can visit the Web site and search the other postings to determine who else might be researching the same family or subject as you are.

The Web site for RootsWeb is valuable to the family history researcher. The site has many active research groups dealing with specific surnames. This is a tool that can put you in touch with others who might be relatives or have information about your surname of interest.

Some Web sites have bulletin boards where you can post questions or a regularly scheduled live chat that you can participate in. The people who participate in these chats might be knowledgeable about a family name or locality and can further your research considerably. It is wise to watch and listen to the communication between participants for a while to see the etiquette and format of the chat. Don't be intimidated by these chats. You can become comfortable with this medium with practice. Remember that we are all beginners at something!

What is a mail list?

A mail list is a means of communicating with other researchers about a specific subject without having to be available for a live chat. Most of the USGenWeb county sites have a mail list that you can subscribe to. Mail lists come in two basic formats. One is a "mail mode" list, where all messages posted to the list in a specified period of time, usually daily, automatically get forwarded to you as individual e-mails. If twenty people post messages, you get twenty e-mails. This gives you the advantage of being able to delete the impertinent ones and keep just the ones of interest to you. However, this can also be overwhelming. I signed up for the Rogers family list and received more than two hundred e-mails the first day! I quickly unsubscribed from that list. Make sure that you read the instructions on how to do that when you subscribe. I spent several frustrating days unsuccessfully trying to unsubscribe from one list until I went back to the e-mail I received that confirmed my subscription. It contained the information I needed to get myself removed from the list.

The second type of list is the "digest mode," where all of the messages posted in a given period get consolidated into one e-mail that gets forwarded to you.

In some cases a Webmaster is out there somewhere tending the list. He may filter out all messages that are not on topic and only include the ones that meet the set criteria. Since these messages are more likely to be reviewed by human eyes before being forwarded, you might get fewer irrelevant messages than in mail mode.

Some lists are carefully monitored by a Webmaster, who may return a submitted message to the sender indicating why it was not posted to the list (e.g., irrelevant subject matter, inflammatory language, or simply bad taste). The only disadvantage I have found with digest mode lists is that if you want to save just one of the messages included in the master e-mail, you must copy it to another file before deleting the master e-mail. This is a small inconvenience in exchange for receiving only one e-mail from the list.

How can I best use these lists?

The first rule for success with any list is to format your questions in an efficient and effective manner. Read some of the messages that are posted, and you will quickly see how many people post vague questions that cannot easily be answered. Scrutinize the messages posted and learn from the more experienced researchers. Successful postings are no accident—they are well thought out and logically asked.

If you are posting a query looking for information on your family to a surname list, keep the message as brief as possible while still providing pertinent information. An example of a good query is

Tip

> Looking to share information on the Linus (ca 1800–1875) & Hannah (WESCOTT) ROUNDS family of Addison County, Vermont. Known children are Orville (1828–ca 1864); Frederick (1831–?); Spencer (1833–1906), married Malona CARPENTER; Betsey/Phebe (ca 1830–?); Elisha (1823–1902), married Sally/Sarah HALLOCK; & John (ca 1844–?).

This query provides a potential contact with all of the necessary information to place the individuals in a time and place. It also indicates the information you have on each of the family members. By giving all of the known children, not just your direct line, you enable other researchers to connect to your family line through one of the siblings. Your goal is to make your posting meaningful to the largest number of researchers.

An example of an ineffective query is

> Looking for information about Jonathan SMITH in Massachusetts.

This query is far too vague and wide reaching to be effective. In what century did he live? What other information is known? The likelihood that this query would generate any useful replies is doubtful. Some researchers might reply to the sender and explain that the question does not give enough information. Most researchers who read this query will not take the time to reply. Make your requests clear and concise so you will be more likely to get a useful response.

Are there any rules for posting queries?

Yes! When you post a query, make it easy to read or scan for the pertinent data. Notice in the example of the effective query that the surnames *only* are typed in *all* capital letters. This makes spotting the surnames quick and easy. You will come to appreciate this courtesy after you have read many postings. You can quickly see if any of the surnames are of interest to you and skip the e-mails containing those that are not. It is also helpful to include only a few surnames in one query. Break the query up into several postings if necessary. Also, include the surnames, again typed in all capital letters, in the subject line of your message.

Some people type as if they were talking to you, with no punctuation to indicate pauses. This makes reading a query tedious at best. As in other written documents, a comma's location in the sentence can determine the meaning of the entire sentence. Use what you learned in elementary school about grammar and punctuation; you—and your fellow researchers—will be glad you did.

When you post a query that refers to a common surname, be sure to provide enough information for the readers to determine if it is of interest to them. If you query about SMITH families, include where in the world your particular Smiths resided. An effective query might look like this:

> Looking to share information on the ancestry and descendants of Dr. Benjamin Peabody SMITH (1793 in VT to 1851 in Leeds Co., Canada) and wife Lois CRANDALL (1799 in VT to 1882 in St. Lawrence Co., NY). Residences included Royalton, VT; Stockholm, NY; and Kitley, Leeds Co., Ontario, Canada.

As you can see this query provides enough information to help the reader identify the individuals. A posting that simply mentions Benjamin SMITH and wife Lois CRANDALL without giving dates or locations is less likely to be a succesul posting. The effective query might result in responses from other researchers with Smith or Crandall lines in Vermont or in Leeds County, Ontario, Canada, that could prove useful in your research.

Are there tips regarding e-mail etiquette?

Whenever you post to a list or send an e-mail remember this mantra: You only get one chance to make a first impression. This holds true on the Internet as well as in person. The Internet provides a certain amount of anonymity, and unfortunately this sometimes brings out the worst in people. Because they don't know who you are, some people are rude and unthinking when they reply to postings. The term *flaming* is the equivalent to yelling at or being rude to someone in an e-mail. Typing a message in all capital letters is like shouting at the reader. Humor can also be lost without the subtle voice changes or winks that you might pick up in person. Be careful how you word things, since the recipient might interpret them differently than what you intended. This is especially true of jokes or subtle humor.

If you rarely get replies to your postings or if the results are less than helpful, review your entries and compare them to those by others. You will become familiar with the standard practices of e-mail and electronic media with time. Make special note of the postings that you dislike or can't figure out, and avoid the same mistakes and pitfalls in your own postings.

How do I pick a genealogical computer program?

First decide what you need the program to do. Every researcher has unique needs, and no one program on the market meets every person's needs. Some programs have many bells and whistles. Others have features that the professional researcher desires but that the family researcher will never need or want. Consider what you want to do with your information once you compile it. If you want to be able to print it out in a variety of formats such as charts or booklets, you should select a program that offers these options.

The most important thing to remember is that you have to learn how to operate a program before you use it, so starting with a simple, inexpensive one may be your best bet. The most critical feature for any genealogical program is that it be in Genealogical Data Communications (GEDCOM) format. This big title simply means that any program that is in GEDCOM format can talk to and exchange information with any other GEDCOM-formatted program. If the box labeled does not specify GEDCOM format, ask questions. (Remember that not all software sales people are genealogists; you may get a blank stare in response to your question).

Many genealogical magazines and Web sites offer information on software. Do your homework *before* you buy a program so you will be less likely to get in trouble. Also consider that even if the program is GEDCOM formatted, the process of moving information from one program to another is not always seamless and complete. Transferring information from a simple program to a more elaborate one is less likely to cause problems. You really cannot go from a top-of-the-line program to a simple one without losing data. You must consider the fields of information included in each program. (A field of information is a date or location information line.) Some programs hold an entire date in one line or box, while others hold each of the three parts separately. Examples of these date fields are 12 May 1800 and 12 May 1800, respectively. You might lose information trying to transfer data from a program that uses three separate fields into one that uses a single field.

Money Saver

The same applies to location data. Most programs consider the town, county, and state or country as one single piece of information, while more elaborate programs consider each geographic breakdown an additional but separate piece of data. For this reason you are always better off starting with an easy-to-use, easy-to-learn program and moving up as you outgrow the program, if you ever do.

Few people use the same program forever, as new ones come out all the time and existing ones get upgraded to add new features. Talk to others and see what they like and dislike about the programs they are using. If you don't invest a lot of money in a program, you won't feel obligated to stick with it if it doesn't work for you.

Another consideration is technical support for the program. Does the program come with a manual that is understandable? How successful have other users been in talking to an actual person at the support line? Does the program have an online mail list or chat where you can ask questions. Technical support is especially important if you are not computer literate or do have a computer guru in your household.

What about the many other organizational programs available to genealogical researchers?

While many of these programs perform valuable functions, you again need to consider your needs and skill level. One such program, Clooz, is for keeping track of all your research. This program can sharpen your source-citing skills while keeping track of all your information. Since the program allows you to enter all of the information you find along with the source details, it prompts you to look at all of the information and obtain the complete, accurate citation for the data. When I began using Clooz, I had to go back and get missing citation information. I had never realized how much information I had neglected to record until the program showed all those holes in my data.

The drawback to a program like Clooz is that you may have already accumulated so much data that it would take you a long time to get it all entered; you may find that task overwhelming. I set aside a couple of hours each week to enter data from my years of manual documentation. It may take me a while, but eventually some lucky relative will inherit a well-documented family tree!

Sources

FURTHER READING

The Complete Beginner's Guide to Genealogy, the Internet, and Your Genealogy Computer Program, by Karen Clifford. Baltimore, Md.: Genealogical Publishing Co., Inc., 2001.

The Complete Idiot's Guide to Online Genealogy, by Rhonda R. McClure. Indianapolis, Ind.: Alpha Books, 2000.

Cyndi's List: A Comprehensive List of Over 40,000 Genealogical Sites on the Internet, by Cyndi Howells. 2 vols. Baltimore, Md.: Genealogical Publishing Co., Inc., 2001.

The Genealogist's Computer Companion, by Rhonda McClure. Cincinnati, Ohio: Betterway Books, 2002.

Genealogist's Virtual Library: Full-Text Books on the World Wide Web, by Thomas Jay Kemp. Wilmington, Del.: Scholarly Resources, 2000.

Genealogy Basics Online, by Cherri Melton Flinn. Cincinnati, Ohio: Muska and Lipman, 2000.

Genealogy and Computers for the Advanced Researcher, by Karen Clifford. Baltimore, Md.: Clearfield Co., 1995.

Genealogy and Computers for the Complete Beginner, by Karen Clifford. Baltimore, Md.: Clearfield Co., 1992.

Genealogy and Computers for the Determined Researcher, by Karen Clifford. Baltimore, Md.: Clearfield Co., 1995.

The Genealogy Forum on America Online, by G. Morgan. Salt Lake City, Utah: Ancestry, Inc., 1998.

Genealogy On-Line for Dummies, 3d ed., by April Leigh Helm and Matthew L. Helm. Foster City, Calif.: IDG Books, 2001.

Genealogy Online: Millennium Edition, by Elizabeth Powell Crowe. New York: Computing McGraw-Hill, 1999.

Genealogy Online: Researching Your Roots, Web Edition, by Elizabeth Powell Crowe. New York: McGraw-Hill, 1998.

Genealogy Software Guide, by Marthe Arends. Baltimore, Md.: Genealogical Publishing Co., Inc., 1998.

Genealogy via the Internet: Computerized Genealogy, by Ralph Roberts. Alexander, N.C.: Alexander Books, 1998.

The Internet for Dummies: Quick Reference, 3d ed., by John R. Levine, Margaret Levine Young, and Carol Baroudi. Foster City, Calif: IDG Books, 1997.

The Internet for Genealogists: A Beginner's Guide, 4th ed., by Barbara Renick and Richard S. Wilson. La Habra, Calif.: Compuology, 1998.

Netting Your Ancestors: Genealogical Research on the Internet, by Cyndi Howells. Baltimore, Md.: Genealogical Publishing Co., Inc., 1997.

Sam's Teach Yourself eGenealogy Today, by Terri Stephens. Sams, 1999.

Searching for Cyber-Roots: A Step-by-Step Guide to Genealogy on the World Wide Web, by Laurie and Steve Bonner. Salt Lake City, Utah: Ancestry, Inc., 1997.

Turbo Genealogy: An Introduction to Family History Research in the Information Age, by John C. and Carolyn H. Cosgriff. Salt Lake City, Utah: Ancestry, Inc., 1997.

The Unofficial Guide to Online Genealogy, by Pamela Rice Hahn. Foster City, Calif.: Hungry Minds, Inc., 2000.

Virtual Roots: A Guide to Genealogy and Local History on the World Wide Web, by Thomas Jay Kemp. Wilmington, Del.: Scholarly Resources, 1997.

Web Publishing for Genealogy, 2d ed., by Peter Christian. Baltimore, Md.: Genealogical Publishing Co., Inc., 2000.

Your Family Tree Using Your PC, by Jim Oldfield Jr. Grand Rapids, Mich.: Abacus Books, 1997.

EIGHT

Land, Probate, and Tax Records

M any researchers overlook land, probate, and tax records and the valuable information in them when trying to prove ancestral lines. Since land is usually the largest single possession that an individual has at the time of death, using land, probate, and tax records together in genealogy is beneficial.

As always, you must keep in mind the original purpose of a record in order to completely understand and evaluate it. Land records were created at the time of purchase to provide legal protection for the purchasing individual against other claims to the property. The original deed was then copied into the official record of the town, county, or other governmental jurisdiction that had authority over such records. The location of the record varies from state to state. Some land records are held at the town level, some are held at a county or subcounty level, while others are state or federal records depending on when and where the transaction occurred, who had official ownership of the land, and where the land was situated.

LAND AND TAX RECORDS

Reminder

When using land records, always keep in mind that you are not, in most cases, looking at the original record. The original deed is given to the landowner and a copy of the record is filed with or transcribed into the official records. The only time you will have an original land record is if you find an actual deed in family papers, in a manuscript collection, or in the town records collections. The deed is an individual sheet of paper with signatures of the individuals involved and the date it was recorded into the official records, and it usually bears an official seal or stamp. If you come across one that is not marked as recorded, it may never have been recorded at the time of the transfer, so it may not appear in the collection of official records.

Land transaction records may also be included in the original proprietor's records of a town. When a grant was given, usually by the state or the government ruling the geographic area, to lay out a town, the land was divided among a group of individuals referred to as proprietors. Each proprietor was given a set amount of land to improve and build upon. Land was also set off for churches, meetinghouses, and cemeteries within the new township. These land acquisitions usually were not recorded in the land transfer records with later purchases, but separately with town records. Most of these records predate the Revolutionary War, when the United States became a separate country rather than colonies of various foreign countries.

Once a town was established, all land transactions involving the original proprietor's land fell under the rules of land transfers. Some states, such as Vermont and Rhode Island, maintain their land records at the town level, while New Hampshire and Massachusetts do so at the county level. As the population increased, many counties divided their property records into two or more deed districts. Many Massachusetts counties have two or three deed districts within them. This is especially true of high-population counties. Keep in mind that the counties that existed at the time of the transfer of landownership may have been very different than the current counties.

Some post–Revolutionary War land records fall under the category of public domain land. This means that the original landowner was the U.S. government, and land ownership could be granted through many different processes. These included selling the land and giving the land to individuals as bounty land, perhaps in repayment for military service. Both federal and state bounty lands were issued for military service. These lands were mostly in the unsettled western portions of the United States and included a set number of acres based on rank and military service. Most individuals who received these lands never lived on them, but rather sold their interests to others or passed the land title to their children or heirs.

In many federal land purchases, the individual applying to purchase the land was required to be a citizen or to have at least filed a declaration of intention to become a U.S. citizen. This restriction did not apply to military bounty lands. Some military bounty lands were issued by the U.S. or a foreign government as incentives to serve in specific military engagements since landownership was important in nearly every culture. It was used as a means of paying soldiers, thereby helping to establish townships in unpopulated areas and expand the United States westward.

Tax records can be used to establish landownership within an area. Towns or counties assessed taxes on land and other property just as they do today. Inclusion in these tax lists indicates ownership of some type of taxable property, be it land, livestock, slaves, or luxury items. Many town records have yearly tax lists that can provide valuable clues to other family members who lived in the same community, the financial status of an individual, and a time period when an individual may have moved or died. Individuals were also charged a poll tax in many areas and time periods. A poll tax was usually levied on an individual who was twenty-one years of age and eligible to vote within his county, regardless of how much land or property he owned. Most areas exempted individuals over the age of fifty from paying poll taxes. Since women

For More Info

See *Ancestry's Red Book*, edited by Alice Eichholz; *The Handy Book for Genealogists*, by Everton Publishers; and *The Source: A Guidebook of American Genealogy*, edited by Loretto Dennis Szucs and Sandra Hargreaves Luebking.

\di'fin\ *vb*

Definitions

did not nationally attain the right to vote until the passage of the nineteenth amendment in 1920, they do not appear in most poll tax lists, even if they were widows. Some states passed full or partial suffrage laws prior to the nineteenth amendment, so women's names appear in some lists in earlier time periods. No one rule applies to all in most record types for all states. The only hard-and-fast rule is that there aren't any hard-and-fast rules.

PROBATE RECORDS

Probate records contain many references to land ownership or transfers. When a person dies, his worldly goods must be dispersed among his heirs after all debts are paid from the estate. If an individual who does not have a will dies, he is referred to as "dying intestate." His property, both real and personal, must still be divided and his debts paid. Without a will, the deceased has no control over how that disbursement will occur. An administrator (male) or administratrix (female) is appointed by the court having jurisdiction. The administrator then has a complete inventory of the property compiled, as well as a list of debts owed by the deceased and to the deceased. From these values he determines how to divide the property. Many estates were determined to be insolvent, meaning that the value of the property was not enough to pay the outstanding debts or to divide the property among the heirs.

If you have information indicating that an individual owned land but land is not mentioned in the will or the inventory of the estate, you should look to the land records. Many individuals, knowing that their days were numbered, disbursed their land among their heirs, thereby assuring themselves that their wishes would be fulfilled. Many sold land to their children for token amounts such as one dollar or "love and affection." Land transfers to individuals with the same surname might indicate sons or daughters of the individual. Sales of land to males with different surnames might indicate daughters' married names. In many time periods married women could not own land in their own right, so land ownership would transfer to their husbands.

QUESTIONS ON LAND RECORDS

What was the original purpose of a land record?
The original purpose was to secure a new owner's right to a specific piece of land. This protected the owner from claims against the land and protected his interest in it from others who might claim ownership. Having his deed in hand provided protection for his investment of time and effort. Unfortunately, in some instances grants were given for the same piece of land by different states or governments who each claimed jurisdiction over it. This happened in Vermont because both New Hampshire and New York claimed the territory and both states felt free to grant land to individuals and townships.

When you first begin using land records, you may be surprised to find so much legal terminology and rhetoric in these old records. **If you read many land records from the same time period and locality you will see that their format was pretty standard with the wording almost the same in all deeds from a time period.** This was because the legally accepted format was set, and even though the documents are handwritten most appear to have been written in a fill-in-the-blanks manner.

Tip

How can I determine whether my ancestor owned land or property?

Many different documents indicate whether an individual was a property owner. The most commonly used is the U.S. federal census. In later censuses (1900 to 1930), the enumerator asked if the people owned or rented their residences. Some censuses show if they owned it free and clear or if there was a mortgage on the property. While earlier census records (1850 to 1870) may not specifically include the question of home ownership, they do contain a column showing the value of real estate and personal estate. A figure in the real estate column indicates that a person did indeed own property, so you should search land records. Other records that can provide clues to property ownership are tax lists, probate records, state census records, town histories, and maps showing landowners.

Are most land deeds considered primary source records?

Many researchers do consider land records to be primary sources, while others consider them to be secondary. This debate has been ongoing for some time. Since deeds are created at the time of the event—the purchase or sale—and then copied into the town records, some people consider the town records to be transcriptions and prone to errors. As stated before, the original deed was given to the landowner or purchaser, just as it is today. When you purchase a house or land you receive the original deed as proof of ownership, and copies are filed with the governmental division that has jurisdiction over deeds and property. Because the original was not kept by the town or county clerk, you will always see a transcription or copy of the original in those town or county records—probably in a copybook. Before the advent of photocopies, hand transcription was used to make duplicates.

You may have, in family papers or manuscript collections, some original deeds that may or may not have been recorded at the official location. Most deeds bear original signatures, perhaps a wax seal or stamp, and the date and place it was recorded. In many cases fees were due to record these documents, so you may see notations or seals applied to the original to indicate that all fees were paid. This might also explain why some deeds were not recorded. Perhaps the people didn't want to or could not pay the recording fees.

Why have so few land records been lost over the years compared to other record types?

The original deed went to the landowners and were not stored in a town hall or courthouse, where many records have been destroyed by fire or flood over the years. Copybooks were often destroyed in these catastrophes but re-created afterward. All landowners were to take their original deeds to the governing officials to have the deeds rerecorded so that they would be on file and official.

Since it was in a landowner's best interest to have his deed recorded again, most did so to protect their considerable monetary investments. Vital records did not fare as well. Since not having a birth or death recorded in the official records did not jeopardize a person's property or possessions, lost vital records were often neglected after such a disaster.

What special information can be gleaned from land and tax records?

Land records usually provide you with a description of the land involved or a reference to another deed or record that contains the description. If the actual description is included within the deed, the names of abutters, or neighbors may be listed. **This can be valuable information because relatives often lived on the adjoining land.** The names of all of the individuals whose land abuts your ancestor's can provide clues as to migratory patterns, siblings, wives' maiden names, and the like.

Research Tip

Some land deeds explain how the seller or grantee, obtained the land in the first place. Many list the means of acquisition—such as the proprietor's records, inheritance, or bounty land warrants—to show the legal right to sell the property. An example of such a land deed from the Danby, Rutland County, Vermont, land records is transcribed on the following page exactly as I interpreted it from the handwritten record that appears in the town land records.

To obtain a complete description and location for this piece of land I would have to go to the original records of the township under the original grant. Many deeds refer to a previous land sale for the exact description of the land. Others, usually in later time periods, refer to a parcel as it appears on an official town map (perhaps one in the assessor's office).

Can land deeds and probate records ever prove familial relationships?

Absolutely! In many cases where vital records were not kept or destroyed for some reason, **land and probate records may provide the only proof of relationships.** Since probate and land deeds are legal documents, the mention of a person as "my son," "my brother," or "my father" can be considered legal proof of a familial relationship.

Case Study

While researching a Joseph A. Rogers of Vermont, I needed to prove that he was the son of Constant Rogers, and I could find no vital or church record for Joseph's birth. Joseph's marriage record in 1839 did not list his parents' names or his place of birth, and I have never located his death record. Since Joseph and his wife, Annie Delilah Barber, named their first son Constant Hoxie Barber—Annie's father's name was Hoxie—Constant and Love were married in 1811, and Joseph's tombstone lists his date of birth as 1813. The naming pattern of Joseph's children, especially the first son, fit the pattern of the Constant Rogers family. I felt that Joseph's parents might have been Constant Rogers and Love Sanborn Cummings.

As I continued my search, I looked at the indexes for land transactions that involved Constant Rogers. In the index I found a land transaction between Constant Rogers and Noah Ellis in 1813, the year of Joseph's birth. Further research in the indexes showed a land transfer from Joseph A. Rogers to Noah

ABRAHAM IVES TO STEPHEN NICHOLS OF HARWICH— DANBY LAND RECORDS VOLUME 2; PAGE 210

Know all Men by these present that I Abraham Ives of Wallingford in the County of Rutland and State of Vermont Do for the Consideration of ten pounds Silver Money Received to My full Satisfaction of Stephen Nichols of Harwich County and State aforesaid Do Give Grant Bargain Sell and Confirm unto him the Said Stephen Nichols his heirs and assigns for Ever the one half of one whole Right or Shire of Land in the Township of Harwich Said Right was Granted to Samuel Willard by his Name being in the Charter Being on of said of said [sic] Township Granted by the Governor of New Hampshire. To have and to hold the above Granted and Bargained premises with all the privelidges and appurtinances their unto belonging unto him the said Stephen Nichols his heirs and assigns for Ever to his and their owne proper use and Behoof and also for my Self My heirs and assigns Covenant with the said Grantee his heirs & assigns that at and until the insealing of these presents I am well Sealed of the premises and have good Right to Bargain and Sell the Same in Manner and forme above Mentioned and that the Same is free of all Incumberances what so Ever and further more I the Said Grantor Do Ingage to warrant and Defend the Said Granted premises aGainst [sic] all Lawful Claims and Demands what So Ever. In witness where of I have here unto Set My hand and Seal 3rd Day of May 1782.

[Abraham Ives signature]

Signd Seald and Delivered in presence of Henry Spaulding Israel Seelye Recorded Febr ye 7th 1783

Routlee Justice Peace

Rutland County Ss: February ye 7th 1783 personally appeared Abraham Ives and Signor and Sealor of the above Instrument and acknowledged the same to be his voluntary act and Deed Before Thomas

Ellis in 1833. I then focused my research on these two land transactions. The land deed on page 142 was entered in the town land records:

As the example shows, parentage can be proven with a land deed. This deed establishes that Joseph A. Rodgers/Rogers was an heir of Constant, and possibly his son, since Constant was married in 1811 and Joseph was born in 1813. It also establishes Joseph as an heir and the grandson of Samuel and Mehitable Rodgers/Rogers. Further research in the land deeds showed that the land Joseph sold to Noah Ellis in 1833 adjoined the land Noah purchased from Constant in 1813.

What other information can be gleaned from the land deeds?

In some cases an approximate date or time period of death can be established using the land records and the indexes to them. In the case of the Rogers/

THETFORD, ORANGE COUNTY, VERMONT DEEDS BOOK NUMBER 12, PAGE 464

Joseph A. Rodgers to
Noah Ellis

Know all men by these present that I Joseph A. Rodgers of Thetford in Orange County and state of Vermont for the consideration of sixty dollars paid in full to my full satisfaction by Noah Ellis of Thetford in Orange County and State of Vermont have given, granted, bargained and sold and hereby do freely give, grant, bargain, and sell and confirm unto said Noah Ellis his heirs and assigns forever a certain piece of land in Thetford aforesaid as described as follows viz: all the right title or interest that shall or may fall to me as heir to the estate of Constant Rodgers formerly of said Thetford deceased meaning to convey all the interest that may fall to me as heir to the estate of Widow Mehitable Rodgers what was set off to her as her right of dower of the estate of Samuel Rogers late of said Thetford, deceased—To have and to hold said granted premises with all the priviledges and appurtenances thereof to the said Noah Ellis his heirs and asignes to his and their own use and behoof forever and I the said Joseph A. Rodgers for myself and my heirs executors and administrators do covenant with the said Noah Ellis and his heirs and assigns that until the ensealing of these presents I am the sole owner of the premises and have good right and title to convey the same in manner aforesaid that they are free from any incumberance and thereby engage to warrant and defend the same against all lawful claims whatsoever—The true content and meaning of this instrument is to convey all the right title or interest that I have or may have to the above described estate and to quitclaim the same to him the said Noah Ellis and his heirs and assigns forever. In witness whereof I hereunto set my hand and seal this ninth day of May 1833.

In the presence of Harrison Eastman   [Joseph A. Rodgers signature]
                    Stephen Eastman

State of Vermont   Thetford May 9th AD 1833 Then Joseph A.
Orange County   Rodgers signer and sealer of the foregoing
                          personally appeared and acknowledged this instrument be signed, sealed & subscribed to be his free act and deed before me Stephen Eastman, Justice of the Peace.

Rodgers family, no death record has ever been found for Constant or Love (Cummings) Rogers to my knowledge. The last vital record found was for their 1811 marriage in Thetford. One published manuscript indicated that they both died young, but it did not mention any known children. Further research in the land indexes showed that the last land deed found recorded for Constant Rogers was in 1823. No record has been found that bears his name after that date. The deed involving Noah Ellis in 1833 clearly indicates that Constant, and probably Love, are deceased since Joseph is listed as the heir to the estate with no mention of Love's dower right (see page 145).

One important research tactic must be stressed: Pay attention to the exact wording of a document. What the document says as well as what it does not say can be important clues. There being in the 1833 deed no mention of Constant's wife or her dower right indicates that she was probably deceased by that date. Note also that Samuel is referred to as deceased while Mehitable is named as "Widow Mehitable Rodgers," indicating that she was probably still living. Further research showed that Mehitable was living in Eaton, Canada, at the time of the 1833 deed, and she died there in 1840. Mehitable applied for a Revolutionary War widow's pension in 1838, providing even more conclusive proof that she was alive in 1833.

What else should I watch for in land documents?

Again, pay careful attention to the exact wording in every document. Sometimes things that are not said can be as telling as those things that are. Various sentence structures within the document can imply different meanings. Many documents contain antiquated words and phrases that are foreign to present-day researchers. When researching land and probate records in Worcester County, Massachusetts, I came across a document in a probate file that included distribution of the deceased person's land. The document was handwritten and difficult to read. I began by doing an abstract of the names and places mentioned in the document. The document contained the names of the deceased, three men with the same surname as the deceased, and one man with a different surname than the deceased and no indication of how they might have been related. The object of my search was to determine the names of the deceased's children, and it appeared that I would not secure that information with this document, only additional clues. I then decided to do a complete and accurate transcription of the document rather than rely on the abstract. When doing this, be very careful to copy the document exactly as it is written, maintaining all misspellings and lack of punctuation. Doing this type of work requires that you understand every word in the document rather than just the gist of the record. Human nature allows us to read and generally understand a document or text even if we cannot make out or understand every word. **Forcing yourself to do a complete transcription makes you pay closer attention to the details included.**

While transcribing this particular document I came across a word that appeared to be *mowly* or *mowty*, depending on which example I looked at. The word had me stumped for a while, and I incorrectly assumed that it was a word describing some sort of land. Since different parcels of land within the document were referred to as pastureland, wood lots, and hay lots, this term could have been another antiquated term for land use. The word appeared at least four times within the document, and my curiosity was piqued. I grabbed several dictionaries (see the sidebar on page 144) and started browsing the possible spellings that I had read. After searching several basic dictionaries I finally located the word in a genealogical dictionary. The word was *moiety*, and it means one of equal shares of something—one half, one third, etc. That each of

Research Tip

For More Info

> ## GENEALOGICAL DICTIONARIES
>
> - *A to Zax,* by Barbara Jean Evans
>
> - *Abbreviations & Acronyms: A Guide for Family Historians,* compiled by Kip Sperry
>
> - *Concise Genealogical Dictionary,* compiled by Maurine and Glen Harris
>
> - *A Medical Miscellany for Genealogists,* by Jeannette L. Jerger
>
> - *What Did They Mean By That? A Dictionary of Historical Terms for Genealogists,* volumes 1 and 2, by Paul Drake

the four individuals mentioned in the document received a moiety, or equal share, of land indicates that they were probably the heirs of the deceased. Further research proved that the deceased did indeed have three sons, all mentioned in the deed, and one daughter who was married to the fourth man mentioned in the deed. Transcribing every word and understanding the terminology brought to light the information I sought but could have easily overlooked.

When you look at land documents, know that the earliest ones pertaining to an individual may list his previous place of residence. When an individual purchased his first piece of land in a new location, the record might list him as "John Reynolds of Providence, Rhode Island," providing you with another location to research. Also pay close attention to all witnesses that signed on any document; they might have been relatives of the involved parties.

What is a headright grant?

A headright grant is a grant of land provided to an individual who paid for the passage of immigrants to help settle the new territory. The term *headrights* also refers to other benefits given to those who either paid for transportation or provided it to immigrants in newly established territories. These benefits included tax breaks and bounties. Some states that were affected by headrights or headright grants were California, Florida, Georgia, Maryland, Texas, and Virginia, and the headrights or headright grants were given by the country with ownership or possession of the territory.

What is the difference between the metes and bounds survey system and the rectangular survey system?

The metes and bounds survey system is a method of measuring land that uses directions (such as north, south, east, or west), degrees (relative to the angle at which the sides of the land meet), and measurements (of the length of each side). There are not always four sides to a piece of land measured this way; the land may be irregular in shape. This type of survey is common on the East Coast and in the earliest states. This survey system results in land descriptions that read, for example, "23 degrees northwest for 5 chains, then 45 degrees north for 10 chains." Descriptions from this type of survey system sometimes mention the names of abutters to the land being described.

The rectangular survey system refers to the uniform layout of townships in squares and rectangles containing set amounts of public land (land sold or granted by the government rather than by proprietorship). In most cases this land, or township, is divided into thirty-six sections containing approximately 640 acres, or about one square mile (2.6 square kilometers), each. This township square is also divided into quarters, so it has north/south and east/west axis lines that intersect at the center of the square. Each of the resulting quarter squares contains nine sections. These nine sections can be broken down further into quarters, eighths, sixteenths, etc. In this survey system, you'll find legal land descriptions written as, for instance, "the west half of the southwest quarter, section 8, township 38, range 24, containing 80 acres," abbreviated as "W½ of SW¼ S8 = T38 = R24, containing 80 acres."

For additional information on the rectangular survey system and land records, see *The Sleuth Book for Genealogists* by Emily Anne Croom (pages 93–99).

What is meant by dower rights, dower release, or the "widow's third"?

Dower rights (also known commonly as the widow's third) were provided for in the law so that a widow would not be left destitute after her husband's death. A widow was entitled to life interest (i.e., for the term of her life) in one-third of her deceased husband's real estate. In some states, when a man sold his property, his wife had to sign a dower release, thus relinquishing her rights to that property. *Dower* should not be confused with the term *dowry*, meaning the property—real and personal—that a wife brought into a marriage. Once she was married, however, all of her property became her husband's unless they had a prenuptial agreement stating otherwise.

Definitions

Where can I locate land documents?

You must first determine what governmental division had authority over such transactions in the time period in the specific state. You can accomplish this by using one of the many reference books (e.g., *Ancestry's Red Book*, *The Handybook*, *The Source*, *Land & Property Research in the U.S.*, the Family History Library's state research guides) that outline the specifics for any given state. You also need to know if the land record is for a state, county or federal land transfer. Since many land records are county or town documents and these governmental divisions have changed repeatedly over time, you need to pinpoint where the town or county was located at the time of the sale. If you look for a land deed for the town of Lancaster, Massachusetts, for 1700, you need to know that even though Lancaster, established in 1653, is situated in Worcester County today, it was originally in Middlesex County. Since Worcester County was split off from Middlesex County in 1731, all Lancaster deeds previous to the establishment of Worcester County are Middlesex County records.

Reminder

Once you determine who had jurisdiction over the record, you need to find out where the record is currently housed. Again, many of the reference books on land records will help here. Also keep in mind that records are constantly on the move. Many have been microfilmed and are available at state archives, state and local libraries, the Family History Library, and its Family History Centers, county courts, and town land offices. Just because a book published last year states the location of records does not mean that they are still there. This is another reason that using the microfilm can be helpful. Microfilmed records may be more accessible through state and local libraries, the Family History Centers, and other local facilities than the original records are. If you determine that you need to look at the originals, you should verify their location. I find it a good idea to call the holding facility in advance to find out whether the records are readily available and what days or times are best for research. Since some records must be retrieved from storage it is always advisable to check first rather than learning this after you drive to the facility. Ask what restrictions are in place for using the records, whether photocopying is available and allowed, and any other questions you may have regarding records access.

Since archived land records are rarely the original documents, you have nothing to gain by using the original copybooks rather than the microfilmed version, unless the microfilm quality makes reading difficult. Indexes are often on microfilm and can provide many valuable clues as well.

What should I look for in the indexes to land records?

Important

Land records usually have two types of indexes. One is called the grantee/grantor (buyer/seller or direct/indirect) index, and the other is the grantor/grantee (seller/buyer) index. These two indexes cover the same period of time, and you must be sure to look at both. The grantee/grantor index is alphabetical by the name of the buyer, while the grantor/grantee index is alphabetical by the name of the seller. Many researchers make the mistake of looking at only one index, and they may miss many land transactions and opportunities to gather more information.

Many researchers comment on the number of land transfers that appear clustered together in a short time frame. Two brothers might have traded what appears to be one piece of land back and forth several times in a short time period. Closer inspection usually reveals that they were perhaps exchanging pieces of land to consolidate their other holdings. Perhaps one brother inherited land that did not adjoin his other property, so he swapped it, through a sale, for a parcel that did, thereby consolidating his holdings into one contiguous piece of land.

You should list the citations for all parcels included in the index that might pertain to the family in question and look for any patterns that develop. When using a particular set of indexes I noticed that a man sold his property to his daughter for a nominal fee, and then within several months she sold it back to him. This happened several times over several years and was, for a long time, a mystery. Why would they buy and sell the same property within the family so many times? I found the answer in the town and tax records. It appeared that the father fell on hard times and was unable to pay the property taxes on his home. The town demanded payment—this was listed in the delinquent tax lists—but before the town could put a lien on the property he sold it to his daughter, thereby buying himself time to come up with the taxes. He then bought the property back, paid the taxes, and then start the process again whenever the need arose. I found the father listed in the delinquent tax lists for every year that a transaction like this took place—mystery solved!

Where else might I find land deeds besides the land office or town hall?

Land deeds, or transcriptions of them, may be included in probate packets, pension applications, family Bibles, family papers, manuscript collections in libraries and historical societies, and any other place where you might find original documents. Microfilmed or published copies of the records may be available from many sources, and you should use local libraries and microfilm rental companies. If you need a land deed from a distant location, use these microfilmed or published records first to determine your need for the actual document. Since land deeds on file are rarely the originals due to the nature of the record, you might as well use the microfilmed version of the copybooks rather than travel a distance only to view a copybook. Most libraries have the means to print copies from the microfilm or microfiche records, so you can obtain fairly inexpensive copies. If you are unable to print a copy from the microfilm you can always write to the office holding the record to obtain a copy. By using the films and published versions first you will know if you need a copy of a specific document and save yourself the disappointment of getting a copy only to realize it does not pertain to your research subject.

QUESTIONS ON PROBATE AND ESTATE RECORDS

What might I find in probate documents?

Probate documents, also called probate dockets or packets or files, contain many important papers. These papers might include guardianships of minor children, estate inventories, wills, administrations, affidavits, receipts, appointment of executors, lists of heirs, and any number of other records considered by the governmental authorities to be pertinent to the settlement of an estate. Every state or county may have several or all of these records included in the probate record, and some of them may be filed as completely separate documents. Do your research before you head out to locate any type of record, and understand what is and is not included within it.

Some probate or estate files I have used are extremely detailed, laying out many specifics related to the settlement of the estate. One such file was quite interesting because of what the deceased felt necessary to spell out in his will. He left property to his wife—her dower right—but specifically stated that her sons were to provide her with one cow, firewood, and access to the root cellar and the stairway to the second floor. The will then laid out the provisions for these items. The oldest son was to provide the cow, while the younger son was to provide the feed for said cow. If the cow died, the sons were to share equally in the expenses of replacing the cow and feeding it. The sons were then instructed as to how much firewood should be cut, split, and laid within a certain number of feet of the back door for the widow's use. He also instructed the sons as to who must provide the widow with rides to meeting every week and what percentage of harvest would be for her personal use. Do you think the deceased had a trust issue as to whether his sons would take care of his widow? Perhaps the widow was their stepmother. This will left nothing to chance. Interestingly, further research proved that the widow was indeed the mother of the two sons.

What should I do first when using these records?

It is imperative to know whether you are looking at the original papers or a transcription of them. Whether you are using microfilm or paper documents, look at the format of the papers. Are the records in book form on consecutively numbered pages? If so they are not the originals. Most microfilmed probate records were made from the copybooks, not the original probate packets or dockets. A probate packet should be an envelope or file with many pieces of paper that were created throughout the probate process. These papers, but not necessarily all of them, were copied into the books in a standard format, so remember that the books are transcriptions of the original documents and subject to copying errors. When you write to request copies of probate records, make sure to specify that you want copies of the original papers and not the copybooks. It is also important to specify that you want copies of both the front and back of each paper included in the file.

When should I use the copybooks, and when should I refer to the originals?

In some cases you may not have an option. If the copybooks are the only surviving records, you must use them; but if the originals are also available, you should use both. First I use the microfilmed or published indexes to the pertinent probate records. I make a list of all documents of interest to my search. When there are many documents with similar names you may need to weed out the irrelevant ones by checking the records in the copybooks. After you have determined which probate records pertain to your ancestor and done a cursory review of the file using the copybooks, move on to the original packets. The copybooks are handwritten transcriptions of the original papers filed in the packets or files and may contain copying errors and mistakes in names and other important information. Whenever a document is hand copied, there is about a 25 percent chance for error. The packet may have some pieces of paper that were not copied into the copybook. When you look at the original docket papers, pay attention to every sheet of paper, no matter how insignificant it seems. Examine both the front of the paper and any notations on the back as well.

When reviewing one probate file after using the copybook, I discovered a piece of paper that instructed the administrator of the estate to post a notice to let people know that they were to present any claims against the estate by a certain day. This is still done today, although now the notice is posted in local newspapers where the individual lived, worked, or owned property. This piece of paper was in estate records for a farmer in Vermont in 1788. The instructions to the administrator specified that the notice be posted in Danby and Bennington, Vermont, as well as Stephentown, New York. I had not found any other records that indicated this man was ever outside New England, and this was a clue that led to many other records, not just for him but for several other families in the Danby area. I never would have looked across the Vermont border had I not seen that little tidbit of information in the probate packet.

Why not just use the original probate records first?

Since most probate packets, dockets, or files contain many old, folded, and possibly brittle papers, you should handle them as infrequently as possible. By doing your cursory review of the records in the copybooks, you will probably find that some records are not pertinent to your research and you don't need to examine them. Less handling of the original documents helps to preserve them for future generations. Most microfilming was done of the copybooks because of the difficulty in flattening out all of the various-sized and fragile papers in the packets. Another problem with handling the originals depends on the care that some researchers and clerks use. While some probate offices give you one document to review at a time, I have encountered many that let an individual have several papers at once. Documents can inadvertently get mixed up with those from other files or packets and therefore be "lost" forever. I have found several probate packets that were completely empty. Perhaps the documents were accidentally put into another packet or file, or perhaps they were stolen. I may never know what was in the now empty packet for my great-great-grandfather; the surviving copybooks only cover records to 1850, and he died in 1853. Hopefully someday someone will find the missing papers in another packet and bring them to the attention of the clerks. Until then his probate record will remain a mystery. So use the copybooks first and avoid using the originals until you have determined that those records are important to your research, and then handle them as little as possible and with extreme care.

Where can I find probate or estate documents?

Probate documents, like land records, fall under the different jurisdictions within a state. Some probate documents are town records, while others are county records. First determine who had jurisdiction over these records at the time frame of interest to you. There isn't really a simple answer to this question or any other regarding official documents. Laws governing the recording and preservation of any documents change over time, and also when county and state lines are redrawn or laws revised. Keeping this in mind, you should again utilize one of the many reference books pertaining to records locations in the state or area of interest (see page 145).

Research Tip

Some states combine probate records with records for adoptions, marriages, and civil lawsuits as one record type under one jurisdictional umbrella; others divide all of these records into separate classifications. Some states, such as New York, classify them as surrogate court records. Delaware classifies them as orphan's court records, while Louisiana classifies them as succession records. Exactly what is included in these classifications varies from place to place, so you must understand the state and local laws that control them. Reference books such as *Ancestry's Red Book*, *The Genealogist's Companion & Sourcebook* or Everton's *Handybook for Genealogists* are just some of the many available to you.

What else should I watch out for when using probate or estate records?

One important thing to remember is not to limit yourself to the one individual you are researching. If her probate file does not answer your questions regarding family relationships or previous residences, look at other files bearing the same surname. Many times these belong to other family members and may have more definitive information. One such file provided proof of a relationship that had until then eluded me. I was trying to determine whether a particular man, Henry George SUMNER, was the father of one of my ancestors, but the man's will did not specifically name his children. When I looked at several other probate files of people with the same surname in the same general area, I found one that stated that the deceased, George Henry Sumner, left "a legacy of $150 to his niece, Malona CARPENTER, the daughter of his brother Henry." While Henry had not named his daughter in his will his brother's will provided the crucial information. In another such document, a grandfather left money to his granddaughter, thereby providing proof of another family line.

Tip

Also keep in mind the time frame that your search encompasses. **Look well beyond the years surrounding the death of your research subject.** I was trying to prove a relationship between a Stephen Nichols and my ancestor Druzilla Nichols. I located the probate packet of Stephen Nichols in Rutland County in 1788. Unfortunately, he left his estate "to his children and wife" without specifying their names or even how many children he had. I decided to set the research aside and rethink my approach. Several months later I was looking for another probate packet in the same county for another research subject, and I noticed a probate record for another Stephen Nichols about fifty years later than the 1788 file. Curious as to whether this Stephen might be a son of the one who died in 1788, I looked at the file. To my surprise, it was a continuation of the 1788 probate record! Stephen Nichols and his wife, Nancy, had five daughters, and one of them had never married. In 1790, Stephen's widow, Nancy, married a widower with several children, and they had three children together. Nancy died in 1840, and the unmarried daughter petitioned the court for her share of her father's estate. She had lived with her mother and had never received her one-fifth share of Stephen Nichols's estate. When her mother died, this daughter probably wanted to make sure that her portion was not given to any of her stepfather's children. Because of this request to the court, all of Stephen and Nancy's children were listed, including whom they married, where they lived, and in one case even who their children were. The file was a gold mine that proved Druzilla was indeed the daughter of Stephen and Nancy. Do not overlook or dismiss a file due to the time frame as anything can and did happen in the world of estate settlement.

What other information can be gleaned from estate or probate records?

When you look at probate records, pay special attention to the inventory of the estate. Make note of the people who owed money to the estate or that were owed or paid money from the estate. Individuals listed who shared the deceased's surname were almost always related to the deceased in some way, so check them out. Also pay attention to the listing of belongings that were owned by the deceased. Many times the list indicates a certain occupation, religion, or status in life. I have found several inventories that listed shoemaker tools and dye tubs, indicating that the deceased was not only a farmer but possibly a shoemaker. While many farmers may have made shoes for their own family, the dye tubs suggest that this individual made items for others, as dying the leather would not have been necessary for purely functional shoes.

Another inventory listed barrels of different grains, molasses, and whiskey among the deceased's belongings. Books, Bibles, teacups, silver, mirrors, watches, and jewelry can provide you with a picture of the family and their status in life. The list of belongings can sound as though the people taking the inventory walked through the house, listing each room and the goods within it. This can provide a visual idea of the home's contents and whether the deceased and his family had few or many belongings. The inventory often lists specific linens; furniture; the number of spoons, teacups, or kettles; the number of brass buttons on a coat; and many other interesting details. Farm implements, tools, and other work-related items round out the picture of the family and provide you with a historical perspective of an ancestor's life.

Why are tax records important to genealogists?

Tax records can provide information regarding property ownership and real estate that can lead you to other records such as deeds or probate records. An individual's inclusion in these records can also confirm that she was alive and in a certain place at a specific time. Additionally, if you research two men of the same name, you can distinguish them through tax records, since no two men paid taxes on the exact same real and personal property.

How do I access these records?

You can, in most instances, access the tax records as part of the town or county records regarding assessments of fees or taxes, including poll taxes, due from residents to maintain the operation of the church, town, county, or state. In some areas the tax records might be included in the town meeting records, the town reports or the records of the overseer of the poor.

FURTHER READING

A to Zax: A Comprehensive Dictionary for Genealogists and Historians, by Barbara Jean Evans. Alexandria, Va.: Hearthside Press, 1995.

Ancestry's Red Book: American State, County & Town Sources, edited by Alice Eichholz, Ph.D. Salt Lake City, Utah: Ancestry, Inc., 1982, 1989.

The Basic Researcher's Guide to Homesteads and Other Federal Land

Sources

Records, by James C. Barsi. Colorado Springs, Colo.: Nuthatch Grove Press, 1994.

Concise Genealogical Dictionary, by Maurine and Glen Harris. Salt Lake City, Utah: Ancestry, Inc., 1989.

Estate Inventories: How to Use Them, by Kenneth L. Smith. Elverston, Pa.: Olde Springfield Shoppe, 1993.

The Genealogist's Companion & Sourcebook, by Emily Anne Croom. Cincinnati, Ohio: Betterway Books, 1994.

The Handybook for Genealogists, 9th ed., by George B. Everton. Logan, Utah: Everton Publishing Co., Inc., 1999.

Land and Property Research in the United States, by E. Wade Hone. Salt Lake City, Utah: Ancestry, Inc., 1997.

Long-Distance Genealogy, by Christine Crawford-Oppenheimer. Cincinnati, Ohio: Betterway Books, 2000.

Reading Early American Handwriting, by Kip Sperry. Baltimore, Md.: Genealogical Publishing Co., Inc., 1998.

The Sleuth Book for Genealogists, by Emily Anne Croom. Cincinnati, Ohio: Betterway Books, 2000.

The Source: A Guidebook of American Genealogy, rev. ed., by Loretto Dennis Szucs and Sandra Hargreaves Luebking. Salt Lake City, Utah: Ancestry, Inc., 1997.

What Did They Mean by That?: A Dictionary of Historical Terms for Genealogists, by Paul Drake. Bowie, Md.: J.D. Heritage Books, Inc., 1994.

What Did They Mean by That?: Some More Words, Volume 2, by Paul Drake. Bowie, Md.: Heritage Books, Inc., 1998.

NINE

Documenting Sources and Determining the Reliability of Records

T he documentation of facts presented in any family history or genealogy is always a heavily discussed topic. While documenting where you obtained every fact you present in your work is ideal, not all researchers take the time to do it properly, if at all. Many genealogies, biographies, and town and county histories lack even a semblance of source documentation. That does not mean that you shouldn't use these works; just use them with care and a healthy bit of skepticism. Do not take anything at face value, and question every piece of information you receive from others. If you follow this advice you will be less likely to pass on erroneous or undocumented information to other researchers.

Determining the reliability or accuracy of any record or data goes hand in hand with source documentation. Without source documentation a piece of information is only hearsay evidence, not a fact. I once saw the quote "A family history without documentation should be considered fiction." How far you go with your verification of the information depends on you and your persistence. While many records, such as vital records are taken at face value as acceptable fact, even these are often fraught with errors, omissions, and outright falsehoods. Many times knowing who provided the information recorded on any certificate goes a long way in determining its reliability. Clerks only recorded what they were told or personally knew.

What does the term documentation *mean?*
The term means, simply put, that you list where the information you present or use came from. While your source for the information may be a secondary one, such as a book, CD, or Internet database, it is still the *source* of *your* data. Citing, or listing, that source is important to other researchers' ability to evaluate your data and determine its reliability. It also serves as your paper trail as you accumulate data on an individual or family.

If your information comes from a secondary source, you should evaluate the

Citing Sources

original source of the data used to compile it. Getting back to the original record is the goal here. Since most books, CDs, and databases are compilations of previously published data, they may include many mistakes made in the transferring or interpreting of the information from their sources. Understand this, and realize that being printed in a book or viewed on a computer does not make data accurate.

Emily Anne Croom, one of my favorite authors, put this very well in chapter three of her book *Unpuzzling Your Past*, 4th edition, where she listed the following "Strategies for Winning in Genealogy." Some of these are "be systematic, be resourceful, be thorough, be cautious, and be smart: document your facts." These rules, when you apply them to your research, will make you a better researcher. You should look twice at every piece of information you find and evaluate it for its accuracy, how it fits into the puzzle, how likely it is to be true, and whether it conflicts or agrees with other data. Being critical of, and realistic about every piece of information is important to the final outcome of your research. Many researchers have spent years researching incorrect family lines because they took a record at face value and did not verify it with other sources.

When using a published book as the source of information, how do I document it?

When using published records or indexes, your citation should list the title of the book, the author, the publication date, and the publisher's name and location. I try to make photocopies of the information for my files to help prevent transcription errors or omissions. By making copies of the pages that hold data of interest I also have a means of documenting the source. I also add the library in which I viewed the book as an additional piece of information to help should I ever need to refer to the book later.

Whenever you make copies from a book, photocopy the book's title page, which has the title, author, publisher and publication date (in some cases) all on one page. Write the library name and call number on this title page photocopy. Page numbers are usually printed on the book's pages, so page numbers will appear on your photocopies. This way no matter how many pages you photocopy from that book you will have the complete citation for the source.

Timesaver

I also photocopy the pages that list the abbreviations used in the text. Many times I have gotten home and found strange abbreviations in the text. If you do not understand all of the abbreviations, you risk misinterpreting the data or overlooking clues that might help you in your research.

What should my citation include?

Your citation, or the listing of the source of the information, should contain enough information to enable you or another researcher to go directly back to your source to verify the data. Your citation should be explicit enough that anyone else—or you—can duplicate your research without repeating every step you took to get to that piece of information.

To illustrate, let's look at a sample citation for census records. Many researchers use the U.S. federal census records to gather information on their families. You might record the following information found in these records:

Rhodes Braman was born in New York about 1802.

The citation for this type of information is often listed as just "U.S. federal census." The proper citation should be

U.S. federal census; 1860; PA, Wayne Co., Berlin Twp.; pg. 173; line 12; dwelling/family #1101/1101

Using this complete citation (you can also add the roll number of the NARA film) enables another researcher to go directly to the census record to compare the information you have presented, thereby allowing them to verify that you copied and interpreted the information correctly.

When you take information from a census schedule, you should always list the year, state, county, town, and page number. I always add the dwelling/family number as additional information. This makes it easier to find the family again if the page numbers are not readable. If the census was taken in a later time period (1880, 1900, 1910, or 1920), list the enumeration district number (ED#) as well as the page and line numbers.

How do I document family Bible information?

If the information you list came from a family Bible, give the name and address of the person or repository who had possession of the Bible at the time you viewed it. Also include the name of the person who did the actual transcription of the data from that Bible, along with her place of residence and the date she did the transcription. Whenever possible, obtain a photocopy or photograph of the Bible pages that include family data and of the title page showing the publication date and the publisher's name and location. This is valuable information that many people neglect to record.

Why is the Bible's publication date so important?

Whenever you use data from a Bible it is important to know when the Bible was actually published. If the dates written in the Bible are before the publication date you know that the information was recorded not at the time of the event but at some later date. Since such information might have been recorded from memory or family stories or copied from another record, you might have no way to verify its accuracy.

Also look at the handwriting that is in the Bible. Is it all the same? Do the records cover a wide period of time? Does the handwriting and type of ink used change over time, or is it consistent throughout the Bible? The answers to these questions can provide you with many clues as to when and how the information was compiled. If all of the events occurred after the publication date and the handwriting changes over the period of time covered, it is more likely that the Bible was kept up-to-date as the events happened, making the data more reliable.

Oral History

How do I document information acquired through an oral history interview?
Whenever you conduct an interview to collect information you should always record the date and place of the interview along with the full name of the person you interview. Also document the name of the person conducting the interview and the relationship of the subject to the family being discussed. Remember to document all women with both their maiden and married names. When recording such interviews, record all of this information at the beginning of every tape. This way, even if some of the tapes become lost or destroyed, the surviving tapes will have all of the necessary data to document the recorded information.

How do I record the source in my computer genealogy program?
This varies from program to program, but the basic rules of proper citation should be adhered to. Always make sure to *completely* document the source, including the title, author, and publication information for every record. Most computer programs allow for a source notation as well as a note field. The program I use, FormatSoft Family Origins, has a place for the source record, the specific citation, and a note field to enter the exact data found. I enter the source (e.g., book title, U.S. federal census, Vermont vital record) in the source field. I enter the actual citation (e.g., page number in the book; state, county, town, and page number for a census; volume and page number for vital records) and then transcribe the data into a note field that is attached to the fact by the database. When the family group sheet is printed, the source, citation, and note are all printed indicating which information came from which source. Make sure that the program you choose allows for complete citations. Some have limited fields for entering this data, thereby hindering you from a complete entry.

How can I determine how accurate a record is?
This is the million-dollar question asked by many researchers at one time or another. Determining the reliability of any piece of information requires that you understand how, why, and by whom the original record was created. If vital records were created in the town of the event, then the original is located there. If that town reported the records to a state agency, a record will also be there. There is, however, only one original record—the first one created. Since the town records, before photocopies, had to be hand transcribed to be sent to the state, many errors could have creeped into the resulting record. Some records were incompletely transcribed depending on what information the state might have required in any given time period. Always get back to the original record whenever possible. This will assure that your source record is as accurate as possible. No record, whether the original or a copy, is guaranteed to be 100 percent accurate. The information is only as correct as the person who supplied it.

Why should I use the state copies of vital records if they are not the originals?
Many times you may not know what town or county an event happened in, so locating the original record first would be time consuming and frustrating. Use the state copies, when they exist, to determine what town or county submitted the record to the state. Then go back to the original record, either in the town

or county, to compare the data provided. Many of the early vital, town, and church records are available on microfilm in local libraries, archives, and through the Family History Library and its Family History Centers around the world. Check your state, county, and town libraries for copies of these records. Use the state copy of vital records as an index to and finding aid for the original record. By utilizing these secondary copies and records on microfilm you will not handle as many original records, thereby preserving them for the future. Use microfilms whenever possible.

Why do people's ages seem to vary greatly from one record to another, especially in the census?

One important fact to remember is that before the early 1900s few people had possession of actual birth certificates. Most based how old they were on what someone else told them. Knowing one's specific date of birth was not that important to day-to-day existence. There were no child labor laws, driver's licenses were not the norm, and if you were able to work you did, regardless of your age in many cases. Not until Social Security, state licensing regulations, labors laws, and school attendance requirements came into effect did people generally possess certified information on births.

Many individuals born in the late 1800s and early 1900s did not realize that their births had never been officially recorded until they needed a copy of their birth certificates for Social Security, military enlistment, etc. To determine their ages, they used other records, such as school records and the 1880 U.S. federal census. Individuals who were eligible for the first round of Social Security benefits had to have been born between 1870 and 1880. The Social Security Administration had the 1880 census indexed for all households with children ten years old or younger (born 1870 to 1880) to make verifying the ages of persons applying for benefits easier. Many of these individuals had no birth certificates to prove their eligibility.

The census records are especially unreliable for determining an individual's age. There is no way to know who actually provided the census information, how knowledgeable they were, or whether they were just guessing at the ages. The data recorded could have been provided to the census taker by any member of the household—even a child—or a neighbor. Because of this the names, ages, places of birth, and other data are sometimes incorrectly listed. This means that you should look at all of the available census records and any other records you can accumulate to get a better picture of a person's statistics.

How do I document my source if it is a CD or an electronic database?

Whenever you use a CD or computer database, it is important to determine where the information originally came from. What information was compiled to create the CD or database? Most CDs will list the books, indexes, or other records that are included in the information provided. Some actually tell you which of these sources provided a specific piece of information.

Some researchers cite the source of the information as the CD number, such as Family Tree Maker CD #125. If you are going to use this type of CD, be sure to list the compiler or the publishing company as you would for a book, and cite the publication date as well. If CDs are reissued with additional information they bear either a new number or the original number, confusing the issue of which edition you are citing.

Here is an example of citing a CD source. After finding the immigration date for an ancestor, the following information is noted:

Antonio Bruno; age 6; arrived New York 3 December 1888 on the vessel Letimbo; manifest #188; port of embarkation was Sorrento; last foreign residence was Castrovillari

A proper complete citation for the source of this data is
Family Tree Maker CD #353: Passenger and Immigration Lists: *Italians to America 1880–1893*; Learning Co., Inc., 1999.

The entire listing of the source and full citation provides other researchers with exact information as to which edition of this CD was used. If you simply cited *Italians to America* it would be unclear as to whether you used a CD, online version, or the printed books as your source. Since mistakes are inherent whenever information is transferred from one source to another, the specifics are important.

How accurate are the linked pedigree databases on Internet sites such as Ancestry.com and FamilySearch?

While it is certainly exciting to find information on one of these sites, be careful to determine the exact source of the data as well. Most of the compiled family trees, whether Ancestry World Tree, Ancestral File, or any other, all have basically the same sources—individuals who post their research or lineages online. **The information is only as good as the original research and the care taken by the person who submitted it.** Since most of these databases have no place to list or document sources, you have no way of knowing where the information originated without contacting the submitter. Most contact information consists of an e-mail address, and we all know how often those change.

Warning

I admit to using these databases quite often but with a healthy dose of skepticism. I use them only as clues to further research. I attempt to contact the submitting individual if the information is something that I have been seeking for some time. I am naturally curious about where they found the information; I want to carefully evaluate its accuracy. I have had several occasions when I found long sought after data online and made contact with the researcher. It is wonderful to communicate with others interested in the same research as yours.

One such find was especially fortuitous. I had searched for several years for the maiden name of the wife of my third great-grandfather Hoxie Barber with no luck. I was working in a Family History Center and learning to use the new FamilySearch program and needed to do a practice search. I just pulled the name Hoxie Barber out of my head and typed it into the search criteria. Imagine my surprise when a record came up on the screen! It stated that it was a brief record, but I followed the screen instructions anxiously. Another researcher had posted information regarding the Emery family. It seems that her third great-grandmother was the sister of Hoxie Barber's wife, Nancy Emery. I now had at least a clue as to Nancy's maiden name. I contacted the individual, and she mailed me all of the research and documentation that had produced her information. You never know who might have knowledge of your research subject. It is important to utilize every possible resource available to you—with care.

How do you document such data?

This can be a tough one since the databases are all different and some provide little information other than an e-mail address for the submitter. I list the source as the particular database I am using, then the citation includes whatever information is provided by the database. I also include the date that the search results were produced. This is especially important since these databases change on an almost daily basis as researchers submit their data and it gets added to the database.

The importance of recording as much information regarding the submitter as possible should be noted here. While you may find only one entry for a specific piece of data today, you may get several other "hits" a month from now. If you look at every hit and review the source information, you may find one that still has an active e-mail address or provides a more reliable source for you to follow up on.

I conducted a search and was excited to find a reference to a Francis Akey on a Family Tree Maker disk. When I tracked the information back to the source, I discovered that the information was originally my own! I had shared the research with a cousin who subsequently submitted the data for publication. I was no further ahead or behind, but I looked at the sources a lot more carefully from then on. It also made me more careful about documentation of my sources because I had since disproven some of the original data I had shared. As always, you must determine where the original information came from *before* taking it as fact or passing it on to others in the form of your research.

What about compiled databases other than individuals' submitted pedigrees?

In this twenty-first century we have many resources available to us that were not available even twenty years ago, and that can be overwhelming. Many of the sources that have been used for many years in book format are now being translated into electronic databases. Some of these are compiled onto CDs, while others take shape as databases accessible online or on a computer somewhere. Many companies make these available by subscription or for free. Remember that paying for the information does not make it accurate or above reproach!

When you find data in one of the electronic formats, make sure you look for the original source of the data. Most databases have some sort of explanations of how they were compiled and where the information was accumulated. In most cases the source is books originally published many years ago that are now out of copyright and in the public domain. This means that most databases compiled

Important

from previously published data have been compiled from secondary sources. Any mistakes in the books are also included in the "new" database along with any errors that occurred in the translation from print to electronic form. You could be many generations away from the original source, and each level between the original and the one you are using can contain errors or omissions. As long as you are aware of this and take it into consideration as you evaluate the data, you will be less likely to take another person's word for a presented fact.

Once you have found a piece of information online look for additional information about the source. If the source is a previously published book, locate the book to see where the author's data was found. I utilize many of these online databases as my personal library card catalog.

Here is an example of how a database's contents can vary from the source information. An electronic database provided the following listing:

Perkins, Elizabeth died 2 Feb. 1801 at 74 years

The database listed the source of this information as the Massachusetts Town Record books to 1850 for the town of Ipswich. Looking at the original book the entry reads

Perkins, Elizabeth, wid. Will[ia]m, Feb. 2, 1801.

I then tried searching the database for other individuals listed in the Ipswich deaths in the same book to determine how complete the other entries were. Less than half of the printed listings were included in the database. I then looked for marriages. Using page 21 of the printed book, I searched the database for any marriages listed and found none! Not one single marriage printed on page 21 shows up in the online database even though Ipswich is listed as being included within the database.

This example shows how unreliable the database information can be. While the database lists the source as "Massachusetts Town Records to 1850, Town of Ipswich," it does not list what edition the printed book was (perhaps another edition contains Elizabeth's age at death but not that she was William's widow) or if all of the records within the book are included in the database. As stated before, the source presented should lead you directly to the original source used to compile the database. This one does not appear to do that.

What other problems with accuracy and reliability are there with online and CD databases?
The major problems that I have heard discussed over and over are the incomplete source information, misinterpreted information, and what is or is not included within any given database. You must look realistically at these resources.

Remember that when you don't find someone in an index it does not mean that they are not in the record, or even in the index. While spelling differences are commonplace, most researchers unfamiliar with electronic databases might become very frustrated when using them. Remember that computers are literal machines—they look for exactly what you input. If the entry does not appear that way in the database, you will not find it via that search.

An exception to this rule is the Family History Library's International Genealogical Index. This program searches for the surname by the way it sounds phonetically, not by the literal spelling. I use this database on occasion to determine what other spellings I should search for. While you might think you have covered all possible spellings there can always be another one you have not thought about or encountered.

Example

I had searched for the surname Wait under what I thought was every possible spelling (Waite, Wate, Whate, Wayte) until I did a search on the IGI. Two additional spellings showed up: Weight and Wacht. Using these two additional spellings, I had success finding the family in other online and printed indexes. Neither of these two spellings shows up when doing a Soundex search on Wait (see chapter four for explanation of Soundex).

What does "misinterpreted information" refer to?

Whenever original records are translated from handwritten documents to typed or electronic versions, inaccuracies in how the written record is interpreted are likely. Two individuals can look at the same record and see two different things. Reading any handwriting, never mind the old style of handwriting, is a purely subjective task. The transcriber must have a working knowledge of the handwriting from the time period to effectively and accurately interpret the records. Most of the online and book resources are typed, not scanned images of the original record, so you view another person's interpretation of the original record. This applies to everything that is not in handwritten format.

Another record that is used quite often is the copybook for probate and estate records. Remember that knowing how an original record was created helps you determine what is an original or primary record and what is a secondary one. Probate records are usually made up of many different documents on various pieces of paper that are filed in a probate packet or file. Most, but not necessarily all, of the papers contained in the file are transcribed into a copybook. Most microfilmed probate records are of the copybooks, not the original files. Knowing this, use the copybook to do a cursory review of a record and determine if it is the record or individual in question. Then you can examine the original packet or file. Mistakes and omissions may have occurred when the papers were copied into the book.

When recording your source and citation for such records, be sure to note if the origin of the information is the copybook or the original packet. When you look at someone else's citation you often can tell by the citation which version was used. Copybook citations usually list a volume and page number, while those for probate packets or files usually just include a file number, for instance, "Rutland County, Vermont, Probate File #98."

What other things should I watch for in citations and sources?

The more sources and citations you follow up on the more aware you will be of the inadequacies that are prevalent in both published and online sources. Many years

Case Study

ago I had found a record of interest to my research. I checked the source and citation of the information and found that the author listed "Ipswich, Massachusetts, vital records" as the source. The citation contained no volume or page number, so I decided to look at a microfilmed copy of the town records. After going through the entire roll of film, I had still not found the record that was cited. I decided to look at the published book *Ipswich Vital Records to the End of the Year 1849* at the local library. The record appears in the book. Why was it not on the film, and where did the individual get the information presented?

It took a while to unravel the puzzle, but I finally did (remember my stubborn streak?). The published books in the official series for Massachusetts vital records to 1850 were compiled using not just the vital records from the original town books, but also records from tombstones, church and court records, and personal records (some indicating Bible records) in the possession of individuals. The printed book indicates which information came from the sources other than the original vital records, but the person citing the source neglected to note this designation.

What should the proper source and citation have been?

The source should have been listed as

> *Ipswich Vital Records to the end of the year 1849:* vol. 1; 1910, Essex Institute, Salem, MA.

This citation makes it very clear that the information came from a secondary source, the printed books, which led me back to the original gravestone record. Using the gravestone records I was able to find additional family members not listed in the books or the microfilmed originals.

I have also seen people cite their source as, for example, "Mt. Holly vital records," when the actual record was transcribed from the state copy of the record. The statewide index notes that the town of Mt. Holly submitted the record to the state and lists the volume and page number of the original record. The accurate source would be the "Vermont vital records index" since that is where the person copied the data. The citation "Mt. Holly, Vermont vital records; vol. 2; page 35" would be an accurate citation if they had actually looked at volume number two, page 35 of the Mt. Holly records and transcribed the data from the original source. Careful citations are important in relaying accurate information on your research.

Is there any listing of examples for proper citations?

Emily Anne Croom's book *The Sleuth Book for Genealogists* has both a chapter (chapter four, "Documenting Research") and an appendix (appendix B, "Guide to Documentation: Examples of Style") that are quite extensive outlining documentation and citing of sources. Croom thoroughly covers citing sources from books, journals, electronic media, newspapers, letters, family papers, public records, and more.

Appendix A of the book *First Steps in Genealogy*, by Desmond Walls Allen contains a chart showing proper ways to cite the various sources that most researchers use. I have found this chart useful when I am researching; it constantly

For More Info

reminds me of what information should be included in the citation. Allen also states, "It's better to write too much about a source than too little." Amen!

Another great tool is the software program Clooz. Utilizing the program and entering research finds make for an educational experience. Since the program prods you to enter particular information regarding the source you quickly notice any inadequate citation information. It was a humbling experience the first few times I tried entering data. It has also made me much better at completely citing my sources. As with anything, practice makes perfect.

Do you have any other words of advice on sources?
I stress the importance of researching the record type before you use the record for research. Having a clear understanding of how, why, and when a record was created goes a long way in knowing if you are looking at a primary, secondary, or later copy of any given record. Many wonderful genealogical magazines and books are currently available, along with educational and instructional articles on the Internet to help you learn as much as possible about the records you will use. Look for these articles on any of the genealogical Web sites available to you. Look for links that indicate learning center, learning library, or how-tos, and follow all of the links that indicate there is more information about the particular source you are using. This will go a long way in increasing your knowledge and understanding of the myriad of records now available to you.

Sources

FURTHER READING

The BCG Genealogical Standards Manual, by The Board for Certification of Genealogists. Salt Lake City, Utah: Ancestry, Inc., 2000.

Cite Your Sources, by Richard Lackey. University of Mississippi Press, 1980.

The Complete Idiot's Guide to Writing Your Family History, by Lynda Rutledge Stephenson. Indianapolis, Ind.: Alpha Books, 2000.

Evidence! Citation and Analysis for the Family Historian, by Elizabeth Shown Mills. Baltimore, Md.: Genealogical Publishing Co., Inc., 1997.

First Steps in Genealogy, by Desmond Walls Allen. Cincinnati, Ohio: Betterway Books, 1998.

Organizing Your Family History Search, by Sharon DeBartolo Carmack. Cincinnati, Ohio: Betterway Books, 1999.

Producing a Quality Family History, by Patricia Law Hatcher. Salt Lake City, Utah: Ancestry, Inc., 1996.

The Sleuth Book for Genealogists: Strategies for More Successful Family History Research, by Emily Anne Croom. Cincinnati, Ohio: Betterway Books, 2000.

Unpuzzling Your Past, 4th ed., by Emily Anne Croom. Cincinnati, Ohio: Betterway Books, 2001.

TEN

Newspapers, Periodicals, and City Directories

Idea Generator

While many researchers use vital, probate, land, and census records, many other records are often overlooked as valuable sources of information. This chapter addresses some of these records and how they can be useful in your research. Many research problems have been solved using the more untraditional sources.

When we think of our ancestors, we must think of them as having been living, breathing human beings who led lives just as we do. They did not live in a vacuum any more than we do today. If you think in terms of all of the places, organizations, and people that you have contact with on a daily basis and of the places that records are generated, it should open up many avenues for research.

Many men and women belonged to church groups, vocational groups, and fraternal organizations; these groups may have surviving records, providing you with much insight into your ancestor. Think in terms of all the "slots" that your ancestor would fit into. Consider his occupation, ethnic group, political or religious affiliation, education, and membership in clubs or social groups. This list can be almost endless.

NEWSPAPERS

In research newspapers are usually used to find death notices, obituaries, or articles pertaining to disasters. **Have you ever taken the time to read the editorials, articles, and advertising in old newspapers?** This type of information can provide you with a feeling and understanding of the day-to-day life of your ancestor. What events, both local and worldwide, occurred, and how might they have affected your ancestor? What were the prevailing views, both political and social, at the time that may have impacted her life? These and many more questions can be answered by reading the entire newspaper, not just the death notices. Another part of the newspaper that can provide many details, especially

Idea Generator

SOME ITEMS TO LOOK FOR IN NEWSPAPERS

- obituaries, death notices, and funeral listings

- marriage or engagement notices

- notices regarding estate settlements

- classified ads (to get a sense of prices, rents, and incomes)

- social columns, fraternal organization meetings and articles, etc.

- articles at the times of graduations, 50th wedding anniversaries, 100th birthdays, etc.

- news articles regarding accidents, sudden deaths, and natural disasters

- ads for local businesses, hospitals, and products of the time period

- news articles listing local people serving in the military (especially during wartime)

- articles on local sports (professional, school, or minor league clubs)

for women, is the social column. Many papers listed society functions, local citizens' vacations and travel, as well as information about people who visited relatives or friends in town. These columns can provide you with names and residences of out-of-town relatives. Many small-town newspapers still have such columns. I visited a family in Nebraska in the early 1970s, and an article stating that I had arrived for a visit was in the paper the first day I was there. Several times during my two-week visit, the newspaper mentioned who I went to visit and how I was enjoying myself, and it announced when I went home—and I am certainly not a celebrity.

One important fact of the newspaper business is that advertising rates are based on circulation. What better way to increase circulation, especially for a small-town newspaper, than to include many people's names? If your grandchildren were mentioned in the paper—for their school accomplishments, engagement, or marriage—wouldn't you buy several copies to send to other relatives? The more names and stories about individuals they include, the more newspapers they sell. This is especially relevant to the many ethnic newspapers that existed in the late nineteenth and early twentieth centuries. These ethnic newspapers were prevalent especially in larger cities and had many articles pertaining to an ethnic group's culture and social activity. These newspapers also ran advertisements that highlighted special foods, services, etc., that were unique to a specific ethnic group.

In what time period did death notices begin to appear?

This item began appearing as a regular feature in the early twentieth century, although notices of deaths appeared even in the early 1800s in some locales. Look at several different newspapers over a period of time to determine if death notices were included. Remember to look at all of the available newspapers for that locale and time period. Some may have been political, agricultural, or social, and each had its own specialties. Death notices may not have appeared in the political or agricultural newspapers unless the deceased was well known in those circles. Small local newspapers were more likely to publish reports of social events and marriages or deaths of the average citizens.

Keep in mind that while a newspaper might not have published death notices or obituaries per se, it may have included news of funeral services or accidental deaths. This was true for my husband's great-grandfather, an Italian immigrant. He died on 18 July 1926 in Springfield, Massachusetts, and family stories indicated that he was struck by lightning. When I searched the Springfield daily newspapers for his death notice or obituary, I found none. I looked in both the morning and evening editions as city papers sometimes listed deaths in only one edition. The newspapers at that time had a short index on page 1 or 2 and I used those to go right to the obituary pages on the microfilm. This can be a big mistake because you will miss many other articles of interest appearing on other pages.

Case Study

As I rewound the microfilm a picture on the front page caught my eye. It was the same picture of my husband's great-grandfather that I have on my dining room wall! Two Springfield residents had died in a freak summer storm. Upon reading the story I learned that Saturno Montanari was not struck by lightning; he was struck by a tree branch that had been felled by lightning. The tree branch hit him squarely on the head, crushing his skull. Not a great way to die, but since it was unusual it made the front-page news—picture and all. I never found a death notice or obituary for Saturno, but the article provided far more information than any death notice would have.

Another jewel that solved a research problem was a small news article that appeared in the *Rutland* (Vermont) *Herald* in 1841, far earlier than death notices were commonly published. I had found in a local graveyard a tombstone for a woman and her sister that piqued my curiosity. I was searching for my great-grandmother's birth mother but didn't really have a first name to go on. Since my great-grandmother was born in about 1840 and had a stepmother in 1850, I had a small time frame to consider. The tombstone caught my eye because the two sisters named Caroline and Malona Sumner had died the same day, 11 February 1841. My great-grandmother's name was Malona, and one record that I found, her marriage record, listed her mother as Malona, not Alma or Wilma (the names listed on the census records during her life). I looked for a death notice or article since I thought an accident or illness must have taken both sisters on the same day. I found no article, no death notice, no mention at all of this unusual event. Since the tombstone listed both women under their maiden name, it did not prove that Malona Sumner had been married to Calvin Carpenter. Could my great-grandmother have been an illegitimate child? I found no birth record for her. I decided to look at the newspapers again, and I found a very small notice that read: "Bristol, Vermont. The first double funeral was held from the church in Bristol with the noted Kittridge Havens from Boston, Massachusetts, officiating at the funeral of Miss Caroline Sumner and Mrs. Malona Carpenter, wife of Calvin Carpenter." Problem solved. The notice did not explain the sisters' deaths, but at least it proved the marriage of Calvin and Malona and gave me a new line to follow. I still wonder why her maiden name, not her married name, appeared on the stone—perhaps Calvin's in-laws didn't approve of him.

What other news items should I look for?

Look for articles that appeared around the time of major events in the family. Did any family members celebrate a fiftieth wedding anniversary, celebrate a seventy-fifth or one hundredth birthday, graduate from college, or get inducted into an organization or political office? All of these events might have appeared in articles with pictures, guest lists, lifetime stories and achievements, and other tidbits not found anywhere else.

One article on the occasion of a fiftieth wedding anniversary provided information on a bride's and groom's parents and their places of birth. It also listed the clergyman who performed the ceremony and the church in Canada where it took place. All of the siblings of the couple, both living and deceased, were named in the article along with the names and residences of all the couple's children, grandchildren, and great-grandchildren. Since many of these events took place "somewhere in Canada" according to living relatives, finding the article with more detailed information was crucial to the advancement of the research. More details were provided when the woman turned one hundred years old about twenty-five years later and another family party was chronicled in the same newspaper. That article also noted that her husband had died after sixty-one years of marriage and gave his place of burial in Canada. This led to the finding of their graves in a remote town in Ontario, Canada.

What information can an obituary or death notice provide?

When using any type of record, especially a death notice or an obituary, squeeze every possible bit of information from it. Most people read an obituary and don't evaluate it line by line. Read the following obituary to see what you can learn:

Technique

Frank S. Bertocchi

Frank S. "Pappy" Bertocchi, 83, of 1325 Columbus Ave. was found dead in his home late last night. Medical Examiner W.A.R. Chapin said death was due to a cardiovascular failure. Mr. Bertocchi was a retired auctioneer and known to many in this area as "Pappy." He was born in Renazzo, Ferrarei, Italy, and had lived in Springfield since childhood. He was a member of Our Lady of Mount Carmel Church. He leaves a step-son, James Balboni of this city; two brothers, Randolph of West Springfield and Leo Bertocchi of this city; two sisters, Mrs. Catherine Gavoni of this city and the former Romilde Bertocchi of West Springfield. The funeral will be held

Wednesday morning at 8 at the F. M. Forastiere and Sons Funeral Home, with a blessing at 9 in Our Lady of Mount Carmel Church. Burial will be in St. Michael's Cemetery. Friends may call at the funeral home tonight from 7 to 10 pm.

This obituary provides many important pieces of information that can lead to other records that may reveal a possible year of immigration and perhaps the names of his parents. First, the church and cemetery mentioned, as well as the funeral home, should be investigated for records (see chapters three and eleven on these records). The library might have information on auctioneers in the area or perhaps a city directory with an advertisement for his business. Another valuable record is the medical examiner's file. Since the medical examiner is named, an autopsy or investigation probably provided the conclusion as to the cause of death.

Additional information is not as obvious but just as important. The obituary states that Mr. Bertocchi was eighty-three years old and had lived in Springfield since childhood. He died in 1956, so he had probably lived in Springfield since at least the mid to late 1880s. Since in the late 1800s and early 1900s most young men were working by the time they were in their mid teens, "childhood" indicates that he was younger than twelve or thirteen years of age when he arrived in Springfield. Since he was eighty-three at the time of his death, his length of residence there would have been about seventy years. Subtract 70 from 1956 and you get 1886. This may not be the exact date, but it's a pretty good place to start.

The death records for Mr. Bertocchi's two brothers and two sisters might provide the parents' names. Since we know that at least three of these siblings were alive in 1956, we can begin with that year in our search for death records. Frank was eighty-three, so his siblings were probably more than sixty years of age as well. His sister Catherine was married to a Gavoni by 1956, so a marriage record before that date might also give additional information on the parents of Frank and his siblings. It is interesting to note that his other sister is listed as "the former Romilda Bertocchi of West Springfield." This statement does not indicate if she is alive or deceased or to whom she was married. Perhaps she was divorced and did not want her ex-husband's name listed. Just one more clue to use to look for additional records.

The information that Frank was born in "Renazzo, Ferrarei, [Ferrara] Italy," can aid in determining his lineage further back than his parents. Renazzo is a small village within the town of Cento in the Ferrara Province of Italy, so this narrows down the research location considerably.

What other helpful information can you find in newspapers?
Many newspapers have a page that lists community services, churches, and schools within the geographic area. These can provide you with many new avenues for research. If a town had only one Catholic church and your ancestor was Catholic, you might find church records with more information on him.

Knowing what fraternal organizations were active in that specific locale and time period can also provide you with clues to other records.

An interesting item in newspapers is the advertisements. I have located among the advertisements family groceries and fruit markets, churches, and even companies my ancestors worked for. It is also interesting to see the products shown for housework and medical care and the clothing. Including some of these advertisements with your family history will make it much more interesting. Along with the advertisements, look at the classified ads. These ads will provide you with a sense of home valuations, available jobs, and types of items bought and sold in that time period. I came across an interesting ad in a 1788 newspaper in which I was looking for a mention of a death. The ad was a notice of estate filing for my individual and announced that all claims against the estate had to be presented before a certain date. It confirmed that the death had occurred before the date of the paper and after the date on the will. The same column of ads included an ad for a runaway apprentice of another ancestor. The ad listed the young man's age, height, weight, and clothing, and it stated that if the apprentice was returned his "master" would pay a reward and "forgive the indiscretion" of the apprentice. What an interesting item to add to the genealogy.

Idea Generator

Two interesting finds were in *The Morning Call* (San Francisco) in 1885 under "Physicians":

> A Private Sanitarium for Confinement and
> diseases of females: Dr. Hall, 426 Kearny st.

> Li Po Tai's Chinese and Herb Sanitarium
> removed to 727 Washington street, two doors
> below the old place.

Locating hospitals, sanitariums, and asylums can lead you to other records for your ancestors. This is especially important for the periods when tuberculosis and other such ailments felled many individuals. Some of these hospitals and sanitariums had records of patients and of burials on the institutions' grounds that may prove valuable to you. The two examples above are obviously specialty hospitals that would have been used by only portions of the population.

What else should I look for?

1. If your ancestor was an athlete or a policeman, fireman, or other public official, look for news and sports articles, police notices, court reports, etc., to see if he was mentioned. Also watch out for those ancestors who were on the wrong side of the law and just might have shown up in the court records or police notices. These articles are colorful and add a new dimension to your family history. Sometimes I wish that my ancestors hadn't been so law abiding— I'd love to "adopt" one of these interesting characters!

2. Articles covering funerals might have appeared in the week or two following a death. I have found notices from the family of the deceased thanking the people who had sent flowers and notes of condolence. These notices actually

contained names and cities of residence of the individuals—even more research clues. Again, check any social columns to see if any out-of-town relatives or friends traveled to the funeral.

3. While researching a family in the San Francisco newspapers from 1900, I came across some interesting lists. The daily paper listed all of the individuals who arrived in San Francisco on a particular day and gave their names, previous residences, and the means by which they had arrived (e.g., boat, train). The paper also listed all of the boats, both cargo and passenger vessels, that arrived at the harbor on a given day. While I found no index to these lists, it might be interesting and useful to look through them if your ancestor was in San Francisco for the 1900 or 1910 census or in the San Francisco city directory in that time frame.

4. While looking for a death notice or obituary for a woman who died of old age in San Francisco in 1910 I was unsuccessful. Since she did not die an accidental or newsworthy death, I didn't hold out much hope of finding a news article. Don't count anything out! On the front page of the newspaper, the headline "Mrs. E. A. Cootey, Who Died Leaving 108 Descendants" caught my eye. Below the headline was a photograph of Mrs. Cootey and then another bold headline that stated "52 Grandchildren Mourn Her Death. Six Grandsons to Act as Pallbearers at Funeral for Aged Woman."

The article took up one complete column of the front page and chronicled the family back to Vermont and the Revolutionary War. It included the names of all thirteen of her children, the wars her ancestors fought in, and when her daughter had moved to California. It stated that her thirteenth child, George H. Cootey, was the first of her children to die. He had served in the Thirteenth Minnesota Regiment in the Spanish-American War and died of smallpox contracted while he was in the service. It also stated that Mrs. Cootey received a pension from the U.S. government for his service. The article gave the maiden names of her mother and grandmother along with the names of her father, grandfather, and great-grandfather. It also listed the married names of her daughters and all of the children's residences. It told when she and her husband had moved from Vermont to California and which daughter she lived with there. Needless to say, this was far better than any death notice. Her husband's death was noted in a mere two lines in the paper the next year. No one in this woman's family had ever seen a picture of her, so the article provided not only a wealth of information but also a photo of an ancestor.

Are there any indexes available for newspaper articles, death notices, and obituaries?

Many of the smaller local papers have indexes that were compiled by local libraries and societies and list all names and articles of interest. Some larger papers, like *The New York Times*, have published indexes for death notices during certain time periods, but as a rule you will find no indexes or just basic ones listing the pages that deaths, sports, etc., appear on. There are, of course, exceptions to this rule. The Sutro Library in California has a valuable card index to the San Francisco papers for news articles (mostly pre-1900). Since my research subject was the Cootey family, an unusual name, I decided to try the index. The article I had found on Mrs. Cootey was not included in the index, but several articles about a Patrick H. Cootey were. How many Cootey families could there have been in San Francisco? The indexed articles turned out to be about a missing whaling ship called the *Amethyst*, whose captain was a Patrick Cootey. The articles began in December 1885 and continued until the report of finding the wreckage in September 1887. The entries were fascinating and included interviews with the Cootey family (the same family I was researching), rescue personnel, and fellow whaler captains regarding Patrick Cootey's skills as a navigator and how highly regarded he was among his peers. It also chronicled Cootey's life as a whaler captain in Boston, Massachusetts, his marriage to a woman from the Sandwich Islands, and his trek westward by sea.

Where can I find archived newspapers?

Newspapers are housed in many different facilities. Libraries (local, county, state, and university), historical and genealogical societies, and even newspaper offices may have archived newspapers from the local area.

The United States Newspaper Program (USNP) has in each state a library that is the designated repository for surviving newspapers in that state. The USNP has a Web site <http://www.neh.gov/projects/usnp.html> that lists the coordinating library in each state. Look on this Web site for a link to your state of interest to determine if they have posted a list of newspapers that are available and for what years. If the state you are interested in does not have a link or indicate what library has been designated as the official repository, check with the state library in that locale. If it is not the designated facility, the staff should be able to provide that information. Also check the many resource books available for each state. *Ancestry's Red Book*, for example, lists newspaper holdings for each state.

Internet Source

How do I gain access to newspapers from a distance?

You have several means for accessing these wonderful sources. One way is to contact the local library to determine if they have either copies of the original newspapers or microfilmed copies available. Many local libraries and societies will look up information in their holdings (sometimes for a fee) and steer you to another facility that has what you need if they do not. To determine what newspapers might be located in certain facilities, check *Newspapers in Microform, United States*, which is a list of microfilmed newspaper holdings that libraries have reported to the Library of Congress. It was published by the Library of Congress in 1973 and is available in many libraries. Another valuable publication is the *Gale Directory of Publications and Broadcast Media*, which is published yearly. It is broken down first by state and then by city or town. This directory lists a newspaper's establishment date and contact information. Other resources are *History and Bibliography of American Newspapers, 1690–1820* by Clarence S. Brigham and *American Newspapers, 1821–1936*, edited by Winifred Gregory. These titles list both in-print and defunct newspapers.

Some newspapers have been in publication for many years, while others have had short durations in print. Making sure that you use all available newspapers is important to a thorough search.

Once you have determined what library has the newspapers you are interested in, you may be able to borrow microfilm copies through the interlibrary loan program. Talk to the reference librarian in your local library to see if she can obtain these copies for you. When interlibrary loan has been ruled out, try the USGenWeb <http://www.usgenweb.com> for the state or county of interest to see if any individuals will look up information for you, free or for a fee. Hiring a professional researcher in the geographic area of interest can also prove valuable to your research. Or you can make a trip to the location and do the research yourself, which I always find to be more fun although it's not always possible.

For more information regarding newspapers, you can consult the many genealogical books available, including *Long-Distance Genealogy* by Christine Crawford-Oppenheimer, *The Genealogy Sourcebook* by Sharon DeBartolo Carmack, and *The Genealogist's Companion & Sourcebook* by Emily Anne Croom.

PERIODICALS

You have almost as many periodicals as you do newspapers to pursue in your research. Many organizations, libraries, and businesses have published periodicals over the years. Historical and genealogical societies have been publishing articles pertaining to specific families, geographic locations, and research sources for many years. The *New England Historical and Genealogical Register* has been published for more than 150 years (1847 to the present) and provides many researchers with valuable information on their ancestries. Other long-running periodicals available to today's researcher include *The American Genealogist* (1922 to the present*), The New York Genealogical and Biographical Record* (1870 to the present), *Essex Institute Historical Collections* (1859 to the present), and *The William and Mary Quarterly* (1892 to the present). These publications can provide you with data from ongoing or completed research projects, updated genealogical information, additional sources to search, and historical backgrounds on certain time frames and localities.

How can I locate these periodicals?

You can use several sources to look for periodicals in any specific geographical area, for any time frame, or on a research specialty. *Ancestry's Red Book* lists periodicals under each state and tells where these collections are housed, what years they cover, and what unique information they might contain.

Many of the state and county Web sites for libraries, the USGenWeb, state historical societies, etc., also provide information regarding periodicals of interest to researchers. Several of the subscription Web sites contain databases that index periodicals. The most often used index to periodicals is *Periodical Source Index* (PERSI), created by the Allen County Public Library in Fort Wayne, Indiana. Available in printed format, on CD, and online, PERSI contains an index to many of the older and current genealogical and historical periodicals. Some individual organizations, such as the New York Genealogical and Biographical Society and the New England Historic Genealogical Society, have published indexes to their publications, both in print and on CD-ROM. Some have even produced CDs that contain not only indexes but an entire run of a publication. Many local and state libraries, historical societies, and genealogical societies have collections of periodicals relating to their particular research specialties or geographic area.

Another index worth checking is the *Genealogical Periodical Annual Index*, which began publication in 1962, when it included about seventy-five genealogical periodicals. It is published annually and now encompasses more than 350 English-language genealogical periodicals indexed by surname, locality, and topic. The index also includes published book reviews that may lead you to a book you had not known about. The index should be available in your local library—the genealogical section or the general reference section—or online at <http://www.heritagebooks.com/library/>.

What other types of periodicals are available?

Some of the most widely used periodicals of interest to family historians are those published by family associations. Since such a publication specializes in one or more specific surnames, these can be very helpful. Much like some of the present-day electronic message boards and Web sites, these publications help researchers with a common interest network. Articles address topics such as certain family groups, states of residence, and research questions and answers. **By making contact with others tracing the same surname, you might find transcribed Bible pages, cemetery records, family photos and papers, and cousins that will provide you with additional information.**

Hidden Treasures

County and state historical or genealogical societies list in their monthly or quarterly publications family reunions, lectures and educational opportunities, recent publications, acquisitions, and more. One county that I was doing extensive research in is several states away from my home, so using its facilities would have been difficult. Upon reading one of their past publications I realized that membership in the county historical society provided me with many benefits. As a member I could post queries in the newsletter, get free lookups in their records, and be apprised of all new records that were deposited in the library they maintained. Not bad for a mere ten-dollar annual membership fee! The newsletter has provided me with a better understanding of the history of the county and towns, the families that have lived there over the past two centuries, and the current activities. I also found a notice regarding a family reunion for a surname that I was researching for a friend. We traveled to the reunion and met many wonderful people who are all related to the original settler in that county. One of the gentlemen took us to the cemetery where the ancestors of my friend were buried. To say that we would never have found it on our own is an understatement. It is on a hill, behind a pasture full of cows, and not visible from the dirt road. Networking with these organizations through their publications is a valuable tool in the research process.

How can I access periodicals not available to me locally?
You can borrow many periodicals, in paper or on microfilm, through interlibrary loan. You can obtain photocopies of specific articles (sometimes for a fee) through the state, county, or local libraries that have the periodical of interest to you, as well as from the Allen County Public Library (whose staff created PERSI), Genealogy Department, P.O. Box 2270, Fort Wayne, Indiana 46802; <http://www.acpl.lib.in.us/genealogy/persi.html>.

CITY DIRECTORIES

This underutilized source can make researching in larger cities much more productive by providing information about where in the city your ancestor lived. The city directory was actually a precursor to present-day telephone books. Before telephones were widespread in the population, a city directory listed the residents of a geographic area. Like the telephone book of today, not all residents were listed in the directory. Most listings are of the head of the household—usually a man or a widow—children that were employed outside the home or in school, and businesses within the area covered. Some directories cover individual cities or towns, while others cover the city and the adjoining suburbs and rural areas. Countywide directories also exist for some locations.

Important

Why is this record important to my research?
All directories are valuable tools for the researcher. **They can help fill in data for the years between census enumerations and show the movement of families within or out of the area.** They can provide employment information for an individual and cue research in employment records, retirement records, and business advertisements.

While the bulk of the directory is in alphabetical order by surname, the cross-street directory section lists streets in alphabetical order, addresses in numerical order for each street, and then the primary resident at each address. The cross-street directory goes by several different names, including street listing, residential list, crisscross directory, and householders index. It is actually a census of sorts and can provide you with the names of others living nearby your ancestor. The listing also shows where streets intersect, so you can pinpoint additional neighborhood streets to look at. Most of our ancestors lived within a few blocks of their relatives, so this can be a valuable tool.

What time periods do the directories encompass?
The time periods vary by geographic location. Boston, Massachusetts, has directories that date back to the late 1700s and continue today. As stated before, some of these directories might include just the city or the surrounding area. Others may be county directories, suburban directories, or voter registration directories. Always keep an open mind when you see the word *directory*, since the many different types encompass many different subjects that might interest you.

What is the source of the information contained in directories?
The answer to this question varies by the type of directory. A voter registration directory might have been compiled from the official voter registration list at the city, town, or county level. A basic city directory might have been in much the same manner as the U.S. census; by door-to-door solicitation of data. Because of this, city directory information may or may not be completely accurate.

What other information can be gleaned from city directories?
Perhaps the most underutilized portions of directories are the listings of churches, schools, cemeteries, clergymen, craftsmen or tradesmen, undertakers, and banks. Always look at the table of contents at the front of the directory to see what subjects are indexed in it. I have seen listings of fraternal organizations, associations, census statistics, lawyers, public and private libraries, courts, medical examiners, and many other items of interest.

When you locate a marriage record that lists the officiating clergyman's name, you can use the city directory to find his religious affiliation and steer your search for additional family records. Just knowing what churches existed in the community when your ancestors lived there can be helpful. Many times the churches list the ethnicity of the parishes, such as Italian, Irish Catholic, Russian, or Jewish Orthodox. Especially larger towns or cities currently may have many churches serving one religion. Which ones existed when your ancestor lived there, perhaps one hundred years ago? Is the church still operational? If another church of that denomination was open in that time frame and still is, it may now have the other church's records in its facility.

Cemetery listings show what cemeteries were in use in that time period. Some listings also include a cemetery's affiliation with a particular church, again leading you to church records for your family. Schools, both public and private, are also listed, giving you clues to even more records to search.

Additionally, **many of the directories have a street map somewhere within the volume.** This can help you learn what streets were in the area, where they crossed each other, and what topographical features—lakes, rivers, railroads—were in the area. Comparing the map from the directory with a present-day map can reveal streets that no longer exist, that have had name changes, or that were associated with specific industries. The town of Ipswich, Massachusetts, for instance, had a factory and a neighborhood of homes where most of the factory workers and managers lived. The mill owned all of the homes and rented them out to the mostly Polish workers who came to the United States and worked in the mill. Hence, the popular nickname for the area was Pole Alley.

Using the map in conjunction with the surname listings and the cross-street section of the directory can help you document ethnic neighborhoods. When you look at the surnames and the streets or areas of town the specific groups lived in, you will see why areas were called Little Italy or Irishtown. Knowing where these ethnic neighborhoods were located can give you additional insight into your family history research and how people might have met and married each other. It also provides insight into another era and culture that may no longer exist. The cultural and ethnic makeup of your ancestors' neighborhood

Idea Generator

might explain some of the traditions, recipes, and cultural influences that shaped their lives and yours.

What can I learn from the alphabetical listings of individuals?

When you use the main portion—the listing of the residents—of any city directory, look up all spellings you can think of for a name. It is amazing sometimes how many different ways one surname can be spelled. Being thorough in this search will pay big dividends. If the name has a prefix such as *di*, *O'*, or *Mc*, look for the name without the prefix as well.

Once you find your individual, look at all of the others with the same surname and note where they reside. Do any of the twenty-five people listed with the surname Wilcox live at the same address? This may indicate a familial relationship (e.g., brothers, uncles) and provide you with additional research subjects. Pay close attention to individuals with the same surname living on the same street as well as in the same house; these may be additional relatives.

What does an entry in the city directory include?

While entries vary slightly from one directory to another, most have the name of the individual and possibly his wife's name, his occupation, his employer, his employer's address, and his residential address. If a person owned a business in one town but resided in another, he might be listed in both directories with the information cross-referenced. The following Malden, Massachusetts, directory entry is an example of this:

Martin, Joseph, (Catherine), Martin & Smith Insurance Co., 12 Main st, residence, Everett.

This entry tells you that Joseph Martin owned a business in Malden at 12 Main Street but his residence was in the town of Everett. These entries are helpful for locating someone who owned a business and changed residences often. By using the more stable fact, the business, you can find the residential information as well.

What do all of the cryptic abbreviations stand for?

Look for the abbreviation list (listed in the table of contents of the city directory) when using this type of record. Understanding every abbreviation is important to getting the most information from the directory. Some directories abbreviate the names of employers, such as CVC for Chapman Valve Company and USA for U.S. Army. Knowing who your ancestor's employer was will help you find company or employment records. The abbreviations that precede the residence notation tell you about the status of that individual at that address. To illustrate, look at the following listings for people who lived at the same address:

Balboni, Angelina, clk 392 Main bds 17 Whiting

Balboni, Anthony, (Balboni Bros) 6 Sanford bds 17 Whiting

Balboni, Charles, emp 175 N Main h 17 Whiting

Balboni, Louis, (Balboni Bros) 6 Sanford bds 17 Whiting

Anthony and Louis were in business together at 6 Sanford (Street, Avenue, or Road). Three of the above individuals are listed as "bds 17 Whiting," which in this directory means "boards at 17 Whiting." Charles is listed as having a house ("h") at 17 Whiting, so he is the owner or the head of the household in this example. The possibility that the other three individuals are related to Charles is pretty good. When an adult child lived with his parents but attended school or was employed outside the home, he was usually listed as boarding or rooming at the parents' address.

Because each directory might have its own unique set of abbreviations, make sure that you know what every abbreviation in a directory stands for. I find it easiest to photocopy the abbreviation listing *before* I make copies of any other pages. This way when I get home I won't discover abbreviations or acronyms that I can't understand. Some abbreviations stand for small villages within town or city limits, as in the following entry:

Important

Boston, Massachusetts—Brown, Jeffrey emp USA bds 25 Melrose JP

In this example Jeffrey Brown was employed in the U.S. Army and he boarded in the Jamaica Plain section of Boston. This can be helpful information when you research in a large city such as Boston.

What other unexpected information might I find in these listings?

While every directory is different, you might unexpectedly find a death date for an individual or an entry indicating where a person moved. The entry might look like this:

Fayes, Antonio J. deceased Oct. 28, 1878
Fayes, Antonio J. Mrs. widow, h Washington near Jewett

Clearly Mrs. Antonio J. Fayes is the widow of Antonio, and having his date of death is useful as well. Sometimes the entry will read as follows:

Fayes, Mary (widow of Antonio J.) h Washington near Jewett

Either way, it provides you with additional information. If Mary had been listed as "Fayes, Mary h Washington near Jewett," you would not know if she was a daughter, sister-in-law or widow of Anthony J.

The city directory might also include information regarding where a person moved. This entry is an example:

Pendleton, Nathaniel G. Mrs. rem to New York City

This entry in the 1915 Northhampton directory tells you that the individual has removed ("rem") to New York City from the town of Northampton, Massachusetts. This type of entry is common since the directories were compiled annually or every two to three years and the previous list was used to compile the current list. The person collecting the information visited each residence, much as the census takers did. When a different person no longer lived at an address, the enumerator might have asked the new resident where the previous resident went. An answer such as "he moved to New York City" was then noted next to the name on the previous list. Information that pertains to an individual's move usually only appeared in one directory, lending evidence to the assumption that the previous directory was probably used to compile an updated one.

How else might the city directory assist me in my research?

If you research an individual who lived in a larger town or city and the census record is not indexed or the individual does not appear in the index, the city directory can help you considerably narrow down your search area. When I was trying to locate James Balboni in the Springfield, Massachusetts, census index for 1920, he did not appear. Other information indicated that he lived in Springfield from 1914 until 1965, so where was he? Using the Springfield City Directories from 1913 through 1924 (the year he got married), I located him in every available directory listed at the same address in each one. Since I knew that he should be in the 1920 census, I checked the alphabetical listing of streets in the 1920 city directory to see what ward Colten Street was in. Since most cities are broken down by wards and precincts in the census, locating the ward information meant that I had to look through only half a roll of census microfilm instead of twelve rolls! James Balboni was exactly where he should have been, at the address where he was listed in the directories, he just did not get indexed in the census. Using one record (the directory) to help utilize another (the census) makes a search much easier and less frustrating.

Like the census index, people sometimes do not appear in the directories. Don't allow one missing record to throw you off course. Compare the information from every available directory for the locality to get the most information and assistance.

What problems might I encounter when using city directories?

The most common complaint is the abbreviations. As stated before, make sure you know what every abbreviation stands for and how the directory is laid out.

Notes

Also note that **the year listed on the directory is usually the publication year and not necessarily the year information was collected.** This means that if you use directories to help you locate an individual in a census—especially the mostly unindexed 1910 census—look at several directories both before and after the census year to be sure you know where the individual lived. If the individual appears at the same address in the pre–and the post–census year directories, find out what ward or precinct that street was in for each of these years. Wards and precincts changed often as populations grew. If the street of interest was in Ward Four in 1908 and in Ward Six in 1910 and 1912, check both wards in the 1910 census. This is necessary because the directories do not say when the ward line changed, so it could have changed before or after the census.

What information will the street listings in the directory provide?

This part of the directory, sometimes made into a completely separate directory, lists the street addresses in alphabetical order rather than the individuals. Different directories refer to this section differently; it may be called the cross-street directory, the residential directory, the street directory, etc. Whatever the name, look for it in every directory. Some large cities might list only the street names alphabetically, what ward or precinct a street is in, what streets intersect it, and where the street begins and ends. It might not include the residents' names due to the volume of entries. An example from the Springfield, Massachusetts, 1917 directory shows the following:

Colten, from 33 Wilbraham Rd. south to 28 Beacon. Wards 4 and 6.

10	vacant store
	38 Monroe St. intersects
39*	Conway, James J. flour food and grain
41	Brown, John H.
45	Meyrick, Harry K.
47*	McCleary, John & Sons slate roofers
52	Wrightmeyer, William L.
53	Collins, William, tailor
54*	Alport, Lisle I. scrap iron
133	Weeks, Charles B.
	136 Tyler St. intersects
145	Massei, Tommaso
145	Montonari, Chaturo
146	Stanton, Augusta J.
150	Lucia, Pasquale
154	Artioli, Augusto
155	Stoboda, Frank J.

* A business is at this address.

This sample, while not complete, shows some of the details of the street listing. You can determine the ward, the streets that intersect or cross Colten, as well as who lives next door to or in the same neighborhood as your ancestor. When using this directory listing for Colten Street, I noticed that an Augusto Artioli lived on the same street as and just a few doors away from Chaturo (should be Saturno) Montanari. Saturno's sister married an Artioli, and Augusto turned out to be Saturno's brother-in-law. The alphabetical surname listings would not highlight this close living arrangement of Saturno and Augusto, so an important clue would have been missed without the street listing. I looked at the entries on the listing for Tyler Street, which crossed Colten near Saturno's house, and located even more relatives who lived in the neighborhood. Use every available piece of information and part of the directory, and you will reap the rewards! Like the censuses, the directories provide you with a snapshot of the neighborhood makeup at a given point in time.

Where can I find these directories?
Many public, state, and county libraries have at least some of the directories for their areas. State libraries may have the broadest collection since they hold

information on the entire state. The largest collection is housed in the Library of Congress in Washington, DC, but the Library of Congress does not lend these through interlibrary loan so research must be done at the Library of Congress.

Some states maintain a comprehensive collection. Massachusetts holds such a collection in the Special Collections Room at the Massachusetts State House. Check to see if your state library or state house has such a collection. You will save time if you research in a collection that covers more than just one locality, since individuals often moved around. Some larger libraries, such as the Boston Public Library, have directories for other states and cities as well as for their own geographic area.

Microfilm Source

Many city directories are also available in microform in libraries or through the Family History Library. Some are on microfilm, while others are on microfiche (small microfilm sheets rather than reels). The National Archives regional facilities may also have city directories for certain time periods to make searching the census in larger cities a little easier. Since the 1910 federal census is unindexed for all of the New England states, these directories are valuable for researching those records. You can use the directories to pinpoint the ward the street is in and then use the published finding aid to determine which roll of film that ward is on. When possible, utilize the interlibrary loan system to borrow these directories for use in your local library or Family History Center.

Sources

FURTHER READING

American Newspapers, 1821–1936: A Union List of Files Available in the United States and Canada, by Winifred Gregory. New York: H.W. Wilson Co., 1937.

Gale Directory of Publications and Broadcast Media. Detroit, Mich.: Gale Publishing. Published yearly.

Genealogical Periodical Index. Bowie, Md.: Heritage Books. 1962. Published yearly.

The Genealogist's Companion & Sourcebook, by Emily Anne Croom. Cincinnati, Ohio: Betterway Books, 1994.

The Genealogy Sourcebook, by Sharon DeBartolo Carmack. Los Angeles, Calif.: Lowell House, 1997.

History and Bibliography of American Newspapers, 1690–1820, by Clarence S. Brigham. Westport, Conn.: Greenwood Press, 1976.

Locating Lost Family Members & Friends, by Kathleen W. Hinckley. Cincinnati, Ohio: Betterway Books, 1999.

Long-Distance Genealogy: Researching Your Family History From Home, by Christine Crawford-Oppenheimer. Cincinnati, Ohio: Betterway Books, 2000.

Newspapers in Microform, United States, by the Library of Congress. [1973–].

Periodical Source Index (PERSI). Fort Wayne, Ind.: Allen County Public Library Foundation, 1988.

ELEVEN

Cemetery and Funeral Home Records

Cemetery and funeral home records are perhaps some of the most fascinating records available to you. While cemetery records are used regularly, the associated funeral home records are often overlooked by genealogical researchers. Many funeral homes have kept meticulous records dating back to years before the turn of the twentieth century. I have discovered that with a little—OK sometimes a lot—of research these records can be found and reviewed to provide additional information that you might not expect. I have also been told by funeral home directors that funeral homes rarely go out of business; they are usually sold or absorbed by another funeral home in the area. Because of this, the records may still be available for a now defunct business.

Who else but a funeral home owner would know all of the cemeteries in an area, the funereal customs and practices at any given time in history, and possibly the names of other relatives of the deceased? I am always amazed at the amount of information I can access through these businesses. Most undertakers also have a comprehensive knowledge of religious customs for the population they serve.

What is the difference between an obituary and a death notice?
A **death notice,** usually published in a local or regional newspaper, provides basic information about the deceased, including the date of death, funeral arrangements, and church services. This information is provided to the paper by the undertaker or funeral home, and the notice is fairly brief. It is intended to inform people as to when and where the funeral services will be held.

An **obituary** is a longer written piece containing information about the individual's life as well as funeral arrangements. This information may include place of birth, parents, spouse, children, grandchildren, employment or affiliations with organizations, and military service information. Far fewer obituaries than death notices appear in any given newspaper due to their length, but obituaries can be valuable. They are more likely to appear in smaller local newspapers than in those for larger metropolitan areas.

\di'fin\ *vb*

Definitions

CEMETERY RECORDS

What can I learn from cemetery research?

In many cases a family cemetery plot is like a family Bible. If several individuals who are buried in the same plot have the same surname, the odds are good that those people were all related in some way. How a plot is laid out, who is buried next to whom, what plots adjoin it, and what other surnames appear within the plot are important clues to further research.

Once you find a plot where one of your ancestors is buried, record all others buried in the plot, as well as all others with the same surname buried near the plot. In most cases you will find birth and death dates (or death dates and ages at death), so you can use this information to look up death records, obituaries, death notices, and other records. How were these people related? Try to determine the familial connection to uncover additional research avenues to pursue.

Is it safe to go to cemeteries alone?

Warning

It is never a good idea. Even if you can't find someone who enjoys walking amongst the dead, you should have another living person in the vicinity. I have heard stories of individuals falling down, breaking an ankle or leg, and encountering wild animals—or the occasional strange human being—in cemeteries. Better safe than sorry.

I have gone to a cemetery alone on only one occasion (it only takes once). I took my dog with me for company and tied him on a rope to a nearby tree. He started to growl, and the hair on his back stood up. I couldn't see what he was upset about, but I untied him and held his rope. (He is a 105-pound Akita/shepherd mix, so he is pretty intimidating.) After several minutes I saw an individual wearing camouflage gear approach from under an overgrown bush. Since I was out in the middle of nowhere carrying my purse and camera gear, I felt especially vulnerable. I instructed the individual to stop, but he ignored that, so I threatened to let the dog go. The dog was barking loudly and pulling at the rope, so I knew he would protect me, or at least keep the guy busy so I could get to my car and mobile phone. The man obviously did not want to take on my dog and left in a hurry. I quickly retreated to my car, having learned a valuable lesson due to my carelessness. Now I never go into a cemetery alone or without my cell phone. Someone was obviously watching over me that day since that was the first time I had ever taken the dog with me. He earned his treats that day!

How can I read a worn stone?

Important

This is one of the most commonly asked, and debated, questions I get from researchers regarding cemeteries. **First of all do *not* use any substance on a tombstone.** This includes chalk, flour, cornstarch, and shaving cream. Researchers have used these and countless other products to try to enhance the carving for legibility. All of these examples contain chemicals that can harm the tombstones or will leave a residue that may encourage the growth of lichen (the moss that grows on many old tombstones) or attract insects to take up residence in or on the tombstone.

Many people think that a monument made out of stone is indestructible. Just one visit to an older graveyard will dispel this belief. Stone, like any other natural and many man-made materials, can be damaged or destroyed by the elements or human interaction. Many marble tombstones have been damaged over the years by well-meaning individuals who tried to clean the white marble. I have spoken with people who remember going to a cemetery as children and using bleach and wire brushes to clean the marble gravestones before the Memorial Day celebrations. Bleach, not to mention wire brushes, does irreparable harm to a gravestone and speeds up the stone's decay.

Another procedure used in the early twentieth century to read tombstones was to place chalk on its side and rub it across the raised portion of the carving. Putting pressure on the face of a gravestone should be avoided. Many of the chalks available today are synthetic and contain dyes or chemicals that will remain on a stone permanently, thereby defacing it. I saw in a historic cemetery in Rhode Island a gravestone that has been permanently damaged because someone used blue synthetic chalk on it. The blue dye has remained on the stone for many years and may not ever come off.

One of the best ways to enhance the carving on any stone is to use a mirror. Hold the mirror at an angle and reflect the sun across the carving at various angles to allow you to read previously illegible carving. Try holding the mirror at different angles and reflecting the sun across the stone from either side and from the top. You will be amazed at how much you will be able to read. Casting shadows across the carving, no matter how shallow, makes viewing the stone and clarifying the carvings more productive. Keep a small hand mirror in your cemetery backpack for this.

Another method to make the carving stand out is to spray a fine water mist on the stone. This works especially well on dark slate and unpolished granite markers. I keep in my cemetery backpack a spray bottle containing distilled water, which is available in pharmacies and stores that carry contact lens supplies. (The water produced in a dehumidifier is also distilled. Since I run a dehumidifier in my basement, I have an ample supply of distilled water without having to buy it.) Using distilled water ensures that you do not apply to the stone chlorine, fluoride, or other chemicals that are sometimes in tap water, bottled water, or well water. Rainwater is highly acidic and should not be used.

How do I clean a stone to make it more readable?

If a stone has lichen, moss, dirt, or bird droppings on it, take extreme care when attempting to clean it. Only remove what you absolutely need to to read the inscription. A soft toothbrush and the water from your sprayer will do a decent job. Simply spray the substance with a small amount of water and rub gently with the toothbrush bristles. As long as you do not put pressure on the toothbrush, you should be able to get some of the material off the carving without damaging the stone. Do *not* scrape off the substance, as this will damage the stone. A toothpick or a wooden cuticle tool can be used very gently to clean the inside of the letters or carving.

What tools should I carry for my cemetery research?

The items I carry in a backpack for my cemetery trips include

- Spray bottle filled with distilled water.
- Disposable surgical or rubber gloves to keep my hands clean and prevent poison ivy.
- Trowel and small garden rake for clearing vegetation around a gravestone.
- Pruning shears to cut away any unwanted brush.
- Variety of toothbrushes, toothpicks, soft nylon bristle brushes for cleaning the stone.
- Dark trash bags. To remove stubborn lichen and dirt, I spray on a little water and slip the bag over the stone, let it sit for a few minutes, and then try again to remove the material. The water and heat soften the debris. Trash bags also keep your backside dry if you sit on them instead of the damp ground, and they also make great makeshift ponchos or raincoats when the need arises. And most important, always remember to leave the cemetery in better condition than you found it.
- Foam kneeler (like the ones gardeners use) to protect your knees. You will spend a lot of time on yours knees in a cemetery!
- Roll of bright orange or yellow plastic ribbon (to tie on plant stakes).
- Insect repellent (I like the individually wrapped towelettes).
- Sun hat, sunglasses, sunscreen, and a foldable rain slicker with a hood (good for not only sudden showers but when insistent bugs ignore the insect repellent!)
- 12″ (30cm) square mirror tile (bind the edges in electrical tape so they won't be sharp).
- Clipboard with attached pencil or pen and paper.
- Small tape recorder and extra tapes and batteries.
- Bright orange scarf, hat, and gloves. (This is my "I am not a deer" outfit!)
- Retractable 50′ (15m) measuring tape for measuring stones, distances between stones, etc.

I keep these supplies permanently packed so I need only to grab my garden stakes (3′ [91cm] plant stakes, to which I tie yellow or orange ribbon for marking graves), a bottle of drinking water, my camera, and my mobile phone or walkie-talkie before heading out to a cemetery. Make sure you count your stakes before you start sticking them in the ground to assure that you leave with the same number you brought. I keep a full-length mirror in the trunk of my car for occasions when it is needed. I often wonder what a police officer would think if he had to search my car! Think about it—surgical gloves, garden tools, stakes, toothbrushes, and mirrors!

Using the garden stakes with the bright ribbon attached has proven very successful. When I first enter a cemetery I do a cursory walk around to see what the layout is like, and I record the findings on my tape recorder. I carry the stakes with me and stick one in the ground next to any stone that I want to look at later. (I use an old tent bag with an attached strap to carry the stakes with me, keeping my hands free. You can use any long narrow bag for this. I originally used metal stakes, and they got quite heavy. You can get bamboo or lightweight wooden stakes at a local garden center.) Then I get my backpack and my notes and proceed to record on my clipboard the information I've found. I must add that my backpack and my clipboard are the most offensive color I could find—day-glo orange. After once spending more than an hour at dusk looking for my pack, which of course I had laid down on the ground somewhere, I decided brighter was better. I have never lost it again.

Should I make a gravestone rubbing?

Making gravestone rubbings was a common practice in the early twentieth century; it is now discouraged or prohibited. Individuals placed paper or fabric over the stone and used wax or other substances to rub on the paper over the stone thereby producing a copy of the relief portion of the stone. As a result, many stones were damaged by the wax or the pressure put on the fragile stone.

Many states have banned the practice of gravestone rubbing altogether. Unless you have been trained in preservation and know how to determine if a given stone is sound enough to withstand rubbing, you should never do so!

If I cannot do a rubbing, how can I permanently document the stone?

Photographing the tombstone is a wonderful way to document its existence. You get not only a record of the stone's type, shape, colorations, and inscription, but also a record of its placement in its surroundings. I always take a picture of the stone up close and from a distance. I can then find the stone again later by relating it to the stones and scenery around it.

Taking the picture may require some flexibility and ingenuity on your part. Depending on the time of day, the position of the sun or the stone, and the type of camera you are using, you have to remember certain things. First, if you must use a flash, do not take the picture directly facing the stone or you will obliterate all of the shadows and make the resulting picture useless.

Idea Generator

The mirror technique is helpful when taking a picture. However, it requires a larger mirror and perhaps a second person to achieve positive results. Use a full-length mirror to reflect the sun at an angle across the face of the stone, and try several different angles until you find a good placement. This is where the second person comes in handy. One person works the mirror and the other watches the stone and takes the photograph. Again, make sure the flash is turned off or you will undo all of the shadowing created by the mirror. You will be positively amazed at the results using the mirror.

Not enough sun, or it is in the wrong position for success? Try using another light source. A bright flashlight or headlights can sometimes produce enough light to enhance the carving.

Another technique that has worked for me involves a large piece of white cardboard and a roll of aluminum foil. Lay the white cardboard on the ground in front of the stone. Move it around until you find the best position for reflecting light across the stone, and take your picture. If the white does not make it bright enough, try covering the cardboard with foil (I find that the heavy-duty foil holds up better) with the shiny side up.

Another means of documenting the stone is to draw a diagram of it. I often make a drawing of the stone's shape and indicate the height and width measurements. Having a rough sketch of the stone's detail can help you when the pictures come back. This is one problem that digital cameras solve. You can actually look at the picture when you take it rather than having to wait until the film is developed and printed to see if the picture is acceptable. If I am in an area and will not be back to for some time, I take my pictures and have them developed locally, using the one-hour processing. This way if I need to retake any shots I am still in the area to do so. Nothing is more disappointing than getting home and finding out that the pictures did not come out. I have also used a video camera to document the cemetery. This solves the problem of unpredictable pictures and enables you to record a narrative as you film.

What should I look for in the cemetery?

As stated before, pay attention to all of the burials in and around the plot. Is there a family monument? What names appear on it? What other markers are in the plot? Look for Civil War stars, DAR markers, military markers, and fraternal organization markers. If any of these items appears within the plot or as a decoration on a tombstone, you will know to check other record sources.

Check out the layout of the cemetery. Does it have an older section and a newer one, or does it appear not to be in current use. These are important things to note. If the cemetery is still in use there may be an office or maintenance building on the site. Try to determine who has jurisdiction over the grounds. If the cemetery is mowed and appears to be tended, some local government office, church, or private organization must have responsibility for its care. If the cemetery appears to be abandoned, go to the town hall to determine who has authority over the grounds. Is it a town cemetery or a private cemetery? The historical society might also have information about older cemeteries and transcriptions of the tombstones.

What other things should I note about the cemetery or tombstones?

Look very carefully at the inscriptions or carvings on all stones. What symbols are carved on a stone that might indicate a fraternal organization, religious affiliation, occupation, or ethnic identity? Copy all wording carved on the stone as well. This includes poems, relationships to other individuals (e.g., Mary, wife of John Hubbard), cause of death, and age at death. A multitude of information can be gleaned from tombstones, and it may not seem important or apparent at first glance. Document everything you see as well as placement of the stones as they relate to other stones in the plot or area. Look for corner markers that indicate the outside edges of a plot; this will help you determine which stones are within the family plot and which are outside of it.

Look for unusual terminology on tombstones. There are many clues in the words carved on a stone. Not only what is said but how it is said is important. I have seen several terms, that at first I thought I understood, but later found out that their meanings were not what I had assumed. The terms *relict* and *consort* appear on a woman's gravestone. While at first I thought "How terrible

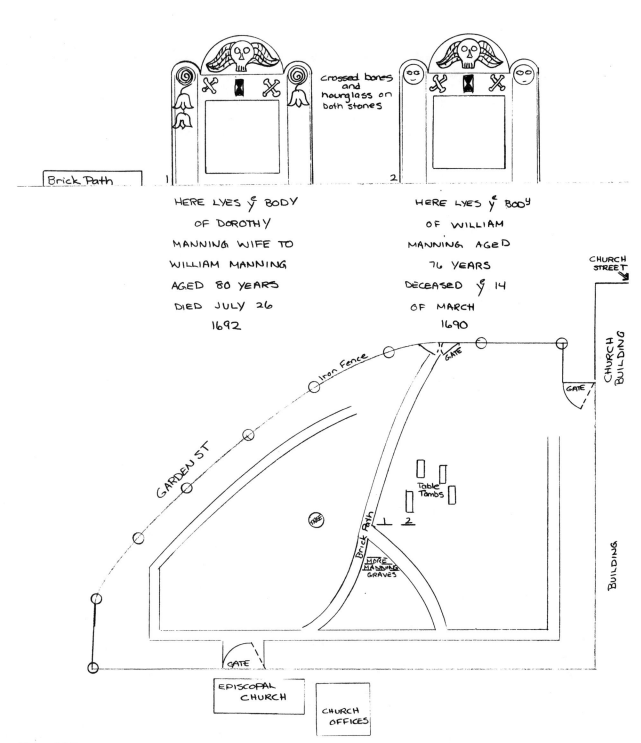

Figure 11-1
Diagram of the Old Burial Ground in Harvard Square, Cambridge, Massachusetts, showing the location of the graves of Dorothy and William Manning.

to refer to her as a relict!" I learned that the term meant that she was a widow when she died. This is information useful in determining when her husband died. The term *consort* indicates that her husband was alive at the time of her death.

\di'fin\ *vb*

Definitions

INTERESTING TERMS FOUND ON WOMEN'S TOMBSTONES

Relict: deceased was a widow at the time of her death

Consort: woman's husband was still living at the time of her death

Another such term was an abbreviation that I found, and it took me a while to learn its meaning. *N.B.* stands for the Latin term *nota bene*, or note well. It is like a footnote or a postscript on a letter and indicates additional information that should be noted. The particular gravestone said at the bottom, "N.B. buried on her left arm is a child that was still," indicating that her child was buried with her and she probably died in childbirth. Since I had never found a death record for this individual, this was new information to me.

For additional guidance to terminology and iconography on tombstones, see *Your Guide to Cemetery Research*, by Sharon DeBartolo Carmack.

What should I ask at a cemetery office?

Some questions you need to ask are Who is buried in the plot? Who is listed as the owner or buyer? When was the lot purchased or first used? When was the last burial? The answers will provide you with clues as to the time frame the cemetery plot was in use by your ancestor's family. Also check to see if other plots in the same cemetery are owned by the same person, other individuals with the same surname, or other related family surnames in your ancestry. Many extended families bought plots in the same cemetery, especially in smaller towns where there were fewer cemeteries.

Ask the person in charge if there is a contact name on the records. Is a local relative responsible for the plot? Does anyone plant or leave flowers there on a regular basis? In small towns the cemetery office staff and maintenance workers know a lot about the goings-on in their cemetery.

What other information might be included in the cemetery office records?

Some cemetery offices actually have copies of obituaries, death certificates, interment certificates, and other such information within the files. One cemetery file had a list of the individuals who had sent flowers to the cemetery at the time of the funeral to be put on the grave. Another cemetery provided me with a piece of information that had eluded me for some time. I had found in California the burial place for a man and had his dates of birth and death as carved on the stone, but I could find no death record in the town, county, or state he was buried in. When the cemetery clerk checked the records, she informed me that the individual had died in New York while on vacation, and the file held a death

Sources

certificate and other papers from New York indicating that the body was sent to California for burial. I would never have looked for his death on the East Coast, since he lived his entire life west of the Mississippi!

What other information might I get from the town offices that will assist in my cemetery research?

Some town or county offices have listings of all the cemeteries within their boundaries and lists of who has the records for or control over any individual cemetery. Some cemeteries are associated with churches, while some others are town cemeteries. If the cemetery is associated with a church, locate the church and its records.

Municipal cemeteries may have incomplete records depending on how carefully the information was recorded over the lifetime of the cemetery. At one cemetery I spoke with the caretaker, who explained how the cemetery was laid out, in what time period certain sections were in use, which section included only single gravesites, and which sections had double or quad plots in them. When I asked about the record for burials he just shook his head and said that he had taken over the records for the cemetery only five years before and had only those records. When I asked him where the previous records were he said that they did not exist as far as he knew. The previous caretaker had held the job for nearly forty years, and when he died suddenly it was discovered that all of the record books were empty. Apparently the previous caretaker had not recorded anything. No records were found from his nearly forty-year tenure as cemetery caretaker.

What should I do if the cemetery office or officials do not have records for early burials?

Many municipal cemeteries have lost records over the years or, like in the previous example, never had complete records. When you encounter this type of problem, do not give up. **Check with the local library, historical society, and undertakers to see if transcriptions of the tombstones were ever done.** Many such books were compiled in the early 1900s and may be the only record of a cemetery whose stones have either been destroyed or become unreadable. If you exhaust all of these avenues without success, you may have to do a cemetery transcription yourself. Record everything you find, including the layout of the cemetery; any fences or stone walls that go around or through it; the number and types of stones within the cemetery; and all of the names, dates, and epitaphs on the stones. Be sure to record the stones in the proper order. Who is buried near an individual can be important information. Create a map, no matter how crude, showing the layout of the cemetery, any topographical points of interest (e.g., large boulders, trees, paths), and where the stones are located in relationship to them.

Also make note of which section contains the oldest stones. Is it the section near the front of the cemetery, near the road, or at the back? This could indicate where a church, meetinghouse, or other facility might have been in a previous century.

Idea Generator

Does the layout of a cemetery provide any clues?

The layout can show you the evolution of the cemetery over the years of its existence. Many cemeteries have the oldest stones in the front, and the stones become more recent the farther back in the cemetery you go. You might also notice changes in the styles and materials of tombstones, carving, and iconography that will provide you with additional information as to the time frames that are included within its boundaries. Some cemeteries have annexes, or sections that were added on to the original cemetery when it met capacity. Some annexes are adjoining plots, while others are in another area all together.

Another thing to watch for is an old cemetery that appears to be laid out in neat rows with all the stones facing the same way. This is not the way cemeteries were normally laid out in the seventeenth and eighteenth centuries. In an intact old cemetery, the stones are in a haphazard pattern. I have seen cemeteries with family plots that form a circle rather than a square or rectangle and cemeteries with stones going every which way.

Some cemeteries have been relocated from other places. In some areas, cemeteries near rivers suffered during severe flooding and were subsequently moved to safer locations. How carefully the stones were replaced to match their original orientation is hard to determine. Many clues are lost and false clues are provided when stones are placed out of order. This is where the transcriptions from previous eras come in handy. Some transcriptions were recorded before the cemetery was moved, while others document which stones were moved to the current location and from where. Just knowing that the stones were moved makes you more aware of possible errors in the current placement pattern.

How can I locate cemeteries in an area?

Some map books, geological or topographical survey maps, and mapping programs indicate some, if not all, cemeteries within the scope of the map. Look at early histories of the town or county for any cemetery listings and clues to their locations. Check with a local undertaker. I have been surprised over the years to find that undertakers know about cemeteries long since forgotten by the town's residents. Look for locations of churches or meetinghouses, since many had cemeteries associated with them. Some cemeteries on private property (e.g., the family farm) are listed in deeds that indicate their existence at a certain time and note their existence with each subsequent land transfer. This varies in different parts of the country, but it is worth a look.

For the late nineteenth and early twentieth centuries, check a city directory for the names and locations of cemeteries, undertakers, churches, etc. Some early vital record books (such as the printed *Massachusetts Town Vital Records to 1850*) list the cemeteries that were used to compile the records included in the book. This will provide you with a list of all cemeteries and churches that were in use for that specific town. This is great but often overlooked information.

Many local historical and genealogical societies have compiled lists of the cemeteries within a specific geographical area and where the transcriptions can be found. The Vermont Old Cemetery Association published the book *Burial Grounds of Vermont* in 1985, and it outlines all of the known cemeteries in the state, divided by county and then by town. It provides first and last burial dates, condition of the cemetery, directions to get to it, and where any lists of burials or transcriptions might be found. It also includes the name and address of the person who compiled the list for that county.

Sources

Look in your local or genealogical library for books on cemetery locations and transcriptions. The Essex Society of Genealogists compiled the book *A Guide to Cemeteries in Essex County, Massachusetts*, similar to the Vermont volume, that indicates the location of each cemetery within Essex County as well as if and where transcriptions can be found. Many groups or individuals have produced indexes or files regarding the burials, especially those for veterans. These might take the form of card files, books, or simple lists, and they are worth looking for. Ask the individuals working in the library if such lists exist.

Many county historical societies have collections of transcriptions for cemeteries within their area which were compiled by members over the years. Many of these are included in manuscript collections. The New England Historic Genealogical

---

CITY OF NEWBURYPORT, MASS. ————————GRAVES REGISTRATION RECORD

1. Name of deceased ....
   (Surname)   (First)   (Middle)

2. Name of Cemetery ....Place ....
   (City or Town)

   Grave Number .... Location...
   (Section, path, lot, etc.)

   Date of burial in this Cemetery ....Grave No. on Blue Prints ....

3. Marker placed? .... By Post No. ....Headstone—Family—Govt. ....
   (Date)

4. Were remains buried elsewhere? ....Date ....

   Place ....
   (Cemetery, location, section, path, lot, etc.)

5. Branch of Service ....Organization ....
   (Army, Navy, Marines)   (Company, Regiment, Vessel)

6. Born ....Died ....
   (Place and Date)   (Place and Date)

7. Cause of death ....
   (Killed in action, died of wounds received in action, accident, illness, etc.)

8. Was deceased member of Veteran Organization? ....
   (Post, camp, garrison, etc.—Location—American Legion, etc.)

9. Name and address of next of kin ....
   (Name, Relationship, Address)

10. Undertaker ....
    (Name and Address)

    ....

REMARKS: (Over)   Post No. .... Graves Registration Officer.

Figure 11-2A
This card shows what the Newburyport Public Library in Newburyport, Massachusetts, uses to document veterans' graves within the town. The back of the card is on page 192.

11. Is Government stone permitted in this Cemetery? ....

12. Type of Government stone ....
        (Bronze, granite, marble, upright, flat)

13. Name and address of organization making this report ....
....

14. If deceased received any decorations, medals, citation etc. Note: ....
....

15. Date of enlistment ....

16. Date of discharge ....

Figure 11-2B
Example of a graves registration record, back.

Society in Boston, Massachusetts, has a large manuscript collection of New England cemetery inscriptions for use by its members. Check the manuscript collections in local and state libraries and archives to see what you might find.

Other organizations to look for are state or county cemetery associations. Many states, such as New Hampshire, Rhode Island, Vermont, and Wisconsin have old cemetery associations. Many groups do wonderful work documenting, maintaining, and in some cases repairing the forgotten and neglected cemeteries.

The Association for Gravestone Studies (278 Main Street, Suite 207, Greenfield, Massachusetts 01301; <http://www.gravestonestudies.org>) is an international organization that maintains a quite extensive library. While they do not have a complete transcription of every cemetery, they do have many resources documenting the carving styles, symbolism, and carver information. The amount of data they have studied and written about that concerns gravestones and cemeteries is positively amazing!

Some of the books that can help you locate and understand cemetery records include *Ancestry's Red Book*, Sharon DeBartolo Carmack's *Your Guide to Cemetery Research*, and *Cemeteries of the U.S.* When I look for a book specific to a state or to cemetery information, I visit Amazon.com at <http://www.amazon.com> and search under "cemetery." The last time I did this more than 660 books showed up in the search results. Amazing! Also check the USGenWeb at

<http://www.usgenweb.com> for additional resources in the state of interest. Some of these county sites actually include photographs of the tombstones!

What other indexes are available?

The National Archives has an index to gravestone applications for veterans. This index is on twenty-two rolls of microfilm: Publication M1845, *Card Records of Headstones Provided for Deceased Civil War Veterans, ca. 1879–ca. 1903.* The applications included were submitted to the Department of Veterans Affairs by individuals, usually relatives, in the process of applying for a grave marker or tombstone for a veteran's grave. Most of the applications included in this index are for Civil War veterans and may include information valuable to you, such as dates of military service, dates of enlistment or discharge, place of burial, dates of birth or death, rank, and the name and address of the individual making the application. Check with a regional NARA facility to see if they have this index in their collection.

To obtain a copy of an application, call the Veterans Affairs office in your state, or you can obtain the request form online at the Department of Veterans Affairs National Cemetery Administration's Web site at <http://www.cem.va.gov/hmorder .htm>. Headstones and markers can be requested for veterans' unmarked graves. Memorial markers may also be requested even for veterans whose remains are not buried in a cemetery (i.e., the veteran was buried at sea, lost in battle, cremated and had his ashes scattered, or buried in an unknown location).

UNDERTAKERS' RECORDS

What might I find in an undertaker's records?

Undertakers' records vary over different time periods, but they can be valuable resources for family historians. Some such records contain information about where a person died, relatives' names, obituaries, burial places, and so much more. On one trip to Vermont I was looking for a grave site for a man who had died in Barnard, Windsor County, Vermont. His death certificate listed a cemetery nearly fifty miles from his home as the place of burial. After searching the cemetery for several hours and finding no office, caretaker, or grave for the deceased, I decided to give up. As I drove out of the cemetery I noticed that the funeral home across the street was the one listed on the death certificate. After getting up the courage to knock on the door, I was greeted by a young man who seemed more than pleased to see what he could do for me.

I presented him with the death certificate, and he checked it against his records of burials in the cemetery across the street. The individual did not appear in the cemetery records. Now we were both confused. How could this be? He looked at the date on the death record and stated that his grandfather had run the funeral home in that time period. He called his grandfather at home, spoke to him for just a minute, and then looked at the certificate again and ended his conversation. His grandfather had told him to look at the burial information again. It stated that the deceased was "entombed" in that cemetery, not interred. The cemetery across the street was the only one in the area with a tomb at that time, and since the funeral home did not do burials during the winter or early spring, the deceased would have been placed in the tomb until burial could take place later in the spring.

He sent me to the town hall to find out where the body had been removed to in the spring of 1922. The disentombment certificate indicated that the burial had taken place in May 1922 in the deceased person's hometown of Barnard! I proceeded to the cemetery there and found the burial. You have to read certificates with a knowledgeable eye to pick out these details!

What other records does an undertaker have?

You never know until you ask! At the town hall in a small town in New Hampshire, I was told that it had no cemetery information at all. When I inquired as to who would have it, I was told to go to the funeral home at the bottom of the hill. I proceeded to the funeral home and went in. I was greeted by a solemn-looking man in a conservative black suit. When I told him what I was looking for, he gave me a big smile and invited me to have a seat. He left the room and returned with several wooden card files. The files contained a listing of every known burial within the town and what cemetery it was in. We discussed the records for nearly thirty minutes before I thanked him and got up to leave. I apologized for taking up his time, and he responded, "I enjoy talking to people who are actually glad to see me." We both had a good laugh, and I left with a newfound respect for the undertakers of the world.

Another wonderful piece of information from an undertaker's record has led to other records of value. A death certificate from New York City stated that the individual died from "asphyxiation from illuminating gas." While homes were indeed lit by gas lamps in the early 1900s, it seemed strange that the cause of death was not listed as accidental asphyxiation. Further research led to the original undertaker, and his record listed it as a suicide. How could this be? The undertaker we spoke with thought that because the individual was Catholic the suicide information might have been left off the original certificate to enable the family to have a Mass and burial in the Catholic cemetery.

What additional records are created by the undertaker or funeral home?

Most funeral directors have a form for gathering information about the deceased in preparation for services and composing the death notice or obituary. This form or questionnaire usually includes the name, age, address, and death information for an individual but also contains information regarding his place of birth, parentage, occupation, military service, cemetery name and location of grave, and a list of surviving relatives, including parents, children, siblings, aunts, uncles, and grandchildren. The clergyman's name and church are documented, as well as any organizations or societies the deceased was associated with. The names of the pallbearers and the music played at the services might also be listed. The following "worksheet" was provided to me by a local funeral home as an example of this questionnaire.

FRANK S. ROBERTS & SON FUNERAL HOME
ROWLEY, MASSACHUSETTS 01969
(978) 948-7763

Name					
Residence					
If Non-Resident, Give City & State					
Place of Death					
Date of Death					
Sex	Color	Single	Married	Widowed	Citizen
Husband of (Maiden Name)					
Wife of					
Age of Husband or Wife if Alive					
Birthplace of Deceased		City		State	
Date of Birth		Age			
If Veteran, Specify War & Unit		Service No.			
Entered Service		Discharged			
Rank or Rating		Education			
Occupation		Soc. Security			
Place of Business					
Date Deceased last worked					
How long in hospital		In City		In U. S.	
Doctor		Last Visited			
Cause of Death					
Informant		Tel.			
Informant's Address					
Father's Name					
Father's Birthplace					
Mother's Maiden Name					
Mother's Birthplace					
Cemetery		City			
Funeral at					
Date		Hour		A.M.-P.M.	

Figure 11-3A
Example of a funeral home's questionnaire and record, page one.

Another record created by the funeral home is documentation of the official disposition, removal, or transportation of the body to the crematorium or its final resting place. The Commonwealth of Massachusetts form is in three parts, and the forms are bound in a book. The stub portion of the form remains in the book, which when filled completely is turned over to the town or county department of health. The second portion is sent to the town where the death occurred, and the third section (which actually has a top and bottom part) is sent along with the body or remains

Sources

SURVIVING RELATIVES AND ADDRESSES

Father

Mother

Husband

Wife

Sons

Daughters

Brothers

Sisters

Grandchildren (No.)

Newspaper Notices

to the town where the deceased is buried. After the burial the receiving town fills in the bottom portion and returns it to the town where the death occurred.

What other records can funeral home records lead to?
Whenever you locate a death that was not by natural causes, try to access the coroner's or medical examiner's records. When a death was the result of suicide, murder, accident, or questionable circumstances, there might have been an in-

SERVICE DETAILS

Clergyman   Call for

Church

Pallbearers

Orders & Societies

Music

Grave No.   Plot No.

Range No.   Section No.

Lot Owner

```
              N
    W  [          ]  E
              S
```

CREMATION INFORMATION

Date   Place

Disposition of Ashes

Figure 11-3C
A funeral home's questionnaire and record, page three.

vestigation into the cause of death. The state, county, or town medical examiner might have come in to determine the exact cause of death. Most death certificates from the twentieth century include information as to whether an autopsy was performed. The autopsy report might be included in the medical examiner's report detailing the cause of death.

I recently had an opportunity to obtain one such record from New York City. An individual had died in Manhattan on Christmas Day in 1950 in a car accident,

Case Study

Figure 11-3D
A funeral home's question-naire and record, page four.

WORK SHEET

Check each item as accomplished.

.....Casket.................................$...................	.....Outside Case Delivered.......$...............
.....Vault...................................$...................	.....Cemetery Equipment.............$...............
.....Opening Grave....................$...................	.....Grave Marker......................$...............
.....Hair Dresser........................$...................	.....Clothing..............................$...............
.....Death Certificate................$...................	.....Burial Permit......................$...............
.....Newspaper Notices..............$...................	.....Telephone & Telegrams.......$...............
.....Flowers...............................$...................	.....Door Spray.........................$...............
.....Bearers................................$...................	.....Lodges Notified..................$...............
.....Hearse Hire.........................$...................	.....Police..................................$...............
.....Extra Limousines..................$...................	.....Flower Car..........................$...............
.....Clergyman...........................$...................	.....Prayer Cards.......................$...............
.....Church Expense...................$...................	.....Acknowledgment Cards.......$...............
.....Air Freight...........................$...................	.....Organist.............................$...............

INSTRUCTIONS
Visiting Hours
_____

_____

Hair Styling
_____

_____

Coloring
_____

_____

_____

_____

_____

_____

_____

_____

_____

_____

_____

according to family stories. The death certificate indicated that the cause of death was multiple fractures, internal injuries, hemorrhage, and shock. That sounded like the results of a car accident, but the death certificate did not specifically state that.

The medical examiner's record clarified the missing details of the death and provided me with wonderful additional information about the deceased individual. The file contained a page listing his name, age, place of birth, color, parents, marital status, residence, and place of death and the name of the individual who identified the body. That person was his cousin, and the file also included the cousin's address in New York City. The file contained a five-page autopsy report with more information than I really wanted to know, some of it being pretty graphic. It did, however, provide a physical description of the deceased that read, in part "Adult white, well developed and nourished, somewhat muscular and obese white male 5'6" long. There is sparse dark brown hair on the head, slightly grey streaked. Bushy black eyebrows. Grey eyes." The report then went on to describe the body and the extensive injuries. The report ended with the statement "Struck by towing truck, 12-25-50 at 125th St. bet 3rd Ave. & Lexington Ave." Mystery solved. Another notation on the document listed that testing for alcohol was done and that no alcohol was present, thereby ruling out the individual's being drunk at the time of the accident.

When should I look for medical examiner's records?

You should follow up on these records if the death was by accidental or questionable means. If the death certificate lists the death as an accident, suicide, or unknown, look for these records.

I found a death certificate listing an individual's cause of death as drowning, but with no further indication as to whether it was an accident or the result of an accident. Since the man drowned on Thanksgiving Day in 1900 and left a wife and three small children, I naturally looked in the local newspaper for a story. There was no mention of the death in either the news or the death notices. The newspaper information indicated that it had been too warm for him to have been skating and too cold for him to logically have been out boating. So why was this tragedy not recorded in the paper when minor automobile accidents for that day were listed? A look at the medical examiner's report provided the answer. It seems the man had come home drunk and had fallen face first into the river behind his home and drowned. Not something that the family wanted published in the paper, I would assume.

Some books (for example, *Coroner's Reports, New York City, 1823–1842*, published by the New York Genealogical and Biographical Society, 1989) have transcriptions of some medical examiner's or coroner's records that are fascinating reading. Though they are brief, they provide a great deal of information regarding family members that were interviewed or who provided information about the deceased.

Some examples from *Coroner's Reports, New York City, 1823–1842*:
- Ayers, Jethro Johnson—drowning, age c. 47, a carpenter by trade. His daughter is Freelove Purdy, wife of Johnson Purdy. (10 Oct 1839)
- Bailey, Mary—suicide by arsenic, b. England, age 45, married in England to Thomas Bailey, an Englishman. They have been in the U.S. 6 yrs. and have 5 children, the eldest age 15. (26 Mar 1840)
- Bailey, Mary—choked on a piece of lobster, b. Ireland, age c. 40. Mary Feeney is her mother. (24 Oct 1842)
- Farrell, Phillip—taking of laudanum by mistake, b. New Jersey, age c. 7 yrs. Mother of the child is Elizabeth Farrell. The father of the child has

been in the Marine Corps of the U.S. Navy and was discharged last Monday. About 2 years ago he married another woman and kept her, with 4 children. (19 Sep 1840)

- Frew, Jane—injuries inflicted by John Lyons, b. Scotland, age 34. (3 Dec 1837)
- Fuller, Harriet—accidentally burned to death, b. New York, age 1 yr., child of Joseph and Lydia Fuller, of 22 Broom St. (7 Nov 1838)
- Gaffney, Mary—visitation by God, b. Ireland, age c. 45 or 50, a widow with no children (29 Jan 1939)

As you can see, these records are full of information that can help, or even entertain, you. The cause of death for Mary Gaffney and the information regarding Phillip Farrell's father are interesting, at least.

Where can I find coroner's or medical examiner's records?

These records may be in the municipal archives of the city or in the county or state archives. Determine whether the coroner was a local, county, or state position at the time of the death you are researching, and try to determine if the records are in an archive or still in the city or county of original jurisdiction.

What if the undertaker or funeral home is no longer in business?

First look at a city directory or business listing for the time frame the undertaker was in business to determine what other, if any, undertakers were working in the area at that time. Since many undertakers and funeral homes began operation in the mid 1800s and continue today, most are listed in city or suburban directories. Interestingly, many early undertakers were also listed as cabinetmakers in the census and city directory records. I have a copy of a bill for my great-grandfather's funeral that shows the business was not only an undertaker, but also an insurance agency and furniture dealer. **Also check local newspapers from the time period and look for advertisements.** Once you have determined what other undertakers were in business at the same time, see if any of them are still in operation today. Since undertakers rarely go out of business but get absorbed or purchased by another, the records in many cases have been preserved. While the records may not be easily accessed, in many cases they do exist. Some funeral homes' and undertakers' records have been deposited in historical societies and manuscript collections as well. Many genealogical societies have either originals or transcriptions of some of these records. It is worth a try to locate such records.

Also look in the local library for directories of funeral homes and undertakers. These specialized directories were printed by many different companies during the twentieth century and are usually referred to as the *National Yellow Book* or *American Blue Book of Funeral Directors*; they vary in title and format by publisher. Many different publishers produced these, and most of the books are held in the reference section of the library, along with other professional directories specific to occupations.

Idea Generator

How do I determine what undertaker or funeral home handled the funeral arrangements?

In some states the name of the undertaker or funeral home is listed on the death certificate. This practice began for the most part in the late 1800s and continues today. If the undertaker's name does not appear on the death record, look for the death notice or obituary to see if it is stated there. The cemetery or church may also have a record of who provided the services at the time of burial. If all of these avenues prove fruitless, you can always check the city or business directories for those years to see who was in business at the time and take it from there. You might also look at a few other death records from the time frame and see what undertaker is listed.

In the mid to late 1800s and early 1900s most wakes were held in the deceased individual's home, and in many cases, unless the law forbade it, the deceased was prepared by family members. This changed when embalming became commonplace or required by law. Some undertakers performed the embalming procedure in the deceased's home as late as the 1940s in some areas. Gradually over time, wakes and funerals were held in funeral homes more often than in private residences, although some undertakers still perform these services in the home of the deceased upon request.

Sources

FURTHER READING

Ancestry's Red Book: American State, County & Town Sources, rev. ed., edited by Alice Eichholz. Salt Lake City, Utah: Ancestry, Inc., 1992.

Beautiful Death: Art of the Cemetery, by David Robinson and Dean Koontz. New York: Penguin Books, 1996.

Celebrations of Death: The Anthropology of Mortuary Rituals, by Peter Metcalf. New York: Cambridge University Press, 1992.

Cemeteries & Gravemarkers: Voices of American Culture, edited by Richard E. Meyer. Logan, Utah: Utah State University Press, 1992.

Cemeteries of the U.S.: A Guide to Contact Information for U.S. Cemeteries and Their Records, by Deborah M. Burek, ed. Detroit, Mich.: Gale Research, Inc., 1994.

The Cemetery Record Compendium, by John D. and E. Diane Stemmons. Logan Utah: Everton Publishers, 1979.

Church & Tombstone Research, by John W. Heisey. Indianapolis, Ind.: Ye Olde Genealogy Shoppe, 1987.

Churchyard Literature: A Choice Collection of American Epitaphs, With Remarks on Corpses, Coffins, and Crypts: A History of Burials, by Penny Colman. New York: Henry Holt and Co., 1997.

Early New England Gravestone Rubbings, 2d ed., by Edmund Vincent Gillon. New York: Dover Publications, 1981.

Ethnicity and the American Cemetery, edited by Richard E. Meyer. Bowling Green, Ohio: Bowling Green University Popular Press, 1993.

Famous and Curious Cemeteries, by John Francis Marion. New York: Crown Publishers, Inc., 1977.

Gravestone Chronicles, Volumes I and II, by Theodore Chase and Laurel Gable. Boston, Mass.: New England Historic Genealogical Society, 1997.

A Gravestone Preservation Primer, by Lynette Strangstad. Walnut Creek, Calif.: AltaMira Press, 1995.

Gravestones of Early New England and the Men Who Made Them, 1653–1800, by Harriett Merrifield Forbes. 1927. Rev. ed., New York: Center for Thanatology Research and Education, Inc., 1989.

The Last Great Necessity, by David Charles Sloane. Baltimore, Md.: John Hopkins University Press, 1991.

Markers: The Journal of the Association for Gravestone Studies. Continuing periodical. Greenfield, Mass.: Association Gravestone Studies.

Monumental Inscriptions and Obsequies of Various Nations, by John Robert Kippax. 1876. Reprinted by Heritage Books, 1994.

Monuments and Their Inscriptions: A Practical Guide, by H. Leslie White. 1977. Reprinted with some corrections by Society of Genealogists. London, England: 1987.

National Yellow Book of Funeral Directors 2001. Youngstown, Ohio: Nomis Publications. Published yearly.

Puritan Gravestone Art I & II, edited by Peter Benes. Dublin, N.H.: Boston University and the Dublin Seminar for New England Folk Life, 1977 and 1979.

Tombstones of Your Ancestors, by Louis S. Shafer. Bowie, Md.: Heritage Books, 1991.

Your Guide to Cemetery Research, by Sharon DeBartolo Carmack. Cincinnati, Ohio: Betterway Books, 2002.

TWELVE

Terminology: Genealogical Terms and What They Mean

A ny new family history researcher must learn all of the terminology that flies around when the discussion turns to genealogy. Like any other hobby (or should I say obsession), genealogical research has more than its share of unique terms, abbreviations, acronyms, and references. Many of these confusing terms are explained in the following pages.

We have all heard words or terms that we do not understand. While we can always look up an unknown word in a dictionary, most specialized terms and abbreviations pertaining to genealogical research do not appear in your everyday dictionary, no matter how complete it is. Because of this, you will need additional dictionaries for your research. **Several genealogy-specific dictionaries on the market not only explain antiquated terms and phrases but also most of the genealogical terminology you will encounter.**

Some of these books are *A to Zax: A Comprehensive Dictionary for Genealogists & Historians*, *What Did They Mean By That?: A Dictionary of Historical Terms for Genealogists*, *Ancestry's Concise Genealogical Dictionary*, *A Medical Miscellany for Genealogists*, and *Abbreviations & Acronyms: A Guide for Family Historians*. All of these books must be consulted during the research process to help you fully understand every record you find. I have also used *Black's Law Dictionary* for legal terminology that appeared in probates and land records. Understanding all of the terms and phrases is imperative to successful research.

For More Info

Abbreviations You Might Encounter

abt = about	ct. r. = court record
ae = age	d = died, death
b = born	d/o = daughter of
bap/bp = baptized	dau = daughter
c/ch = child, children	dea = deacon (of a church)
cnbl = cannot be learned	desc = descendant
c.r. = church record	div = divorce

Abbreviations You Might Encounter (continued)

doc = document

d.s.p. = *decessit sine prole* (died without issue)

d.y. = died younget al. = et alii (and others, among others)

fl = flourished (was alive)

fmc or fwc = free man/woman of color

g.r. = gravestone record

g.s. = gravestone

h = husband

ibid = in the same place (repeat references)

i.e. = in other words

inf = infant

int = intention (marriage)

liv = living

m = married, marriage, month

mul/m = mullato (color of person)

N.B. = *nota bene* (note well/please note)

N.S. = New Style calendar

op.cit. = *opera citato* (in the work cited)

O.S. = Old Style calendar

q.v. = which see, reference

rem = removed (moved)

res = residence

s/o = son of

sic = copied exactly from original

unm = unmarried

viz = namely

w = wife

wid = widow

widr = widower

yeo = yeoman (farmer)

m/1, m/2 = married first (married second, etc.)

wit = witness

[See also page 68, chapter four.]

FORMS

Ahnentafel

German word meaning "family table." This type of chart is a numerical listing of all ancestors who would appear on a *pedigree chart* (see page 205) with numbers assigned according to sex and parentage. Person number 1 can be male or female, but from that point on males are always even numbers and females are always odd numbers. To determine an individual's parents' Ahnentafel numbers, simply double the individual's number to get the father's number and double the individual's number and add 1 to get the mother's number.

Example

1. Seneca Baker ROGERS (1885–1959)
2. Hoxie Constant ROGERS (1842–1929) [father]
3. Teresa Rebecca STEARNS (1847–1924) [mother]
4. Joseph A. ROGERS (1813–1853) [paternal grandfather]
5. Annie Delilah BARBER (1817–1894) [paternal grandmother]
6. Harvey STEARNS (1800–1853) [maternal grandfather]
7. Rebecca BROWN (1804–1864) [maternal grandmother]

Hoxie Constant Rogers is number 2. He is therefore the father of Seneca Baker Rogers (number 1) and the son of Joseph A. Rogers (number 4) and Annie

Delilah Barber (number 5). Using this system, parentage can be determined by the number assigned to the individual.

Census Extraction Forms

These forms were created to make copying of census information easier and more thorough by providing all the applicable columns for a census year so complete documentation is assured. While these forms may seem like a good idea that will save you money on census record photocopies, they can impede further research. Extracting just one family group from a census record isolates those individuals from the neighborhood that they lived in. Seeing our ancestors in the context in which they lived provides a better picture of their world. Also, whenever you hand copy any information from one place to another, you have a 25 percent chance of making transcription errors. When you get the information home and something seems wrong or incorrect, you will not know if you copied it incorrectly or if it was listed that way in the original record. A photocopy of the record itself will save you time and serves as good insurance against transcription errors.

Census Overview Forms

These forms are helpful to you after you have acquired several census records for an individual or a family unit. By transferring certain information to this form from each census year, you create an overview of the data for that family over a period of time. Inaccuracies in ages and inconsistent information regarding birthplaces, names, and other facts become obvious when the information is on one sheet of paper.

Family Group Sheet

This form lists one family group including a father, a mother, and their biological children regardless of whether the couple was married. If either parent was married previously and children were born of that union, you should have a separate family group sheet for that family. Adopted children can be listed on the family group sheet with their adopted parents *as long as it is clearly marked that they were adopted*. This is crucial information if a medical history is needed for the child.

Pedigree Chart

This standard format chart that lists your ancestors, such as your parents, grandparents, and great-grandparents. This is your bloodline, and it does not include siblings or cousins. All of the people on a pedigree chart are directly responsible for your existence. If any one of these individuals had not existed, neither would you.

Research Log Sheet

This form is a log or listing of all sources that you have consulted in your research. You can compile your research logs by surname, locality, or research facility. You can customize the format to suit your personal requirements. It is

WHERE TO GET FORMS

Census extraction and overview forms

- National Archives and Records Administration

- *Unpuzzling Your Past*, 4th edition, by Emily Anne Croom

- *The Unpuzzling Your Past Workbook: Essential Forms and Letters for All Genealogists*, by Emily Anne Croom

- *The Weekend Genealogist: Timesaving Techniques for Effective Research*, by Marcia Yannizze Melnyk

Family group sheets and pedigree charts

- Everton Publishers, (800) 443-6325 <http://www.everton.com>

- Ancestry, Inc. (800) 531-1790 <http://www.ancestry.com>

- Family History Library and its Family History Centers

- *The Unpuzzling Your Past Workbook*, by Emily Anne Croom

- Most genealogical software programs

- Online for free at sites like FamilyTreeMagazine.com

Miscellaneous forms

- *The Unpuzzling Your Past Workbook*, by Emily Anne Croom

- *The Weekend Genealogist*, by Marcia Yannizze Melnyk

- *Organizing Your Family History Search: Efficient & Effective Ways to Gather and Protect Your Genealogical Research*, by Sharon DeBartolo Carmack

important to record all of the sources you consult even if they produced no useable information. By recording such negative results you avoid wasting time consulting these sources again for information that you know is not there.

RECORD TYPES

What is a vital record?

A vital record is created by the governing officials in an area to document a birth, marriage, or death. The governing body can be a town, county, state, or territory, depending on the geographic location and the time frame of the record.

What is a source?

A source is anything that provides you with information on your ancestors. Whether you obtain information from a book, an official record, the Internet, a CD database, an individual, your personal knowledge, or any other source, you must properly document the origin of the information. Note specifically where you obtained the information—title of the book, publication date, page numbers. Since many books, CDs, and databases are merely compilations of data found elsewhere the proper citation of their sources is important to evaluating their accuracy.

What is a citation?

The source of your information, when recorded along with the information, is called the citation and clearly indicates the source. A proper citation should enable you or another researcher to find the original source directly, without having to go through all of the steps you took to find it in the first place. For information obtained from a census record, the citation should include the year, state, county, town, and page (or enumeration district number, when applicable); just "U.S. federal census" is not sufficient.

These sample citations appear in the book *The John Round Family of Swansea and Rehoboth, Massachusetts* by H.L. Peter Rounds (Gateway Press, 1983).

Fact: Amey Round died 8 March 1844 at Gloucester, Rhode Island.

Citation: Gloucester Cemetery Records, Rhode Island vital records.

Fact: Abner Crossman was of Oyster Bay, New York.

Citation: Bristol County, Massachusetts, deeds; vol. 91; page 427.

Fact: Isaac Round was on the Tax Lists for Rehoboth for 1759, 1765, and 1769.

Citation: Tax Lists published by Bowen (vol. 4; pp. 95, 103, 111).

If you were to record these events in your genealogy or database, your proper citation would be of the book by H.L. Peter Rounds, including publication date and page numbers, unless you personally looked at the original sources that he cited. The author cites the record that he saw to establish the fact. Until you have looked at the same record, you cannot know if his citation and information are accurate or erroneous.

What are primary and secondary sources?

A primary source is the *first* record of any event and is usually created at or near the time of the event. Most primary sources contain information provided by a person or persons involved in the event. This usually makes the information reliable providing that they were truthful in giving it. While some primary sources are church records for baptisms, marriages, and burials, other primary sources are civil documents required by the governing authorities. A birth, marriage, or death may have two primary source documents. A birth may be documented on an official birth record recorded in the town or county office and on a baptism record recorded in the church. The same is true for marriages and deaths: Church records contain the marriage certificate and burial information, while civil records with the local authority include the marriage license and the death record.

A marriage record or a marriage license is an example of a primary source. It lists the individuals getting married, and the information contained in the record is likely to have been provided by those two individuals.

A secondary source is a later or subsequent record of the event. Since most states did not require recording of vital records at the state level until well into the late 1800s and early 1900s, most statewide records for events prior to that time are compilations of previously recorded primary sources. Knowing and understanding the laws governing the records in the geographic location and time period will help you determine if a record is a primary or secondary source.

To understand the difference between primary and secondary sources, consider Massachusetts, where all vital records (births, marriages, and deaths) are recorded at the town level. This has been true since the earliest time periods. In the 1840s a law was passed requiring all towns to send a copy of all vital records to the state level for recording. While the state record is considered an official record, it is not a primary source. Mistakes may have been made when the record was transcribed onto the state-required forms, and some of the information may not have been required on the state copy thereby making it unreliable and incomplete at best.

Statewide records and indexes are wonderful tools for you as you try to locate original records for your ancestors. Use the state indexes and records to determine what locality or official provided the original information to the state and then seek out those original records. (See chapter three for more information about vital records.)

Are family Bibles considered primary or secondary sources?

The answer to that is that the Bible is a primary source, although the information can be secondary. First you need to determine when the Bible was published. This information is usually on the cover page and indicates the earliest possible date that the Bible could have been in your ancestor's possession. Next look at the pages that include your family information. Do any of the dates predate the publication date of the Bible? If so they may have been written in the Bible from memory or copied from a previously prepared document or Bible. This makes the information a secondary source. Another detail to look at is the handwriting. Is it all in the same hand and ink, or does the handwriting change for different events? This change indicates that the Bible was kept up-to-date as events occurred.

It is fascinating to look at the evolution of the handwriting in an old Bible. Many early entries are in a lovely script that deteriorates over time into unsteady handwriting. Then, different handwriting appears, indicating that another individual took over the task of recording that family's records. Watch for these details to get a better picture of how primary or secondary the information might be.

What is a city directory?

City directories are compilations or listings of residents within a given geographic or governmental boundary for a specific period of time. Most city

Figure 12-1
Bible records from the manuscript collection of the New England Historic Genealogical Society. Record #1304 (call number GEN 1 R58).

directories were published yearly or every other year. They are the precursors to the present-day telephone books and list individuals by name, occupation, employer, and address. Like in telephone books, not all individuals living in any specific household are listed. The directories listed the head of the household (and the spouse's name, in later years) and any individuals in school or employed outside of the home.

What is a periodical?

Any publication that is produced at regular intervals of more than a day (i.e., weekly, quarterly, monthly, yearly) is a periodical. This includes some newspapers (weekly or monthly editions), newsletters, and magazines. The most comprehensive index to periodicals is *Periodical Source Index* (PERSI), created by the staff of the Allen County Public Library in Fort Wayne, Indiana. It is available in print, on CD, and on the Internet as well. (See chapter ten for additional information.)

What is a probate record?

A probate record is created during the legal process of validating a will, evaluating the estate's value, appointing an administrator or executor, dividing the property among legal heirs, and executing the final resolution of the estate of a deceased individual. These files may contain wills, inventories of property, distribution of the estate, appointment of an executor of the estate, guardianship of minor children, and any number of other documents depending on the time period, government jurisdiction, and the court that has authority over such matters. (See "Probate Records" in this chapter for additional terms.)

What is a manuscript?

A manuscript is a one-of-a-kind document, volume, or record that is usually handwritten or typed and is not published. Many libraries have papers donated by individuals that represent their entire life's research and may include original documents, family papers, Bibles, diaries, and more. Consult the manuscripts in any library or research facility you visit, since they may contain valuable information. This is especially true in state, county, or local libraries, as well as at genealogical and historical societies in the location where your ancestors lived. The *National Union Catalog of Manuscript Collections* (commonly called NUCMC, or "nuckmuck") should be consulted to locate manuscript collections. NUCMC is a series of books that describe the locations and contents of manuscript collections all over the United States. It has been published since 1962 (for manuscripts cataloged between 1959–1961), and it is now published annually. (See Emily Anne Croom's *The Genealogist's Companion & Sourcebook*, chapter eight, for more details on NUCMC.) *Ancestry's Red Book* also addresses the manuscript collections in each state and should be consulted along with other reference books to see which facilities in your state of interest have such collections.

What is a naturalization record?

The process of becoming a U.S. citizen generates many different documents over a period of time; they are collectively called naturalization records. The content of these records varies depending on the time period and locality within the United States and the laws that were in effect at the time citizenship was applied for and granted.

FACILITIES, PUBLICATIONS, AND ORGANIZATIONS

Seasoned genealogists have developed a language all their own when it comes to the names of organizations and frequently used research facilities. The official names for these organizations and facilities are often long and tedious to say repeatedly. Here is a list of some, certainly not all, that you may encounter. To locate additional organizations, try Cyndi's List <http://www.cyndislist.com> and search on "organizations."

AGBI: *The American Genealogical-Biographical Index.* This index to census, the *Boston Evening Transcript*'s genealogical column, and many other publications including published genealogies were created by the Godfrey Memorial Library in Middletown, Connecticut. (AGBI was previously called the Riders Index.)

AIS: Accelerated Indexing Systems. This group has created many of the published books containing census indexes to the U.S. federal census records.

DAR: Daughters of the American Revolution. This organization documents and records the descendants of Revolutionary War soldiers and patriots. Individuals can become members by proving their descent from one of these individuals. Strict guidelines for the research and documentation make these some of the most sought-after records for genealogists who can trace their lineage back to the Revolutionary War period. The DAR maintains an extensive research library in Washington, DC (see chapter one). You can visit the DAR Web site at <http://www.dar.org/library/default.html>.

FGS: Federation of Genealogical Societies. FGS is based in Austin, Texas, and is comprised of genealogical societies around the world. They produce a yearly conference with instructional lectures and workshops for genealogists. They also publish the quarterly periodical *Forum.* The Web site address is <http://www.fgs.org/>.

GAR: The Grand Army of the Republic. This is a fraternal organization made up of Union veterans of the Civil War. See the Web site at <http://pages.pro digy.com/CGBD86A/garhp.htm>.

IGI: International Genealogical Index. Created by the Church of Jesus Christ of Latter-day Saints, IGI is a compilation of individually submitted records as well as extractions from official records.

INS: Immigration and Naturalization Service. Located in Washington, DC, this organization was created in the early 1900s to maintain records of immigrants coming into the United States. The INS Web site is at <http://www.ins .gov/graphics/index.htm>.

LDS: Church of Jesus Christ of Latter-day Saints. (Latter-day Saints are commonly referred to as Mormons.) They operate the Family History Library in Salt Lake City, Utah, which is the largest single holder of microfilmed records from all over the world. Their collection continues to grow by thousands of rolls of microfilm monthly. These filmed records are available to anyone at no charge. If you use the microfilms at one of the thousands of local facilities (called Family History Centers or FHCs) around the world, you pay a nominal rental and mailing fee. If you have the opportunity to visit the Family History Library (FHL), you can use the film at no charge. You pay for any photocopies that you make, but use of the records and the facility are free and without obligation (see chapter one). The Web site address is <http://www.familysearch .org>.

LOC: Library of Congress. Located in Washington, DC, this is the largest library in the United States, and it holds copies of all copyrighted material published in the United States. It holds the largest collection of family genealogies and city directories in the United States and may have the only copies of some of them. For more information or online access to the LOC catalog, visit <http://lcweb.loc.gov/>.

NARA: National Archives and Records Administration. Based in Washington, DC, NARA also has sixteen regional facilities throughout the United States. NARA holds original and/or microfilmed copies of all federal records including federal census schedules, military service and military pension records, naturalization records, passenger lists, and many other unique records pertaining to the federal government. They do not hold vital records unless the individual was born, married, or died outside of the United States on a U.S. military base. (See chapter one.) The Web site is at <http://www.nara.gov>.

NEHGS or HisGen: The New England Historic Genealogical Society. Located in Boston, this is the oldest genealogical society in the country. The library is private, and membership is required to access parts of their collection including rare books, manuscripts, and the lending library. Nonmembers may use the library facility by paying a day fee, but they are restricted from using any of the previously mentioned items. Their collection of genealogies; town, state, and county histories; vital records; and land and probate records encompasses the entire United States as well as most of Canada. They hold all federal census records for New England and many for other states through 1850. They hold all available state vital records for all of the New England states as well as the maritime provinces of Canada, and the collection continues to grow at a rapid rate. See the NEHGS Web site <http://www.newenglandancestors.org>.

NGS: National Genealogical Society. This organization, in Arlington, Virginia, presents conferences, maintains a library, and offers educational courses and research guidance. Visit the Web site at <http://www.ngsgenealogy.org/>.

NUCMC: *National Union Catalog of Manuscript Collections.* This important reference source lists manuscripts located in libraries all over the United States to make locating and accessing these papers easier for genealogical and historical researchers.

SAR: Sons of the American Revolution. This is a fraternal organization for male descendants of Revolutionary War soldiers. The Web site address is <http://www.sar.org/>.

SCV: The Sons of Confederate Veterans. This is a fraternal organization made up of veterans of the Civil War who served the Confederacy. The Web site is at <http://www.scv.org/>.

Transcript: *Boston Evening Transcript*. This was a newspaper that included a genealogical query column providing researchers with a place to post, and possibly receive a reply to, a genealogical research question. It was published during the early twentieth century in Boston, Massachusetts. It is indexed in the *American Genealogical-Biographical Index* (see "AGBI").

UDC: The United Daughters of the Confederacy. This organization is made up of female descendants of the Confederate soldiers. The Web site can be accessed at <http://www.hqudc.org/>.

WPA: Work Projects Administration (formerly the Works Progress Administration). This agency (1935–1943) was set up by President Franklin Delano Roosevelt as a means of putting individuals back to work and counteracting the effects of the Great Depression. Government jobs were created, and many different projects fell under this agency's jurisdiction. One such project is the Historical Records Survey, which employed several thousand clerical workers who produced many inventories and indexes of records that genealogists commonly use. Some of these are the Soundex and Miracode indexes to the 1900, 1910, and 1920 U.S. federal censuses.

TERMS THAT APPEAR IN RECORDS
Land Records (see also chapter eight)

Bounty Land: Land that is given to an individual in exchange for military service or as a bonus for enlisting in the military.

Conveyance: This word is used interchangeably with the word *deed* and refers to the same transaction.

Deed: Document that transfers ownership, title, and interest in a piece of property.

Dower right: This term refers to a widow's right to a portion, usually one-third, of her deceased husband's property that is then granted to her for her lifetime. It is also known as the widow's third.

Freeholder: This is a person who owns his property rather than renting or leasing it.

Grantee or Grantor: These terms refer to the parties involved in a land or property transfer. The person selling the property is referred to as the **grantor** or seller, and the purchaser is called the **grantee** of the property. Indexes to land records are usually divided into two sections: the grantor-grantee index and the grantee-grantor index. Using both of these indexes help you find and access records for your ancestors regardless of whether they bought or sold property.

Legacy: Property or money left to an individual in a will.

Legatee: An individual who inherits money or property through a will.

Lessee or Lessor: A **lessee** is a person who lives on and/or works a piece of property without having actual title of ownership to that property. The **lessor** is the individual who has ownership of the property and allows, for money or other payment, another individual to reside on or work the property he owns.

Moiety: This term means one-half or some equal share of something, usually in reference to land or property distribution in a will.

Patent: A grant of land given to an individual by the government.

Public domain: This term refers to land that is owned by the government rather than by an individual.

Quitclaim deed: This refers to the transfer of a claim or title to property without a guarantee that it has a clear and valid title.

Surety: An individual who, through money or other items of value, guarantees the truth of some matter or the appearance of himself or another.

Township: A township is a division of land owned by the United States that is divided, using the rectangular survey system, into thirty-six sections or thirty-six square miles. The term is also used to describe a subdivision of a town or county.

Warranty deed: This type of deed contains a guarantee by the seller (grantor) that the property has a clear and valid title. It is the opposite of the quitclaim deed, which does not provide such a guarantee.

Immigration and Naturalization Records (see also chapter six)

Alien registration: Beginning with the Alien Registration Act of 1940, all immigrants living within the United States who had not become citizens were required to register yearly as aliens (noncitizens) with the Immigration and Naturalization Service (INS). The individuals were then fingerprinted and issued a card indicating their status. This procedure continues today, and the alien registration card is commonly referred to as a green card.

Certificate of Arrival: This document shows that the information provided by the immigrant applying for citizenship was verified with the ship's manifest by the Immigration and Naturalization Service. A certificate is then issued and returned to the court of record to be filed with the naturalization record.

Certificate of Naturalization: This document is presented to the immigrant as proof that he is a U.S. citizen. Many of these certificates turn up in family papers. In most cases the information it provides is minimal, but its facts will lead you to the complete naturalization records. Certificates from certain time frames also include a picture of the individual who was naturalized. Get the name of the court, the date, and the petition number along with the name of the individual on this certificate to locate the records. The certificate number is of no significance in locating the naturalization records.

Collective naturalization: The act of granting citizenship privileges and responsibilities to a group of people when a government, by treaty or session, acquires the whole or a part of a territory of a foreign nation.

Declaration of Intention: This is also referred to as the "first papers" filed by immigrants when they apply for citizenship. Depending on the time period, the information contained in this document may be minimal or extensive. The

Declaration of Intention is turned in when the final papers, Petition for Naturalization, are filed. Beginning in 1929 declarations of intentions included a photograph of the applicant.

Deportation: The act of denying an immigrant residence within the United States and subsequently removing him from the country. Deportation could be the result of many factors depending on the time period. Persons arriving at a U.S. port could be denied entry if they were likely to become public charges (handicapped, no means of support, ill, insane), had been convicted of certain crimes, belonged to an ethnic group that was excluded from the United States, or were considered contract laborers. Deportation could also occur after the immigrant had resided in the United States if she was not a citizen and committed certain crimes or failed to register yearly with the INS.

Derivative citizenship: This refers to citizenship granted to the wife and minor children of a man who had completed the process of becoming a U.S. citizen before 1922 (the wife and minors did not have to apply). After 1922, a woman could gain citizenship through her husband's citizenship without having to file a declaration of intention (first papers) or meet the residency requirements.

Emigrant/Emigration: An individual who leaves his country and moves to another location. The act of leaving one country for another.

Immigrant/Immigration: An individual who moves to a new country from elsewhere. The act of settling in a new area from another location.

Manifest: Passenger lists—commonly referred to as passenger, crew, or ship's manifests—are listings of individuals who traveled on board a specific vessel. Most lists were created by the shipping lines at the port of departure and surrendered at the port of arrival.

Military naturalization: The act of granting citizenship to foreigners who served the United States through military service. Usually granted upon honorable discharge from the service. There was no declaration of intention required, and only the petition for naturalization (final papers) was filed. Any residency requirements in effect at the time were waived as well. This benefit applied to soldiers from the Civil War and after. Many male immigrants became citizens by virtue of their service in World War I.

Naturalization: This is the process of granting citizenship privileges and responsibilities to foreign born residents of the United States. Citizenship was not required to remain in the United States, and many early immigrants never became citizens.

Oath of Allegiance: As part of the petition for naturalization, an oath is taken pledging loyalty to the adopted country and renouncing any future obligation or allegiance to the former country.

Petition for Naturalization: Sometimes referred to as the "second" or "final papers," these records were filed with affidavits that declared the applicants had resided in the country and state for the required length of time. The time between the filing of the first and second papers varied but usually took between three and five years.

Repatriation Certificate: This document restored U.S. citizenship to an individual who had forfeited it due to military service in a foreign country during World Wars I and II, marriage to an alien (this applied to American born women until 1922), or by voting in a foreign political election. This restoration of citizenship occurred on or after 13 January 1941 and required the individual to take an oath of renunciation or allegiance before a naturalization court or before a U.S. diplomatic or consular officer abroad.

Any U.S.-born woman who married an alien prior to 22 September 1922 forfeited her U.S. citizenship. She then assumed her husband's nationality. After this law was repealed these women had to apply for restoration of their citizenship either through repatriation or through her husband if he then acquired his U.S. citizenship.

Probate Records (see also chapter eight)

Administrator: The administrator or executor mentioned in a will or probate record is the person appointed to manage or divide an estate of a deceased individual. He may or may not be a blood relative of the deceased. The deceased, if she left a will, might have named someone to be the executor, and he has the right to accept or decline the position. If the executor declines or if the person died intestate (without a will) or did not name an executor in the will, an administrator is appointed by the court with jurisdiction over the estate.

Codicil: A codicil is an addition to an existing will that either adds to or changes some bequests in the original will.

Estate inventory: After a person dies, testate or intestate, and his estate is presented to the court for distribution, the court usually appoints one or more individuals to make a complete listing of the deceased person's belongings, both personal property and real estate. This listing usually includes household implements, farming or occupational tools, livestock, debts owed to the estate by other individuals, and debts owed to others by the estate. The inventory can provide you with an interesting picture of your ancestor and his worldly goods. Sometimes his occupation can even be determined by looking at the inventory.

Intestate: When an individual dies intestate he left no written will explaining how he wanted his estate to be disbursed. The court appoints an administrator to oversee the estate settlement according to laws governing that distribution.

Nuncupative will: A nuncupative (Latin for "to solemnly declare") will is an oral will recited by an individual certain of his imminent death to another person or persons who must record it in writing within a reasonable period of time. These wills were common among people who died from injuries suffered in accidents, military engagements, or circumstances of imminent death and who had not previously recorded a last will and testament.

Surrogate court: This is a court that has jurisdiction over probate cases within a geographic area. Some states, such as New York, refer to the probate courts as surrogate courts.

Testate: When an individual dies testate she left a written or oral will (see **nuncupative will**) outlining her wishes for the disbursement of her estate. The court asks any administrator named in the will if he will accept that position. The court then appoints that individual, or another if that person declines to serve, to disburse the estate according to law and the deceased's wishes as outlined in the will.

Will: A will is a written document signed by the deceased before her death, usually witnessed by one or more individuals, listing the deceased's wishes as to how her estate will be disbursed.

MISCELLANEOUS TERMS

Abstract: This is the extraction of specific pieces of information (such as names, dates, and locations) from a document or record rather than making a complete copy of the entire document. Indexes are a type of abstract commonly used by researchers. The compiler extracted the names from the documents and compiled them in alphabetical order. Many books have been published with extractions of Revolutionary War Pension records, land records, probates records, etc. Using these abstracts can and should lead you to the original document. Doing a complete transcription of that document might provide you with additional valuable information not included in the abstract or extraction.

CD-ROM: This acronym refers to "compact disc read-only memory," which means that the data included on the CD cannot be changed, only read.

Collateral line: This term refers to the extended family of your ancestors. This includes aunts, siblings, cousins, in-laws, etc. These individuals do not appear on your or your ancestor's pedigree chart. To determine whether a relative is an ancestor or a collateral relative, ask the question "If she did not exist, could I be alive?" If the answer is yes, then she is collateral. If the answer is no, such as for one of your grandparents or great-grandparents, she is an ancestor.

Compilation: A listing of information or facts from one or more sources that has been published as one record or listing. Statewide vital records are a compilation of all of the town or county records that are submitted to the state as required by law. Most CDs with genealogical information are constructed using a number of other previously published sources. Compilations are never considered primary sources since they are not the first record of an event or fact.

Copybook: This term refers to a volume or book maintained by a governmental jurisdiction that contains transcribed copies of original documents. Land deeds used in town or county offices are usually in copybooks since the original deed is given to the owner of the land. It is merely recorded in the official records as documentation of the purchase. Many probate records have also been transcribed from the original papers to a book format. Most microfilms of land and probate records available today were made from the copybooks rather than the original records. Since original land deeds are in the hands of landowners and the probate or surrogate court records are packets or dockets containing many individual pieces of paper, the copybooks are easier to obtain and use in microfilming. Once you determine that a probate record in the copybook is a record of interest to you, seek out the original packet or docket. Since mistakes can be made in the copying process and some papers included in the original file may not have been copied into the books, it is critical that you refer to the original and look at all papers, front and back, for information not listed in the copybook and for accuracy.

Database: All databases, whether on CDs or online at a Web site, are indexes to records grouped together by some commonality, such as passenger arrivals, vital records, or census indexes. Databases vary in accuracy and inclusiveness depending on the publisher, the Web site, and the records included in them.

Dewey decimal system: This library cataloging system groups subjects together without designation as to what state they pertain to. Genealogy as a category is cataloged in this system as number 929. Within this 929 designation are subcategories as follows:

929.1	General Genealogy	925.6	Heraldry
929.2	Family Histories	925.7	Royalty, peerage, landed gentry
929.3	Genealogical Sources		
929.4	Personal Names	925.8	Coats of arms, crests, seals, etc.
929.5	Epitaphs or tombstone transcriptions	925.9	Flags

(For further information see appendix B in *The Genealogist's Companion & Sourcebook*, by Emily Anne Croom.)

Digital image: A digital image is any photograph, drawing, document, or record that has been scanned and/or included in a computer database or file.

Freedman: A male who has been emancipated or released from slavery. Any individual who has been freed from servitude.

Freedman's Bureau: An organization created in 1865 by Congressional action to protect and preserve the civil rights of emancipated and freed slaves.

Gazetteer: Any publication that lists in alphabetical order towns (existing and extinct), locations of county seats or governmental divisions, rivers, and places of interest within a geographic location.

Indentured servant: Any person who enters into an agreement in which he or she agrees to exchange time or labor for property, transportation, training, etc.

Library of Congress cataloging system: A system of assigning numbers to categorize books within a collection. Each book or publication is given a letter designating its category, and then a number follows the letter designation. F is the letter for Local History/Genealogy. The numbers range from 16 to 965 and relate to the states of the union beginning in Maine, traveling down the East Coast, across the gulf, through the Midwest, and then through the western states. The numbering somewhat follows the date of entry of the state into the union.

The numbers assigned to each state or region are as follows:

Alabama	F321–335	District of Columbia	F191–205
Alaska	F901–915	Florida	F306–320
Arizona	F806–820	Georgia	F281–295
Arkansas	F406–420	Great Lakes Region	F551–556
California	F856–870	Gulf States	F296
Colorado	F771–785	Hawaii	F965
Connecticut	F91–105	Idaho	F741–755
Delaware	F161–175	Illinois	F536–550

Indiana	F521–535	Ohio	F486–500
Iowa	F616–630	Ohio River Valley	F516–520
Kansas	F676–690	Oklahoma	F691–705
Kentucky	F446–460	Old Southwest and	
Louisiana	F366–380	Lower Mississippi	
Maine	F16–30	Valley	F396
Maryland	F176–190	Oregon	F871–885
Massachusetts	F61–75	Pacific Region	F851–854
Michigan	F561–575	Pennsylvania	F146–160
Mid-Atlantic States	F106–115	Rhode Island	F76–90
Minnesota	F601–615	Rocky Mountain	
Mississippi Valley;		Region	F721
Midwest	F351–355	South Carolina	F266–280
Missouri	F461–475	South Dakota	F646–660
Missouri River Valley	F598	South Atlantic States	F206–220
Montana	F726–740	Tennessee	F431–445
Nebraska	F661–675	Texas	F381–395
Nevada	F836–850	Utah	F821–835
New England	F1–15	Vermont	F46–60
New Hampshire	F31–35	Virginia	F21–235
New Jersey	F131-145	Washington	F886–900
New Mexico	F791–805	West, Trans-Mississippi	
New Southwest	F786–788	Valley	F591–595
New York	F116–130	West Virginia	F236–250
North Carolina	F251–265	Western Florida	F301
North Dakota	F631–645	Wisconsin	F576–590
Northwest Territory	F476–485	Wyoming	F756–770

(For further information see appendix B in *The Genealogist's Companion & Sourcebook,* by Emily Anne Croom.)

Lineal ancestor: These ancestors are related through a parent/child relationship. Your parents, grandparents, great-grandparents, and so on, are your ancestors. If any one of them had not existed, you would not be alive today. This is also referred to as your bloodline.

Testamentary guardian: This individual is named in a will as a guardian of children of a deceased person so that one need not be appointed by the court.

Transcription: This is a verbatim copy of any document or record. No corrections are made to punctuation, spelling, or other errors within the document. Everything in the document is copied exactly as it appears.

FURTHER READING

A to Zax: A Comprehensive Dictionary for Genealogists & Historians, by
Barbara Jean Evans. Alexandria, Va.: Hearthside Press, 1996.

Sources

Abbreviations & Acronyms: A Guide for Family Historians, compiled by Kip Sperry. Salt Lake City, Utah: Ancestry, Inc., 2000.

Concise Genealogical Dictionary, compiled by Maurine and Glen Harris. Salt Lake City, Utah: Ancestry, Inc., 1989.

The Genealogist's Companion & Sourcebook, by Emily Anne Croom. Cincinnati, Ohio: Betterway Books, 1994.

The Genealogy Sourcebook, by Sharon DeBartolo Carmack. Los Angeles, Calif.: Lowell House, 1997.

Land & Property Research in the United States, by E. Wade Hone. Salt Lake City, Utah: Ancestry, Inc., 1997.

A Medical Miscellany for Genealogists, by Dr. Jeannette L. Jerger. Bowie, Md.: Heritage Books, Inc., 1995.

National Union Catalog of Manuscript Collections. Washington, D.C.: Library of Congress, 1962–. Published annually.

Nicknames: Past and Present, 3d ed. revised and enlarged, by Christine Rose. San Jose, Calif.: Rose Family Association, 1998.

The Sleuth Book for Genealogists: Strategies for More Successful Family History Research, by Emily Anne Croom. Cincinnati, Ohio: Betterway Books, 2000.

What Did They Mean by That?: A Dictionary of Historical Terms for Genealogists, by Paul Drake, Ph.D. Bowie, Md.: Heritage Books, 1994.

What Did They Mean by That?: A Dictionary of Historical Terms for Genealogists. Some More Words, Volume 2, by Paul Drake, Ph.D. Bowie, Md.: Heritage Books, 1998.

When Your Ox Is in a Ditch, by Vera McDowell. Baltimore, Md.: Genealogical Publishing Co., Inc., 1992.

Index

Explore your family history with Betterway Books!

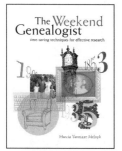

The Weekend Genealogist—Maximize your family research efficiency! With this guide, you can focus your efforts in searching for family documents while still gaining the best results. Organization and research techniques are presented in a clear, easy-to-follow format perfect for advanced researchers *and* beginners. You'll learn how to work more efficiently using family history facilities, the Internet—even the postal service! *ISBN 1-55870-546-5, paperback, 144 pages, #70496-K*

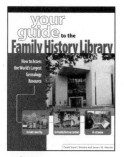

Long-Distance Genealogy—Gathering information from sources that can't be visited is a challenge for all genealogists. This book will teach you the basics of long-distance research. You'll learn what types of records and publications can be accessed from a distance, problems associated with the process, how to network, how to use computer resources, and special "last resort" options. *ISBN 1-55870-535-X, paperback, 272 pages, #70495-K*

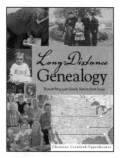

Your Guide to the Family History Library—The Family History Library in Salt Lake City is the largest collection of genealogy and family history materials in the world. No other repository compares for both quantity and *quality* of research materials. Written for beginning and intermediate genealogists, *Your Guide to the Family History Library* will help you use the library's resources effectively, both on site and online. *ISBN 1-55870-578-3, paperback, 272 pages, #70513-K*

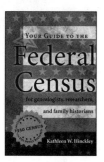

Your Guide to the Federal Census—This one-of-a-kind book examines the "nuts and bolts" of census records. You'll find out where to view the census and how to use it to find ancestors quickly and easily. Easy-to-follow instructions and case studies detail nearly every scenario for tracing family histories through census records. You'll also find invaluable appendixes, a glossary of census terms, and extraction forms. *ISBN 1-55870-588-0, paperback, 208 pages, #70525-K*

These and other fine titles from Betterway Books are available from your local bookstore, online supplier, or by calling (800) 221-5831.